Pandemic Influenza

Emergency Planning and
Community Preparedness

Pandemic Influenza

Emergency Planning and Community Preparedness

Edited by
Jeffrey R. Ryan

CRC Press
Taylor & Francis Group
Boca Raton   London   New York

CRC Press is an imprint of the
Taylor & Francis Group, an **informa** business

CRC Press
Taylor & Francis Group
6000 Broken Sound Parkway NW, Suite 300
Boca Raton, FL 33487-2742

© 2009 by Taylor & Francis Group, LLC
CRC Press is an imprint of Taylor & Francis Group, an Informa business

No claim to original U.S. Government works
Printed in the United States of America on acid-free paper
10 9 8 7 6 5 4 3 2

International Standard Book Number-13: 978-1-4200-6087-4 (Hardcover)

Library of Congress Cataloging-in-Publication Data

Pandemic influenza : emergency planning and community preparedness / editor,
    Jeffrey R. Ryan.
        p. ; cm.
    "A CRC title."
    Includes bibliographical references and index.
    ISBN 978-1-4200-6087-4 (hardcover : alk. paper)
    1. Influenza--Epidemiology. 2. Influenza--Government policy--United States. 3.
Emergency management--United States. I. Ryan, Jeffrey R.
    [DNLM: 1. Influenza, Human--epidemiology. 2. Influenza, Human--history.
    3. Disease Outbreaks--history. 4. Disease Outbreaks--prevention & control.
    5. Emergency Medical Services--organization & administration. 6. Health
Planning--organization & administration. WC 515 P1886 2008]

RA644.I6P366 2008
614.5'18--dc22   2008015483

Visit the Taylor & Francis Web site at
http://www.taylorandfrancis.com

and the CRC Press Web site at
http://www.crcpress.com

Contents

Foreword

We don't know when a pandemic might strike. But we can be sure of two things. Every-thing we do before a pandemic will seem alarmist. Everything we do after a pandemic will seem inadequate. This is the dilemma we face, but it should not stop us from doing what we can to prepare. We need to reach out to everyone with words that inform, but not inflame. We need to encourage everyone to prepare, but not panic.

Michael O. Leavitt
Secretary, Department of Health and Human Services
Pandemic Influenza Leadership Forum, June 13, 2007

Many experts warn that a catastrophic influenza pandemic and its resulting impact are not only likely to happen, but overdue. They agree that if the next pandemic is caused by the currently circulating H5N1 avian (bird) flu, it could be as deadly as or *even more* deadly than the 1918 Spanish flu. That pandemic, caused by the similar H1N1 avian virus, infected more than one-third of the world's population and killed as many as 50 to 100 million people. The massive loss of life caused by the 1918 influenza pandemic is unimaginable. Yet, today, a pandemic with the same rates of infectivity and mortality would result in more than 2 billion infections with 180 million to 360 million deaths worldwide. The Centers for Disease Control has esti-mated that a pandemic could cost the United States alone between $730 billion and $1.6 trillion depending on its severity, a bill far larger than what most corporate and governmental leaders have imagined or are prepared for.

According to the World Health Organization (WHO), the cumulative number of confirmed cases of H5N1 avian influenza as of December 1, 2007, is 335 cases and 206 deaths. The global fatality rate is 61 percent, compared to just 2 percent in 1918. Within 10 years, the H5N1 virus has entrenched in five countries, and has spread to an additional 60 countries. Disease in birds has resulted in the culling of millions of birds worldwide, negatively impacting local economies that depend on open bird markets for food supplies and livelihoods. As a result, some countries have become reluctant to report disease or share viral samples to help scientists track the progression of viral mutation. This information blackout leads many to question whether reported cases and deaths reflect the current situation or are just the "tip of the iceberg." Despite enormous economic losses and horrible statistics, it is hard to find any reports from a major media outlet telling the story. Reports of avian influenza and even isolated reports of clusters of human disease have all but disappeared from the radar. We are in the midst of a "pandemic fatigue."

Where is the rush to prepare?

On November 1, 2005, President George W. Bush sounded the alarm and unveiled the National Strategy for Pandemic Influenza. The document outlines the respon-sibilities that federal, state, and local governments; industry; and individuals have for preparing and responding to a pandemic. Only six months later, the Homeland

Security Council released the Implementation Plan for the National Strategy, which translates the Strategy into more than 300 actions for federal departments and agencies and sets clear expectations for state and local governments and other nonfederal entities. The Plan requires that all federal departments and agencies develop their own pandemic plans based on standardized criteria. Government leaders have visited every state and territory to try and raise awareness and encourage planning at state and local levels. For the first time, there is a joint federal website that provides a "one-stop shop" for information. Unprecedented amounts of preparedness guidance are available on topics such as pandemic planning and the use of physical barriers, masks, respirators, and antiviral medications.

After providing more than $400 million in cooperative agreement emergency supplemental funds intended to help the 50 states, the District of Columbia, three local jurisdictions (New York City, Chicago, and Los Angeles County), five U.S. Territories and three Freely Associated States of the Pacific, state and regional plans continue to be health-centric and fail to include emergency management and the private sector in planning efforts. Many remain in early draft form. Few real exercises have been held to date. States have been provided with more comprehensive guidance and have been asked to re-examine their planning efforts to improve coordination, yet many have turned their attention and resources elsewhere.

Why is there a reluctance to recognize an imminent threat?

It is easy to dismiss these avian influenza events because they have occurred on foreign soil. We are complacent — it's not on our shores or in our backyard, so many see no need to take notice or begin planning. Yet, the threat of an influenza pandemic still remains very serious with no signs of slowing down. The fact of the matter is any of these cases or deaths could have just as easily happened anywhere in North America or in one of our cities.

Pandemics are diseases without borders. The influenza virus will not respect economic, political, and geographic boundaries. National estimates indicate that a pandemic could infect more than one-third of the world's population, killing millions. A severe pandemic outbreak will result in absenteeism of up to 40 percent of the workforce, dramatically decreasing the number of available workers and significantly disrupting the movement of people and goods. When a pandemic occurs, life as we know it will change — in culture and in politics as well as in the prosperity of any nation it touches. We need to be prepared, both personally and professionally, to respond. Our businesses need to know how to stay operational for society to remain functional.

While there is no way to predict when the next pandemic will strike, it is only a matter of time before it does. Knowing the facts is the best preparation. *Pandemic Influenza: Emergency Planning and Community Preparedness* is an amazing resource that you can count on for reliable information. Whether you are an elected official; homeland security, animal, or human health care professional; emergency manager; business owner; student; or a member of the general public, this book offers valuable information that can help YOU.

Dr. Ryan has assembled some of the best experts in the field to guide you in understanding the threat of pandemic influenza and how it can affect you and the people you are responsible for. In this book you'll learn about the history of pandemics and their outcomes, the makeup of the virus and how it transmits disease, and finally what you can do to protect yourself and others. This text pulls it all together, giving you timely and accurate information that you can put into action. It's one of the best sources of information available today.

Unlike a hurricane or wildfire, there will be no resources to move to your aid — the cavalry is NOT coming! Your ability to meet and survive a pandemic depends on you and your plans, and the time to begin planning is NOW!

Lynn A. Slepski, PhD, RN, CCNS*
Captain, United States Public Health Service
Graduate School of Nursing, Uniformed Services University
U.S. Department of Homeland Security

---

* The views expressed here are those of the author and do not represent the official policy or position of the U.S. Public Health Service, the Department of Homeland Security, the Uniformed Services University of the Health Sciences, or the United States government.

Preface

There is a time in the life of every problem when it is big enough to see, yet small enough to solve.

Michael O. Leavitt
Secretary, Department of Health and Human Services

This book is the result of much research, writing, and thoughtful discussion with students, first responders, scholars, and thought-leaders in the field of pandemic influenza planning and preparedness. It comes at a time when emergency managers, public health professionals, clinicians, animal health professionals, and government officials are preparing themselves for the next pandemic. Numerous public health experts are telling us that we are now overdue for one. Pandemic influenza, when it comes, is likely to affect everyone, regardless of who they are, where they are from, what religion they practice, or their political persuasion. Frankly, we all have an equal chance of surviving or dying from an infection with a novel, virulent strain of type-A influenza virus. The pathogen will not observe any laws or borders, nor will it seem to have a preference for its host. In order to face this threat prudently, we must see ourselves and those we serve as universally vulnerable and immunologically naïve. As such, government officials are urging us to prepare our communities.

In the event of an outbreak of a highly pathogenic and transmissible type-A influenza virus, community officials, planners, and responders at all skill levels will be called on to protect the public. Recognition of pandemic influenza will most likely come from public health authorities who have surveillance programs in effect in many parts of the world. However, the President of the United States and the Secretary of the Department of Health and Human Services (HHS) have urged community planners to prepare for pandemic influenza.

A key component of preparedness is planning. The United States has engaged in pandemic flu planning activities, with an emphasis on the public health sector, for several decades. The threat posed by H5N1 avian flu has heightened multi-sector preparedness activities in recent years. The federal government has been engaged in a coordinated, multi-sector, governmentwide planning effort since 2005. In order for us to know how to assemble a functional plan, we have to know how we're going to respond. Pandemic planners must thoroughly examine all the options, pharmaceutical as well as nonpharmaceutical. They must also engage all stakeholders and build partnerships before attempting to assemble a functional plan.

As with any emergency response, most of the responsibility rests with local authorities. Emergency planning and management level responders, health care providers, and community officials at all levels should be involved in the preparation for and response to a possible outbreak of a deadly contagion. These professionals and practitioners are responsible for assembling comprehensive and effective plans to prepare for the challenges of pandemic influenza. They will also generate local plans and guidelines designed to conduct mass vaccination, to transport patients, to enforce isolation and quarantine protocols; to care for the sick, to remove and transport the dead, and to evaluate the progress of any actions taken to ensure response objectives are met safely, effectively, and efficiently.

RECENT HISTORY OF PANDEMIC PREPAREDNESS

Beginning in 2002, states across the United States received funding for preparedness activities through two granting programs: one that is overseen by the Health Resources and Services Administration (HRSA) to prepare clinics, hospitals, and other health care facilities for mass casualty incidents; and the other, which is managed by the Centers for Disease Control and Prevention (CDC) to enhance state public health capacity. Grants for both programs are administered at the state level by each state's public health department. The Department of Health and Human Services (HHS) does not have any grant programs that directly fund local or municipal authorities for preparedness activities.

Starting with fiscal year (FY) 2004 funding, the HRSA and CDC grant programs required all states to develop plans for pandemic influenza and to submit them to the CDC by July 2005. Although the plans were mandated, there were no specific requirements for the content of the plans (CDC, 2004). Although earlier guidance had been developed by the CDC to guide state planning efforts, pandemic planning was voluntary at that time, and the FY2004 requirement did not refer to the earlier voluntary guidance (Lister and Stockdale, 2007). All organizations managed to submit their plans by the July 2005 deadline. In November 2005, HHS published its Pandemic Influenza Plan (HHS, 2005). The second part of the plan, "Public Health Guidance for State and Local Partners," detailed, through a number of supplements, specific activities to help all jurisdictions and health care facilities craft an effective pandemic response. At that time, states were required to have a pandemic plan and were not required to update existing plans with the guidance that had been issued after the 2005 deadline (Lister, 2005). In addition, the Department of Homeland Security and HHS placed a great deal of emphasis on the conduct of exercises and assessments. They also encouraged state public health departments to lend assistance to local jurisdictions as they attempted to formulate their pandemic plans (Lister, 2007). Subsequently, in May 2006, the White House Homeland Security Council published its Implementation Plan for the National Strategy for Pandemic Influenza (HSC, 2006). This weighty document assigned more than 300 preparedness and response tasks to departments and agencies across the federal government, and provided planning guidance for state, local, and tribal entities, businesses, schools and universities, communities, and nongovernmental organizations (HSC, 2006).

In FY2006, Congress provided $6.1 billion in emergency supplemental funding exclusively for pandemic preparedness (Lister, 2007). These funds built upon earlier efforts to plan for public health emergencies in general and pandemic flu in particular. The supplemental funding included $600 million for state and local pandemic preparedness, to be administered by the CDC through the public health preparedness grant program. All states and territories received portions of the pandemic funding according to a formula, and were required by CDC to conduct a variety of activities involving communitywide (versus health-sector specific) planning, exercises and drills, preparedness of sub-state jurisdictions, and others (Lister and Stockdale, 2007). Supplemental funding was made available to states in phases, from the spring through the fall of 2006. An additional $175 million in FY2007 funds was made available in July 2007 (HHS, 2007a).

Since September 11, 2001, Congress has provided almost $8 billion in grants to states to strengthen public health and hospital preparedness for public health threats.

WHERE WE SEEM TO BE NOW

In 2006, all state pandemic plans were analyzed by the Congressional Research Service (CRS). The general assessment showed one dramatic trait: the plans reflect their authorship by public health officials; meaning, they emphasize core public health functions such as disease detection and control. Other planning challenges, such as assuring surge capacity in the health care sector, the continuity of essential services, or the integrity of critical supply chains, which fall outside the authority of public health officials, were sufficiently lacking and require stronger engagement by emergency management officials and others in planning (Lister and Stockdale, 2007). Variability among states in pandemic planning has been noted in another analysis (Holmberg et al., 2006).

Lister and Stockdale had a clear message. They were telling us that when it comes to pandemic response, departments of public health cannot bear all the burden nor can they assemble totally functional plans without the sincere involvement of numerous other stakeholders. Furthermore, as public health authority is decentralized to state rather than federal authorities, it is also decentralized in some states, with local health departments having varying degrees of autonomy, further complicating planning efforts.

The federal government cannot directly dictate to the states what they must do to prepare. However, it can and does establish requirements as a condition of the receipt and maintenance of preparedness funding. There is, and must be, flexibility in those requirements. This allows states and cities to prepare differently for the multitude of threats that they face: terrorism, natural disasters of all types, and man-made, technical disasters. A pandemic, on the other hand, is more likely to affect communities in much the same way. As such, pandemic planning may lend itself to a standardized approach and to more directive federal requirements tied to the funding (Lister and Stockdale, 2007).

So, when it comes to preparedness for pandemic influenza, where does most, if not all, of the money appear to be going? Obviously, it's going to public health organizations — primarily at the state level. Based on the opening discussion, we know that the problem affects all sectors of the community. The stream of funding has done well to infuse the effort within state public health departments, but has done little to activate the remainder of agencies that are needed to assemble a functional plan.

GOALS AND OBJECTIVES

Pandemic Influenza: Emergency Planning and Community Preparedness introduces readers to global and domestic concerns for pandemic influenza and avian influenza. Included is a thorough review of the influenza viruses, the disease they cause, and consequence management considerations. A comprehensive treatment of the subject is needed to promote understanding of the problem and the complex network of international, federal, state, and local assets for dealing with the pandemic threat. Accordingly, readers are introduced to international and federal initiatives and programs that address pandemic mitigation, preparedness, response, and recovery programs.

The primary goal of this book is to give readers an understanding of the threat of pandemic influenza. The book will provide the readers with information regarding the imminent threat of pandemic influenza, its challenges, clinical aspects, its relation to avian influenza (AI), the goals and objectives of the National Strategy for Pandemic Influenza (NSPI), and all the facets of an effective response. The book is intended to provide the reader with an understanding of outbreak containment and response skills, enabling him or her to plan and prepare effectively for an outbreak of pandemic influenza. The book is intended to be used as a reference for students; public health professionals; emergency managers; state, regional, and local planners; health care system emergency preparedness coordinators; and responders at the planning and management levels.

PRIMARY LEARNING OBJECTIVES

- Identify the perils associated with pandemics in general, and pandemic influenza specifically
- Describe the types of influenza and associated implications for human and animal health
- Describe the clinical manifestations of influenza, including epidemiological data, various stages of pandemic influenza, and measures pertaining to prevention
- Identify the principles associated with the National Strategy for Pandemic Influenza
- Describe various factors associated with an outbreak of highly pathogenic avian influenza (HPAI) and the effect it could have on the economy
- Describe the use the pharmaceutical and nonpharmaceutical measures that can be applied in layers in response to pandemic influenza
- Discuss response actions of various emergency services disciplines as they relate to risk communications, social distancing, travel restrictions, and quarantine
- Identify the principles of mass prophylaxis, especially as it applies to mass vaccination and the use of antivirals with an outbreak of influenza
- Explain the importance of rapidly expanding the capacity of the existing health care system in order to provide triage and medical care
- Describe the components of service continuation essential for the private sector to remain intact during a severe pandemic

- Discuss solutions fatality management as it applies to a pandemic situation at its peak

The book is organized into three thematic sections comprised of 10 chapters. The chapters cover a brief history of pandemics, the 1918 Spanish flu, the natural history of the influenza virus, clinical aspects of influenza, avian influenza, international and domestic programs and assets for pandemic influenza, definition of the response to pandemic influenza, service continuation planning, and fatality management. I, along with the other authors, hope that you will find the content useful and that the words here will inspire you to make critical decisions now and apply them toward the creation of a functional plan.

REFERENCES

CDC (Centers for Disease Control and Prevention). 2004. "Continuation Guidance — Budget Year Five, Attachment H, Cross-cutting Benchmarks and Guidance," Cross-Cutting Critical Benchmark #6: Preparedness for Pandemic Influenza. http://www.bt.cdc.gov/planning/continuationguidance/pdf/activities-attachh.pdf (accessed January 11, 2008)

CDC (Centers for Disease Control and Prevention). 2006a. Cooperative Agreement Guidance for Public Health Emergency Preparedness. http://www.bt.cdc.gov/planning/#statelocal (accessed January 11, 2008)

CDC (Centers for Disease Control and Prevention). 2006b. Cooperative Agreement Guidance for Public Health Emergency Preparedness, pandemic influenza guidance supplements, Phase 1 and 2, along with general program guidance for FY2005 and FY2006. http://www.bt.cdc.gov/planning/coopagreement/ (accessed January 11, 2008)

HHS (Department of Health and Human Services). 2005. HHS Pandemic Influenza Plan. November 2005.

HHS (Department of Health and Human Services). 2007a. "HHS Announces $896.7 Million in Funding to States for Public Health Preparedness and Emergency Response," Press release, July 17, 2007.

HHS (Department of Health and Human Services). 2007b. State Pandemic Plans. http://www.pandemicflu.gov/plan/stateplans.html (accessed January 11, 2008)

Holmberg S, Layton C, Ghneim G, Wagener D. 2006. State Plans for Containment of Pandemic Influenza. *Emerg Infect Dis* 12:1414–1417.

HRSA (Health Resources and Services Administration). 2008. HRSA emergency preparedness programs. http://www.hrsa.gov/healthconcerns/default.htm (accessed January 11, 2008)

HSC (Homeland Security Council). 2006. National Strategy for Pandemic Influenza: Implementation Plan. May 2006.

HSC (Homeland Security Council). 2007. National Strategy for Pandemic Influenza Implementation Plan, One-Year Summary.

Lister S. 2005. Congressional Research Service Report: Pandemic Influenza: Domestic Preparedness Efforts. Washington, D.C.

Lister S. 2007. Congressional Research Service Report: Pandemic Influenza: Appropriations for Public Health Preparedness and Response. Washington, D.C.

Lister S, Stockdale H. 2007. Congressional Research Service Report: Pandemic Influenza: An Analysis of State Preparedness and Response Plans. Washington, D.C.

About the Editor

Jeffrey R. Ryan, PhD, is a retired Army lieutenant colonel with an extensive background in preventive medicine, epidemiology, clinical trials, and diagnostics development. Dr. Ryan also served in the private sector, working for a biotech company, Cepheid, where he was a senior business developer and manager for their biothreat government business program. Dr. Ryan has authored more than 40 scientific, peer-reviewed journal articles and is the lead instructor and co-developer of the Pandemic Influenza Planning and Preparedness course, which is taught at the Center for Domestic Preparedness (CDP) in Anniston, Alabama. Currently, Dr. Ryan serves as an assistant professor at the Institute for Emergency Preparedness, Jacksonville State University. His specialty areas include biosecurity, biodefense, medical aspects of emergency management, homeland security planning, and preparedness and terrorism studies.

About the Contributors

John P. Ahrens, MPA, has been with the Fairfax City Fire Department in Fairfax, Virginia, for 24 years. Currently Captain Ahrens serves as a station commander and fill-in battalion chief. He is also the pandemic coordinator for the City of Fairfax, Virginia, and authored their pandemic continuity of operations plan (COOP). He serves as a member of the Virginia Department of Emergency Management's Locality COOP subcommittee. Additionally, he is a member of the National Capital Region's Type 3 Incident Management Team. He was also deployed to East Hancock County, Mississippi, after Hurricane Katrina to provide fire and EMS services. Captain Ahrens has a master's degree in public administration from George Mason University and is currently pursuing a master's certificate in emergency management and homeland security also from George Mason University.

Jane Thomas Cash, PhD, RN, COI, CHS, MEP, began her career as a public health nurse in a county health department specializing in epidemiology and disease surveillance. Over the next 25 years, she continued her work in the academic public health/nursing arena teaching, practicing, and developing courses in epidemiology, biostatistics, health policy and planning, health promotion and disease prevention, communicable diseases, and global emerging infections. Dr. Cash has developed skills and expertise that are essential for working in terrorism and all-hazards disaster planning, training, and exercises. She is a trainer for FEMA's health care programs offered through the Center for Domestic Preparedness. These courses include Healthcare Leadership and Decision Making in WMD Events, Fundamentals of Healthcare Emergency Management, and Pandemic Influenza Planning and Preparedness. Additionally, Dr. Cash is certified in homeland security (CHS) by the American College of Forensic Examiners International (ACFEI) and is a master exercise practitioner (MEP). She is an adjunct professor at the University of Alabama School of Public Health in Birmingham and serves as adjunct faculty at the University of Memphis, Lowenberg School of Nursing.

Jan F. Glarum, EMT-P, retired after 27 years in the emergency response field. He has an extensive background in emergency medical services, fire, and police special weapons and tactics operations. He served as the medical preparedness officer for the State of Oregon Health Division, and executive director of development for the Portland Metropolitan Medical Response System. Mr. Glarum authored the *Homeland Security Field Guide* and is co-developer of the Pandemic Influenza Planning and Preparedness course, taught at the Center for Domestic Preparedness in Anniston, Alabama. Currently, Mr. Glarum works as a consultant for the Department of Homeland Security (DHS) and the Department of Defense, both domestically and internationally.

Onalee Grady-Erickson is the Infectious Disease Outbreak Program coordinator for the State of Minnesota's Department of Public Safety, Division of Homeland Security and Emergency Management. In this role since October 2001, she has extensive experience in developing pandemic influenza planning and preparedness programs for the public and private sectors. Her background includes environmental health, radiological emergency preparedness, all-hazards response, exercise development, emergency management, legislative analysis, governmental relations for the health care industry, and continuity of operations planning. Ms. Grady-Erickson holds a bachelor's degree in biology from the College of St. Benedict and is a certified environmental hygienist and certified emergency manager.

Lori J. Hardin, MFS, is the statewide emergency planner for the Office of the Chief Medical Examiner, under the Virginia Department of Health, a position she has held since January 2003. Prior to her current position, she was the medico-legal death investigator for the Office of the Chief Medical Examiner, Tidewater District Office, and a deputy coroner for Lehigh County Coroner's Office in Allentown, Pennsylvania. Ms. Hardin serves as a member of the Disaster Mortuary Operational Response Team (DMORT), Region III, and was previously a member of the DMORT Weapons of Mass Destruction (WMD) Team. As the Virginia Medical Examiner's statewide emergency planner, she coordinates with 139 independent jurisdictions: all State of Virginia and federal agencies whose roles interface with fatality management as well as various regional teams including the National Capital Region. Ms. Hardin is a commander in the Navy Reserve and continues her military service currently assigned with Joint Forces Command, at the Joint War Fighting Center, Suffolk, Virginia. Her duties include readiness officer, and she acts as a mortuary affairs planner and doctrine developer for the Department of Defense.

Allen W. Kirchner, MD, is a consultant to the U.S. Department of Homeland Security as a subject matter expert in the medical response to chemical and biological terrorism. He co-authored the U.S. government's flagship training course in Pandemic Influenza Planning and Preparedness and has published in the *Journal of Emergency Management* on that topic. Dr. Kirchner received his medical degree from the University of Maryland. He retired after 25 years in the clinical practice of medicine to begin a second career in teaching and writing, and held a faculty position as clinical assistant professor of emergency medicine at the Medical College of Georgia. He also served as director of operational medical support for a large sheriff's office in South Carolina and as a lieutenant and senior SWAT operator in that agency. He instructs at FEMA's Noble Training Facility at the Center for Domestic Preparedness in Anniston, Alabama, and has lectured extensively around the country on this and other homeland security issues.

Martha Griffith Lavender, RN, DSN, is currently serving as associate director of training and education at the Center for Domestic Preparedness (CDP), Federal Emergency Management Agency, U.S. Department of Homeland Security (DHS) in Anniston, Alabama. Dr. Lavender provides executive oversight and management for the emergency preparedness training programs, instructional delivery, and evaluation of the CDP training program, which includes both resident and nonresident course delivery. The program features the only toxic chemical agent training facility for civilian emergency responders in the nation as well as the only hospital dedicated to preparing health care providers to respond to catastrophic/mass casualty events. Dr. Lavender has participated in the development of the National Preparedness Guidance (HSPD 8) through various committees assigned to develop the DHS Target Capabilities for the health care sector. Dr. Lavender received a bachelor of science degree from Jacksonville State University and a master of science in pediatric nursing and a doctor of science in nursing from the University of Alabama at Birmingham. From 1996–2004, she served as dean of the College of Nursing and Health Sciences at Jacksonville State University. In 2001, Dr. Lavender was elected to serve as the national president of the Association of Women's Health, Obstetric, and Neonatal Nursing Association (AWHONN). She has received several awards and research grants for her work including the AWHONN Distinguished Professional Service Award (2004) and the Outstanding Faculty Award by the Jacksonville State University Alumni Association.

Kenneth E. Nusbaum, DVM, PhD, has been at the College of Veterinary Medicine, Auburn University, since 1982, except for a year as a congressional fellow for the American Veterinary Medical Association. After 18 years teaching virology and studying food animal disease, Dr. Nusbaum has re-oriented his efforts to address health needs of the 21st century: emerging and zoonotic diseases, public health education development, and emergency preparedness. Dr. Nusbaum serves on the Public Health Committee of the Association of American Veterinary Medical Colleges, and is a distinguished practitioner of the National Academies of Practice, Veterinary Section, and a diplomate of the American College of Veterinary Microbiologists.

Linda M. Olson, EdD, completed her doctorate in education at the University of North Dakota in Grand Forks, North Dakota. She is an associate professor of family and community medicine and serves as the special projects director of the University of North Dakota School of Medicine and Health Sciences Office of Medical Education. Dr. Olson is currently the director of the Biochemical Organic Radiological Disaster Educational Response System (BORDERS®) Alert and Ready, an innovative education and training program designed to meet the individual and collective ability of all health care professionals to recognize, report, and respond to acts of terrorism, naturally occurring disasters, and/or other public health emergencies. BORDERS is a trademarked program sponsored by the University of North Dakota Research Foundation, Grand Forks, North Dakota.

Lynn A. Slepski, PhD, RN, CCNS, is a career officer in the U.S. Public Health Service. Since 1995, her duties have centered on emergency planning and operations at the national level, most recently functioning in policy positions within the Department of Homeland Security. She has a broad background in disaster response and weapons of mass destruction (WMD), and has been actively involved with pandemic planning at the national, state, and local levels. A graduate of the University of Texas Health Science Center in San Antonio, Captain Slepski earned a master of science degree in nursing from Norwich University. She is nationally certified as a clinical nurse specialist in community health and holds additional certifications as a trauma nurse and health promotion and education coordinator. She received her PhD in the nursing sciences program at the Uniformed Services University of the Health Sciences. Captain. Slepski is a frequently requested author and speaker in the areas of WMD, mass casualty disasters, emergency response and homeland security, the National Response Plan and, most recently, pandemic influenza.

James G.W. Wenzel, DVM, PhD, is a native of Kentucky. He holds the DVM from Auburn University, to which he returned to teach in its large animal clinic; a masters degree from Georgia, where he also completed a clinical residency; and a PhD from the University of Minnesota. He is a diplomate of the American College of Theriogenologists and of the American College of Veterinary Preventive Medicine, in which he also is a member of the specialty in epidemiology. In addition to his professorial duties, he works with branches of the departments of Agriculture and Homeland Security in the training of veterinarians and others for national preparedness, and provides expertise in food animal reproduction and herd health, experimental design and statistics, epidemiology and zoonotic diseases, and bioweapons and veterinary preparedness.

James C. Wright, DVM, PhD, is an associate professor in public health in the Department of Pathobiology and has been at Auburn University since 1985. He received a bachelor of science in biology from Virginia Tech in 1971 and a DVM from the University of Georgia in 1974. After graduating from Georgia, Dr. Wright was in private veterinary practice in Virginia for two years. He then entered graduate school at the University of Missouri in Columbia where he received a master of science and doctorate in microbiology. Dr. Wright joined the Department of Parasitology, Microbiology, and Public Health at Oklahoma State University where he taught veterinary public health and helped conduct vaccine trials for human rabies pre-exposure prophylaxis. At Auburn University, Dr. Wright has been involved in research on vector-borne disease and pre-harvest food safety. He teaches zoonoses and epidemiology in the professional curriculum and has taught electives in population medicine, disaster medicine, cage bird practice, and wildlife diseases. Dr. Wright was elected into the National Academies of Practice and is a diplomate of the American College of Veterinary Preventive Medicine.

Acknowledgments

We would all like to thank our families for taking the time to listen to our ideas and for pardoning us for our extended absences, idiosyncrasies, and preoccupation as we worked on researching and writing this book. We would also like to thank the men and women who proudly and humbly serve their communities as they attempt to prepare for a threat of unlimited potential. Our hope is that they will find this compilation useful as they face the threat of pandemic influenza.

Part I

Defining the Threat of Influenza

1 Past Pandemics and Their Outcome

Jeffrey R. Ryan, PhD

Disease is the retribution of outraged Nature.

Hosea Ballou

CONTENTS

1.1 DISEASE DYNAMICS

I hope the reader will forgive me for starting this chapter off by saying that infectious diseases have "plagued" mankind ever since the beginning of time. Infectious disease occurs whenever conditions are right for a viable pathogen to infect and affect a susceptible host. Infectious disease is the result of complex interactions between the biological agent, the host, and their environment. This is often viewed as a triad (Anderson, May, 1982). The components of the triad and interactions differ for each disease agent and possible host combination (see Figure 1.1A). Some diseases have a complex cycle of transmission and can be dependent upon specific circumstances or requirements of the pathogen and/or each affected animal (host and reservoir). With respect to domesticated animals, the triad is dramatically influenced by animal husbandry and management factors. Vector-borne diseases, like malaria and West Nile fever, are linked to other factors necessary for transmission of the pathogen through a blood-sucking arthropod. Consideration of the different components of this triad is

3

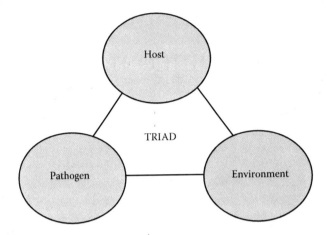

FIGURE 1.1A Disease triad depicting major factors related to infectious disease transmission.

important as an opportunity to reduce disease in the transmission cycle. A common mistake is to focus on only one aspect of the triad for disease control or prevention and to overlook the others.

The host introduces several determinants of disease. Intrinsically, there may be a genetic predisposition to disease. In addition, age and physiological state come into play. The host may not be susceptible to infection. Or, the host may obtain some innate immunity precluding or lessening infection. This resistance can be passive immunity (acquired antibodies), active immunity (previous infection or immunization), or innate resistance. Hosts may be able to support an infection, but may be unaffected by it. In this instance, there is no disease, just an asymptomatic infection. Transmission of most communicable infectious agents will not continue within an exposed group of susceptible hosts if the proportion of resistant hosts in that group is above a threshold level, typically 70 to 80 percent. This level depends upon the agent and factors influencing the likelihood of transmission, such as host density and the infectious dose of the agent. If the host density or the agent dose is significantly high, all individuals in a population may effectively be susceptible to infection even with adequate vaccination.

The etiological agent or pathogen also has some determinants of disease. The agent may not be viable enough to invade host tissues or evade host defenses. The agent may require the host to be in some state of trauma, metabolic state, have nutritional deficiencies, or hormonal imbalances. Naturally, the environment affects disease transmission as it has a dramatic effect on the host and the pathogen. Environmental factors should be considered whenever disease dynamics are being explored. Refer to Figure 1.1B for a listing of some of the possible factors: physical, biological, and socio-economic.

Holistically speaking, diseases have their own biology, often referred to as their "natural history." In 1939, Pavlovsky, a Soviet biologist, described an important concept for public health professionals that he referred to as the "doctrine of nidality." In this doctrine, Pavlovsky explained that each disease has its own "nidus," which

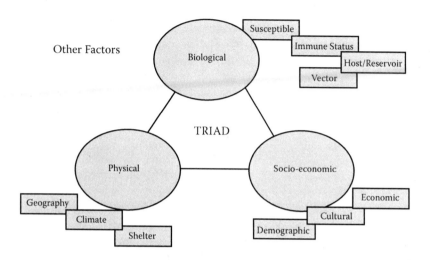

FIGURE 1.1B Other environmental factors that influence infectious disease transmission.

means it has its own nest, home, or habitat. "Nidus" comes from the Latin word meaning focus. The central concept of nidality is that a disease has its own natural habitat in the same way that a species does. Thus, the nidus of a disease "exists under definite conditions of climate, vegetation, soil, and favorable microclimate." Furthermore, pathogens, vectors, and reservoirs are associated in a "biocenose" that is characteristic for a definite geographic landscape. Man acquires a natural–nidal disease of animals (zoonosis) when he occupies or penetrates the particular ecological focus (biocenose) of that infectious agent (Pavlovsky, 1939, with translation, 1966). Typical examples are plague, tularemia, leptospirosis, arboviruses, tickborne relapsing fever, and so on.

Human and animal populations throughout history have been afflicted by major outbreaks of infectious disease that swept through the "known" world mostly in the wake of conquering armies or following trade routes (Anderson, May, 1982). The plague in the 14th century decimated the population of Europe and Asia, with a third of the population from southern to northern Europe dead within four years of introduction of the disease. The Spaniards in their conquest of the very powerful nations of Central America were aided by the smallpox virus that was introduced in naïve populations by Spanish troops and decimated the opposing leadership and armies (Mims et al., 1995). The first veterinary schools in Europe were founded in the 18th century primarily to study and control recurring epidemics of rinderpest (Schwabe, 1985).

In 1969, U.S. Surgeon General William H. Stewart stated that "it's time to close the book on infectious diseases, declare the war against pestilence won, and shift national resources to such chronic problems as cancer and heart disease." But the biological threat and the power of natural selection had been underestimated. The sober reality is that pathogens have shown a propensity to adapt to every antibiotic that researchers develop. With the surge in global travel, these diseases can be spread as quickly as they are identified. The commonly held belief that the war on infectious diseases could be won has been shattered by a score of new or re-emerging diseases that have surfaced in epidemics scattered across the globe over the last 25 years, with some occurring within just the last few years (e.g., SARS, Nipah virus).

Emerging diseases today, as in the Middle Ages and beyond, are cause for popular alert and concern, as shown by the fears generated by bovine spongiform encephalitis and acquired immune deficiency syndrome (AIDS). Highly infectious and lethal diseases now may appear to be controllable, and emerging infectious diseases today have to be considered in the context of decreasing infectious disease-induced mortality during most of the 20th century and the recent increased recognition of novel diseases in human and animal populations, partly due to improved diagnostic capabilities. Emerging diseases can be attributed to either true emergence (i.e., a newly appearing disease agent that had not been present), increased recognition (i.e., a disease agent was present in a population, but has only recently been recognized due to improved diagnostic tests/capabilities), and/or increased incidence of previously recognized disease (because of greater human and animal traffic, greater population densities, increased susceptibility of the host population). Those factors responsible for disease emergence can often be recognized, although intervention altering any of these factors may prove to be difficult, even impossible. For example, recognition of emergence of new influenza strains in Asia will not lead to travel reduction or limitation.

Common diseases that occur at a constant but relatively high rate in the population are said to be endemic. An endemic infection has a natural distribution in a population. For example, plague is endemic in the Four Corners region of the United States, and malaria is endemic in parts of Africa.

An epidemic is an outbreak of a disease that appears as new cases in a human population during a given period at a rate substantially exceeding what is expected, but it is usually limited in its geographic distribution. For example, HIV is said to be epidemic in Haiti and southeastern Africa.

A pandemic is an epidemic that spreads across a large region or even worldwide. Pandemics end when all or most of the population has been exposed to the disease and have either contracted the disease, died from it, or developed a subclinical infection that rendered them immune. The word "pandemic" comes from the Greek *pan* for all and *demos* for people; therefore, literally translated, pandemic means all-people.

It is not the intent of the author for this chapter to give the reader a complete etiology and epidemiology of the various diseases that have afflicted mankind over the ages. Rather, treatment of the subject will highlight a few specific diseases that have been the cause of the most serious global outbreaks and to demonstrate the devastating nature of pandemics and how they have been quelled through advances in sanitation, public health, and medicine. As such, I have selected some of the most insidious scourges that have haunted mankind in recent history: bubonic plague (the Black Death), cholera, AIDS, and influenza.

1.2 THE BLACK DEATH

Plague is a zoonotic disease caused by the bacteria *Yersinia pestis*. Plague has been the cause of three great pandemics of human disease in the 6th, 14th, and 20th centuries (McGovern, Friedlander, 1998). This naturally occurring disease (sylvatic plague) can be transmitted from rodents to humans through the bite of an infected flea (Gage, 1998). Bubonic plague is characterized by an abrupt onset of high fever, painful localized swollen lymph nodes (referred to as buboes), and sepsis due to bacteremia. Septicemic plague often follows untreated bubonic plague. Patients with the bubonic form of the disease may develop secondary pneumonic plague. This complication leads to human-to-human spread by the respiratory route and is the cause of primary pneumonic plague, the most severe and frequently fatal form of the disease (McGovern, Friedlander, 1998).

1.2.1 THE FIRST PANDEMIC

One of the earliest recorded great pandemics, the Plague of Justinian, occurred in the eastern Mediterranean region of the world in 541 AD, during the reign of Emperor Justinian I of Byzantium (Bayliss, 1980). Its origin is not certain, likely Egypt or Ethiopia (or perhaps the steppes of Central Asia), but wherever the disease came from, it followed trade routes and military movements, thus successfully spreading throughout the Empire (Slack, 1989). From historical descriptions, as much as 40 percent of the population of Constantinople (now Istanbul, Turkey) died from the plague. According to Justinian's court historian Procopius, the outbreak struck in the spring of 542 and raged for four months. Procopius wrote that at the height of the outbreak, plague killed up to 10,000 a day in Constantinople alone. No one knows for sure if this account is accurate. However, the overall death toll in the eastern Mediterranean region and the effect on the Roman Army probably put an end to Justinian's hopes to re-establish the Roman Empire to its former glory. Ultimately the Plague of Justinian caused the deaths of 25 percent of the population of the eastern Mediterranean and was responsible for the fall of the Byzantine Empire (Mee, 1990). As many as 100 million Europeans died during this epidemic (Mee, 1990). Repeated, smaller epidemics followed this plague (McEvedy, 1988).

1.2.2 THE SECOND PANDEMIC (THE BLACK DEATH)

In the 14th century, bubonic plague swept throughout Western Europe. In 1346, this pandemic is thought to have originated in China and was brought by the Mongols to the Crimean port of Caffa (now Feodosiya, Ukraine) on the Black Sea, where the Genoese maintained a trading center. The plague spread into Western Europe both along the northern trade route across the steppes and the southern trade route into the Mediterranean. By 1348, plague had already entered Britain at Weymouth (Bayliss, 1980).

Physicians during the 14th century could not provide plague sufferers with an effective treatment. Neither did they understand the epidemiology of plague (McGovern, Friedlander, 1998). At the University of Paris, physicians postulated that a triangulation of the planets Jupiter, Mars, and Saturn, which occurred on

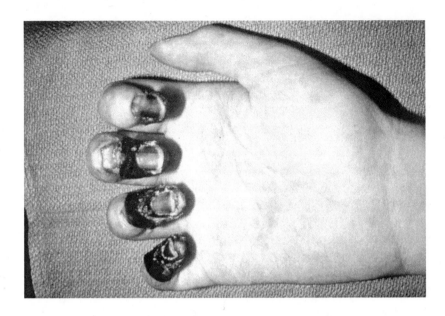

FIGURE 1.2 Right hand of a plague patient displaying acral gangrene. Gangrene is one of the manifestations of plague, and is the origin of the term "Black Death" given to plague throughout the ages. Image courtesy of the Department of Health and Human Services, Centers for Disease Control and Prevention, Public Health Image Library (No. 1957).

March 20 (1345), led to a corruption of the surrounding atmosphere and that this event gave rise to the outbreak (Mee, 1990). This same group of physicians recommended that people consume a simple diet, avoid excessive sleep, get regular enemas, and abstain from sex. Naturally, none of these recommendations had an effect on the incidence of plague.

Some believe that this pandemic got its name, the Black Death, from the septic sequelae of the disease. This was a striking late-stage sign of the disease, in which the sufferer's skin would blacken due to sub-epidermal hemorrhages (purpura) and the extremities would darken with gangrene (acral necrosis). A clinical consequence of septicemic plague is a condition known as disseminated intravascular coagulation (DIC), where blood coagulates in the extremities, causing a gangrene-like appearance noticeable in the feet, hands, and head (see Figure 1.2). Internal bleeding and organ failure ensue; victims would often vomit a black, bloody material just before death. However, according to recent research the term "Black Death" was actually introduced in 1833 (Bennett, Hollister, 2006) and refers to the sense of dread (blackness) and extreme doom brought on by the disease striking a community (Barry, Gualde, 2006).

Regardless of how it got its name, the Black Death took the lives of about 25 million people between the years 1347–1352, which represents about 30 percent of the population of Europe at that time (Mee, 1990). In addition, the Black Death claimed approximately 20 million more people by the end of the 14th century (Mee, 1990). In port cities like Venice, as much as 75 percent of the total population perished.

The plague would penetrate an area, last for about a year, kill about one-third of the population, and move on. While some people killed cats and dogs, thinking them to be carriers of disease, no one ever thought to kill the rats (Mee, 1990). Christians blamed the disease on Muslims, Muslims on Christians, and both Christians and Muslims blamed Jews or witches (McEvedy, 1988). Others blamed themselves and started groups like the excessively penitent Brotherhood of Flagellants, who wandered about whipping themselves (Slack, 1989).

So many people died over such a short period — peasant and noble alike — that workers (serfs) who survived were now able to sell their skills and labors. No longer were serfs tied to the land of the nobility, a third of whom were now dead. The Black Plague created new attitudes toward life and death, changes in religious practice, and economic changes resulting from a loss of laborers. In art, the *Danse Macabre* (Dance of Death) became a popular image. Additionally, literature in national languages (instead of Latin) became the mode of expression. Ultimately, the Black Death led to the demise of the feudal system. It took 400 years for the population of Europe to recover economically and demographically from the Black Death (Cantor, 2002).

1.2.3 THE THIRD PANDEMIC

The third, or modern, plague pandemic began in 1894 in China and spread throughout the world via modern transportation (McGovern, Friedlander, 1998). It was also in 1894 that Yersin applied the germ theory to plague and discovered that *Yersinia pestis* satisfied Koch's postulates for bubonic plague (Butler, 1983). The modern pandemic arrived in Bombay in 1898, and during the next 50 years, more than 13 million Indians died of plague (Cavanaugh, 1974). The disease officially arrived in the United States in March 1900, when the body of a Chinese laborer was discovered in a hotel basement in San Francisco (Risse, 1992); the disease appeared in New York City and Washington state the same year (Caten and Kartman, 1968). New Orleans was infected in 1924 and 1926. Rodents throughout the western United States were probably infected from the San Francisco focus, leading to more infected rodents in the western United States than existed in Europe at the time of the Black Death (Cavanaugh et al., 1982). Therefore, human plague in the United States was initially a result of urban rat epizootics until 1925. After general rat control and hygiene measures were instituted in various port cities, urban plague vanished — only to spread into rural areas, where virtually all cases in the United States have been acquired since 1925 (McGovern, Friedlander, 1998).

1.3 CHOLERA

Cholera is a serious clinical disease and epidemiological syndrome caused by *Vibrio cholerae*, a bacterium (see Figure 1.3). In its severe form, *cholera gravis* is characterized by the passage of high volumes of watery stools (termed "rice water"). The disease causes constant vomiting and purging of the bowels — often as much as several pints in a few minutes. Such dehydration causes violent cramping. The victim's body shrivels so much from the dehydration that he or she is said to appear like a monkey. The victim's blood becomes thick, hampering blood flow, which results in

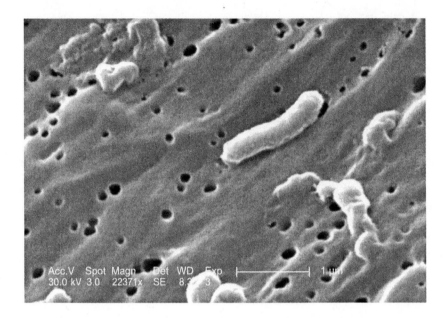

FIGURE 1.3 This scanning electron micrograph (SEM) depicted a number of Vibrio cholerae bacteria of the serogroup 01; magnified 22371×. Cholera can be simply and successfully treated by immediate replacement of the fluid and salts lost through diarrhea. Patients can be treated with an oral rehydration solution, a prepackaged mixture of sugar and salts to be mixed with water and drunk in large amounts. This solution is used throughout the world to treat diarrhea. Severe cases also require intravenous fluid replacement. With prompt rehydration, fewer than 1 percent of cholera patients die. Image courtesy of the Department of Health and Human Services, Centers for Disease Control and Prevention, Public Health Image Library (No. 7818).

the extremities turning black or blue. This massive and rapid purging also leads to extreme dehydration, hypovolemic shock, and acidosis. Death can ensue if prompt and appropriate treatment is not initiated soon after the diarrhea begins. Without treatment cholera kills around 40 to 60 percent of those afflicted (Wilson, 1984).

Infection from *V. cholerae* is spread via the fecal–oral route. Normally, this is facilitated through the consumption of contaminated water where the excreta of infected persons enter the water distribution system. However, *V. cholerae* is easily destroyed by chlorination, heat, or caustic solvents. Perhaps the most distinctive and salient features of cholera as a communicable disease are its epidemiologic behavior by which it tends to occur in explosive outbreaks (often with several simultaneous foci of onset) and its ability to cause true pandemics extensive in place and time (Glass et al., 1982). The occurrence of cholera and its epidemiologic behavior prior to the 19th century are subjects of contentious debate among medical historians, as reviewed by Pollitzer (1959).

1.3.1 Cholera Pandemics

It is generally accepted that seven distinct pandemics of cholera have occurred since the first pandemic was recognized (1817–1823) in the early 19th century (see Table 1.1).

TABLE 1.1
Dates of Occurrence of the Various Pandemics of Cholera

1817–1823
1829–1851
1852–1859
1863–1879
1881–1896
1899–1923
1961–present
1992–present

Source: Kaper J, Morris J, Levine M. 1995. Cholera. *Clin Micro Rev* 8:48–86.

In each instance except one, cholera spread from Asia to reach other continents in pandemics that affected many countries and extended over many years. Medical historians believe that the first six pandemics got their origin from the Ganges delta in Bengal in India (Kaper, Morris, Levine, 1995). This phenomena gave rise to the term "Asiatic cholera." The one exception is the seventh pandemic, which originated from Sulawesi, Indonesia (Wilson, 1984).

Water-borne cholera had been confined to India for at least 2,000 years before appearing in England in 1831. In London, the disease claimed 6,536 victims; in Paris, 20,000 succumbed (out of a population of 650,000) with about 100,000 deaths in all of France. The second pandemic was the first to reach the New World, arriving in Quebec via ships from Ireland carrying immigrants who sustained cases of cholera during the Atlantic crossing (Chambers, 1938a). Spreading from Montreal in June, cholera moved south unchecked over the next 10 weeks to reach, successively, New York, Philadelphia, Baltimore, and Washington, D.C. (Chambers, 1938b). The second cholera pandemic killed 500,000 in New York City (Garrett, 1994). In 1849, there was a second major outbreak in Europe. In London, it was the worst outbreak in the city's history, claiming 14,137 lives, 10 times as many as the 1832 outbreak. Cholera spread throughout the Mississippi River system, killing thousands in St. Louis and New Orleans. It also spread along the California and Oregon trail affecting hundreds as they made their way to the California Gold Rush (Rosenberg, 1987).

The third cholera pandemic (1852–1859) mainly affected Russia, with over a million deaths. However, London experienced an outbreak from 1853 to 1854, where the death toll reached 10,738. John Snow studied the epidemiology of cholera in London during the second and third pandemics. Here, he made key observations that enabled him to deduce that cholera must represent a contagion due to waterborne transmission (Snow, 1855). Koch managed to isolate the etiologic agent from the rice water stools of cholera case patients during the fifth pandemic. Koch referred to them as "comma bacilli" because of their shape; he isolated the same bacteria from cholera patients in India (Koch, 1884). The fifth pandemic affected much of South America, causing large epidemics accompanied by high mortality in Argentina, Chile, and Peru (Laval, 1989). Notably, this represents the last time cholera would affect South America for more than a century (Kaper, Morris, Levine, 1995).

The sixth cholera pandemic (1899–1923) mostly involved populations in the Near and Middle East and the Balkan Peninsula (Pollitzer, 1959). Cholera remained virtually confined to South and Southeast Asia from the mid-1920s until the onset of the seventh pandemic in 1961. The seventh pandemic of cholera, which began in 1961, is notable for several reasons (Kaper, Morris, Levine, 1995). First, this pandemic is the most extensive in geographic spread and in time. Second, all previous pandemics originated from the Indian subcontinent (Pollitzer, 1959), whereas the seventh pandemic originated from the island of Sulawesi, in the Indonesian archipelago. Third, the causative agent of this pandemic involves a new biotype of *V. cholerae* known as El Tor.

Despite what seems like a recount of history, cholera is not a thing of the past. In 1991, a cholera epidemic began in Peru and spread to several South American countries, and, in 1994, an outbreak of dysentery and cholera in Rwandan refugee camps in the Democratic Republic of Congo killed an estimated 25,000 people. Despite advances in medical treatment of case patients and water disinfection systems, cholera continues to cause outbreaks in various countries where basic sanitation and hygiene are still lacking. According to the World Health Organization (WHO), in 2005 there was a sharp increase in the number of cholera cases reported: 131,943 cases, 2,272 deaths, from 52 countries (WHO/WER, 2006). Overall, this represented a 30 percent increase compared with the number of cases reported in 2004. The year was marked by a particularly significant series of outbreaks in West Africa, from 14 countries, accounting for 58 percent of cholera cases reported worldwide. Furthermore, there were a number of countries in the 2005 report where cholera re-emerged after having been absent for several years.

1.4 ACQUIRED IMMUNE DEFICIENCY SYNDROME (AIDS)

Acquired immune deficiency syndrome (AIDS) is a collection of signs and symptoms (a syndrome) resulting from a viral infection that causes specific damage to the immune system. This sexually transmitted disease was first recognized as a medical problem in some homosexual men in California in 1981. The etiologic agent of AIDS is an RNA virus known as the human immunodeficiency virus (HIV-1), which is a retrovirus (see Figure 1.4). A variant of that original isolate, HIV-2, causes a similar illness, but is less aggressive and restricted mainly to West Africa. HIV can be transmitted through blood, bodily fluids, sexual contact, or breast milk. About four to six weeks after infection, the individual starts to develop antibodies to HIV. Most infected individuals seroconvert by three months and are HIV antibody positive; rarely, this takes up to six months.

Continuous high-level HIV replication within the infected host leads to virus-mediated and immune-mediated destruction of a key immune cell, the CD4 lymphocyte. Two decades of study of the AIDS pandemic have provided a wealth of information about the natural history of HIV, leading to the development of highly active antiretroviral therapy (HAART), which has radically improved the prognosis.

1.4.1 EPIDEMIOLOGY

Currently, HIV affects 33 million individuals worldwide. In 2004, the WHO estimated that there were nearly 5 million new cases and 3 million deaths. Sub-Saharan Africa has the greatest burden of disease, with an estimated 26 million infected

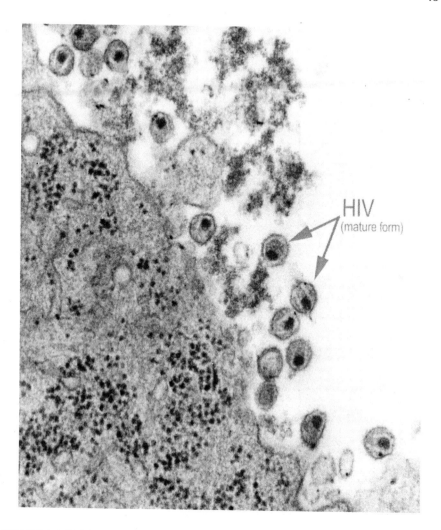

FIGURE 1.4 This highly magnified transmission electron micrographic (TEM) image revealed the presence of mature forms of the human immunodeficiency virus (HIV) in a tissue sample under investigation. The human immunodeficiency virus (HIV), a retrovirus, was identified in 1983 as the etiologic agent for the acquired immunodeficiency syndrome (AIDS). AIDS is characterized by changes in the population of T-cell lymphocytes that play a key role in the immune defense system. In the infected individual, the virus causes a depletion of a subpopulation of T-cells, called T-helper cells, which leaves these patients susceptible to opportunistic infections, as well as certain malignancies. Image courtesy of the Department of Health and Human Services, Centers for Disease Control and Prevention, Public Health Image Library (No. 8254).

individuals. In many southern African countries, 25 to 40 percent of adults are infected; the prevalence is 5 to 15 percent in most other sub-Saharan countries. South Africa now accounts for one-third of deaths worldwide. Originally considered to be a disease of homosexual men, the major route of transmission today (>75 percent) is heterosexual transmission. Approximately 10 percent of new HIV infections

TABLE 1.2
The Latest Statistics on the Incidence of AIDS and HIV in 2007

	Estimate (in millions)	Range (in millions)
People living with HIV/AIDS	33.2	30.6–36.1
Adults living with HIV/AIDS	30.8	28.2–33.6
Women living with HIV/AIDS	15.4	13.9–16.6
Children living with HIV/AIDS	2.5	2.2–2.6
People newly infected with HIV	2.5	1.8–4.1
Adults newly infected with HIV	2.1	1.4–3.6
Children newly infected with HIV	0.42	0.35–0.54
AIDS deaths	2.1	1.9–2.4
Adult AIDS deaths	1.7	1.6–2.1
Child AIDS deaths in 2007	0.33	0.31–0.38

Source: AVERT, 2007 (http://www.avert.org/worldstats.htm).

are in children. More than 90 percent of these children are infected *in utero* or during breastfeeding. Most of these cases occur in Africa, the Caribbean, or Southeast Asia. The incidence in IV drug users varies widely between countries. It is relatively low in the U.K. (<1 percent), but may be up to 50 percent in other areas (e.g., China, Eastern Europe, northeastern India, Vietnam) (see Table 1.2).

Some Other Astounding Numbers about HIV/AIDS

- Since 1981, more than 25 million people have died of AIDS.
- Africa has 12 million AIDS orphans.
- At the end of 2006, women accounted for 50 percent of all adults living with HIV worldwide, and for 61 percent in sub-Saharan Africa.
- People under the age of 25 account for half of all new HIV infections worldwide.
- In developing and transitional countries, more than 7 million people are in immediate need of life-saving AIDS drugs; of these, only about 2 million are receiving the drugs.
- Up to half the people who are living with HIV actually die of tuberculosis (TB), yet it is a preventable, curable disease.
- The number of people living with HIV has risen from around 8 million in 1990 to more than 33 million today, and is still growing. Around 69 percent of people living with HIV are in sub-Saharan Africa.

(UNAIDS. Joint United Nations Programme of HIV/AIDS (2007) http://www.unaids.org/en/.)

A diagnosis of AIDS was a death sentence. However, now with the advent of HAART, HIV-infected individuals can anticipate a normal or near-normal life expectancy. This is particularly likely when the diagnosis is made before serious AIDS-related complications occur (Lewthwaite, Wilkins, 2005). The prognosis is also good in those presenting later, and is improving as knowledge of the disease increases and drug therapies improve. In 10 to 15 percent of cases, however, drug-resistant HIV is transmitted and occasional strains are resistant to all three major classes of antiretroviral drugs. In many cases, resistant virus has a lower replication capacity than wild-type virus, but certain factors can reverse this trait (Lewthwaite, Wilkins, 2005).

The origin of the AIDS virus is unknown. There are a number of plausible theories, imaginative speculations, and some wild ideas ranging from ethnic conspiracy to contaminated polio vaccine. The origin of HIV may never be known. What we do know from this pandemic is that emerging diseases, like AIDS, can come without warning, incubating slowly and insidiously in some facet of human civilization before their full potential is realized. AIDS research has provoked scientists to learn more about the human immune system in 20 years than was gained in the 100 years prior. Despite billions of dollars applied to researching a cure for AIDS, we are still faced with the problem. The development of a good vaccine remains elusive. Like the next disease covered in this chapter, it too involves a highly adaptive pathogen.

1.5 INFLUENZA PANDEMICS

Influenza viruses are among the most common causes of human respiratory infections and among the most significant because they cause high morbidity and mortality. Influenza outbreaks have apparently occurred since at least the Middle Ages, if not since ancient times. Since 1932, when the influenza virus was first isolated in the laboratory, the history of this infection can be recorded and confirmed by laboratory diagnosis. In the two centuries before that time, infections can be identified by the known signs and symptoms of disease and the explosive nature of outbreaks (Patterson, 1985). Influenza presents as a sudden onset of three-day fever, with muscle pain and a degree of prostration out of all proportion with the severity of other symptoms. Secondly, epidemics usually occur suddenly without warning, infecting a large percentage of people, and disappear after a few weeks or months; these epidemics are commonly heralded by an increase in hospital admissions of elderly patients with pneumonia, and an excess of deaths, mainly in the elderly and those suffering from chronic heart and lung disease (Patterson, 1985). From these observations, outbreaks can be identified in the historical record without difficulty, although this identification becomes less secure as one goes back further in time; and reference to influenza can be found in both scientific and lay publications since 1650. More dramatically, pandemics of influenza occur: these appear suddenly in a specific geographical area, spread throughout the world infecting millions, and cause a large numbers of deaths. Evidence of pandemics is also present in the historical record which include 10 probable and three possible pandemics since 1590 AD (Potter, 1998); and allusion to earlier possible pandemics is suggested throughout history (Potter, 2001).

Influenza is an ancient microbe that has appeared in millions of different forms over the millennia, periodically producing devastating epidemics. Among the most famous [is] the Spanish flu or the influenza pandemic of 1918 to 1919, which killed an estimated 20 to 40 million people worldwide — that's more deaths than in World War I (1914 to 1918). (Beveridge, W. The chronicle of influenza epidemics. *History and Philosophy of Life Sciences* 13: 223–235.)

Two conditions must be satisfied for an outbreak of influenza to be classed as a pandemic. First, the outbreak of infection, arising in a specific geographical area, spreads throughout the world; a high percentage of individuals are infected resulting in increased mortality rates. Second, a pandemic is caused by a new influenza virus A subtype, the HA of which is not related to that of influenza viruses circulating immediately before the outbreak, and could not have arisen from those viruses by mutation (Webster, Laver, 1972).

Since 1700, there have been approximately a dozen influenza A virus pandemics (Morens, Fauci, 2007). In the past 120 years there were pandemics in 1889, 1918, 1957, and 1968. The 1957 pandemic caused 66,000 excess deaths in the United States. In 1918, the worst pandemic in recorded history caused approximately 646,000 excess deaths (675,000 total deaths) in the United States and killed up to 50 million people worldwide.

Medical historians believe that the first influenza pandemic occurred in 1510; originating out of Africa and spreading across Europe (Beveridge, 1977). One account suggests that many Spanish cities were "dispopulated" (Garrett, 1994). Four major influenza epidemics were recorded between 1830 and 1848. The 1830–1831 epidemic may have originated in China; then and in 1833 influenza advanced westward out of Russia into Europe. In 1836–1837, influenza diffusion was largely north to south, and in 1847–1848 the disease swept through the Mediterranean to southern France and thence elsewhere in Western Europe (Patterson, 1987). Each of the four epidemics spread rapidly and caused very high morbidity rates. Although case-mortality rates were always low, each epidemic killed thousands of people, with most deaths being among the elderly. Many previous writers have described all four outbreaks as pandemics, but true pandemics, presumably caused by major new viral types, are clearly identifiable only in 1830–1831 and 1833. The status of the 1836–1837 outbreak is unclear, but there was no pandemic in 1847–1848 (Patterson, 1985).

The Asiatic flu of 1889–1890 was first reported in Bukhara, Russia. It was the first named flu pandemic, apparently getting its name due to the believed origin as being Asia. Actually, disease transmission along the silk routes was a common occurrence and belief. Trade activity out of Asia and into Europe, Africa, and the Americas accounts for much of the international spread of epidemics. This is true for scenarios centuries ago and still holds true to this day. By October 1889, the Asiatic flu had reached the Caucasus. It rapidly spread west and hit North America in December 1889, South America in February–April 1890, India in February–March 1890, and Australia in March–April 1890. The strain that was the cause of the Asiatic flu is unknown; however, the virus had a very high attack and mortality rate (Figure 1.5).

L'ÉPIDÉMIE D'INFLUENZA. — Vue intérieure de la tente-hôpital.

FIGURE 1.5 In 1890, an influenza pandemic swept the globe, killing many in its wake. [Credit: National Library of Medicine].

Among factors said by prominent American physicians to be responsible for influenza in 1918 were nakedness, fish contaminated by Germans, dirt, dust, unclean pajamas, Chinese people, open windows, closed windows, old books, and "some cosmic influence." (Garrett, L. *The Coming Plague: Newly Emerging Diseases in a World Out of Balance*. New York: Farrar Straus Giroux, 1994.)

For those readers seeking more information about the dynamics of influenza pandemics prior to 1900, K. David Patterson wrote an excellent book entitled *Pandemic Influenza, 1700–1900; A Study in Historical Epidemiology* (1987). Dr. Patterson conducted years of research examining the historical records from many European countries to look at trends in disease mortality across the globe. His account of those pandemic events is probably the best we have to draw on. What does become clear when one examines the periodicity of these pandemics is that modern man seems to experience a severe pandemic due to influenza about once every 50 to 60 years. Some would consider that once per generation. Generations are typically shorter in duration than once every 50 years. So, what is it about 50 years that we can surmise is happening here? Well, one would have to admit that the world population will be very different in composition 50 years from now. Many of you reading this book will not be alive 50 years from now. The world population — or herd — will have a different immunological makeup or experience than the world population of today.

The same could be said centuries ago. That said, what factors are important, or what seems to set the stage for a pandemic event?

1.6 FACTORS CONTRIBUTING TO A PANDEMIC

History is the source of most of our information on the great pandemics. It is clear that these outbreaks have caused major upheavals in civilization over the centuries. As human populations grew and people encroached further and further into areas that were primarily animal habitats, man was exposed to more and more diseases carried by animals. Humans became susceptible to some of the pathogens animals harbor; these common diseases are considered zoonoses. Zoonotic diseases are those illnesses caused by an infectious agent that can be transmitted between, or shared by, animals and humans. Anthrax, plague, Lyme disease, Rocky Mountain spotted fever, Q fever, tularemia, brucellosis, and influenza are all zoonoses.

With the emergence of a new strain of an infectious agent to which a population's immune system is unfamiliar, conditions may be favorable for the development of a pandemic. This is particularly common with viruses, which undergo rapid and frequent mutations. Through the process of reassortment, or antigenic shift, two different strains of virus may combine to form a new subtype having a mixture of the surface antigens of the two original strains. If the new subtype is sufficiently different immunologically from previous exposures, the immune system of the population may not recognize it, and a pandemic may ensue.

Additional factors to be considered in whether or not a pandemic may occur in a particular circumstance include the following:

- The pathogenicity (the ability of a parasite to inflict damage on the host) of the organism in animals and humans
- The occurrence in domesticated animals and livestock or only in wildlife
- Whether the organism is constantly present (endemic) in an animal population (enzootic) or causing a current outbreak (epidemic) in an animal population (epizootic)
- Whether it is geographically localized or widespread

Other factors include the rate of transmission and the severity of illness. Some diseases, such as Ebola, are so virulent that most of its victims die before they have a chance to spread the disease. In summary, a pandemic occurs when three conditions have been met — a new pathogen or subtype emerges; it infects humans causing serious illness; and it spreads easily and is sustainable among humans.

1.7 CONCLUSION

Plague is a disease of antiquity that is not likely to disappear. Plague's continued but limited outbreaks in many parts of the world attest to its tenacious presence. Since early descriptions, many studies have examined the transmission, epidemiology, and pathogenesis of the disease (Gage, 1998). Plague cycles naturally in a sylvatic cycle, circulating between small mammals and fleas. It may jump from a sylvatic cycle to an urban cycle whereby rodents that dwell in a periurban setting become infected through the bite of an infected flea and then infect and shed other fleas that will come into contact with humans. Once in a human population, plague may be spread through the lungs. Pneumonic plague is highly infectious from one person to another. Plague, as a disease, is deceptive. It goes through quiescent periods lasting for years, during which few or no human cases are detected, leading public health officials to mistakenly declare eradication of the disease. However, plague may suddenly reappear, as it has in India and parts of Africa. The combination of false assurance of its eradication and the failure of public health vigilance sets the stage for the panic that may ensue when enzootic plague spills over from its natural cycle into the peridomestic and commensal rodent populations, bringing plague into closer human contact (Gage, 1998). Poor sanitation, overcrowding, and high numbers of rodents are conditions that enhance urban plague transmission. Thus, outbreaks of plague are indicative of social, environmental, and political changes in the modern world. Due to advances in basic sanitation and home construction, it is unlikely that plague will be the cause of another pandemic.

Cholera rose out of Asia and sparked seven pandemics. One of them continues to rage today. The disease is preventable and easily treated. Despite advancements in basic sanitation and water treatment, cholera kills people by the tens of thousands each year. However, these advancements are not economical or sustainable for all societies. Therefore, it continues to affect the poorest of the poor.

Twenty five years ago, HIV/AIDS threatened adults with homosexual or bisexual tendencies; it now threatens all people. The epidemiology of AIDS has evolved. In addition, the HIV pathogen has shown that it too can adapt to selective pressures placed upon it by medicine. This slow-burning pandemic is unlike any other mankind has faced. The final chapter in the AIDS pandemic story has yet to be written.

In the last years of the 19th century and the early years of the 20th, a series of important scientific discoveries spawned a revolution in biology and medicine and led pioneers such as Hermann Biggs, a New York City doctor, to create entire legal and health systems based on the identification and control of germs. By 1917, the United States and much of Europe had become enthralled by the hygiene movement (Garrett, 1994). Impressive new public health infrastructures had been built in many cities, tens of thousands of tuberculosis victims were isolated in sanatoriums, the incidences of child-killing diseases such as diphtheria and typhoid fever had plummeted, and cholera epidemics had become rare events in the industrialized world. There was great optimism that modern science held the key to perfect health.

Influenza's arrival shattered the hope; scientists still had virtually no understanding of viruses generally, and of influenza in particular. The hygienic precautions and quarantines that had proved so effective in holding back the tide of bacterial diseases in the United States proved useless, even harmful, in the face of the Spanish flu. As the epidemic spread, top physicians and scientists claimed its cause was everything from tiny plants to old dusty books to something called "cosmic influence." It was not until 1933 that a British research team finally isolated and identified the influenza virus. No disease outbreak, however, has had the effect of the greatest pandemic in the history of the human race, the Spanish flu pandemic of 1918.

REFERENCES

Anderson R, May R. 1982. *Population Biology of Infectious Diseases.* Springer-Verlag.

AVERT. 2007. http://www.avert.org/worldstats.htm.

Barry S, Gualde N. 2006. La plus grande épidémie de l'histoire. *L'Histoire* 310:38–60.

Bayliss JH. 1980. The extinction of bubonic plague in Britain. *Endeavour* 4(2):58–66.

Bennett J, Hollister C. 2006. *Medieval Europe: A Short History.* New York: McGraw-Hill.

Beveridge W. 1977. *Influenza: The Last Great Plague: An Unfinished Story of Discovery.* New York: Prodist.

Beveridge W. 1991. The chronicle of influenza epidemics. *History and Philosophy of Life Sciences* 13:223–235.

Butler T. 1983. *Plague and Other* Yersinia *Infections.* New York: Plenum Press.

Cantor N. 2002. *In the Wake of the Plague: The Black Death and the World It Made.* New York: Harper Perennial.

Carten, J. and L. Kartman, 1968. Human plague in the United States. *JAMA* 205: 333–336.

Cavanaugh D. 1974. K.F. Meyer's work on plague. *J Infect Dis* 129(supplement):S10–S12.

Cavanaugh D, Cadigan F, Williams J, Marshall J. 1982. Plague. In: *General Medicine and Infectious Diseases,* Vol. 2: *Internal Medicine in Vietnam,* chapter 8. Ognibene AJ, Barrett O, Eds. Washington, D.C.: Office of the Surgeon General and Center of Military History.

Chambers JS. 1938a. Cholera's first invasion of the New World. In: *The Conquest of Cholera,* pp. 24–44. New York: Macmillan.

Chambers JS. 1938b. Pestilence of 1832 along the Atlantic seaboard. In: *The Conquest of Cholera,* pp. 45–84. New York: Macmillan.

Ewald, P. 1996. *Evolution of Infectious Disease.* Oxford University Press.

Gage KL. 1998. Plague. In: *Topley and Wilson's Microbiology and Microbiological Infections,* Vol. 3, pp. 885–903. Colliers L, Balows A, Sussman M, Hausles, WJ, Eds. London: Edward Arnold Press.

Garrett, L. 1994. *The Coming Plague: Newly Emerging Diseases in a World Out of Balance.* New York: Farrar, Straus, Giroux.

Glass RI, Becker S, Huq MI, Stoll BJ, Khan MU, Merson MH, Lee JV, Black RE. 1982. Endemic cholera in rural Bangladesh, 1966–1980. *Am J Epidemiol* 116:959–970.

Kamal AM. 1974. The seventh pandemic of cholera. In: *Cholera,* pp. 1–14. Barua D, Burrows W, Eds. Philadelphia: WB Saunders.

Kaper J, Morris J, Levine M. 1995. Cholera. *Clin Micro Rev* 8:48–86.

Koch R. 1884. An address on cholera and its bacillus. *BMJ* 403–407.

Laval E. 1989. El cólera en Chile (1886–1888). *Rev Chil Infect* 6:96–99.

Lewthwaite P, Wilkins E. 2005. Natural history of HIV/AIDS. *Medicine* 33:10–13.

McEvedy C. 1988. The bubonic plague. *Sci Am* Feb:118–123.

McGovern T, Friedlander A. 1998. Plague. In: *Medical Aspects of Chemical and Biological Warfare. A Textbook in Military Medicine,* chapter 23. Sidell FR, Takafugi ET, Franz DR, Eds. Washington, D.C.: Office of the Surgeon General, Borden Institute, Walter Reed Army Institute of Research.

Mee C. 1990. How a mysterious disease laid low Europe's masses. *Smithsonian* 20(Feb): 66–79.

Mims C, Dimmock N, Nash A, Stephen J. 1995. *Mims' Pathogenesis of Infectious Disease,* 4th ed. New York: Academic Press.

Morens DM, Fauci AS. 2007. The 1918 influenza pandemic: insights for the 21st century. *J Infect Dis* 195:1018–1028.

Patterson K. 1985. Pandemic and epidemic influenza, 1830–1848. *Soc Sci Med* 21(5): 571–580.

Patterson K. 1987. *Pandemic Influenza, 1700–1900; A Study in Historical Epidemiology.* New Jersey: Rowman & Littlefield.

Pavlovsky E. 1939. Natural nidality of transmissible diseases. Urbana: University of Illinois Press, 1966. English translation.

Pollitzer R. 1959. History of the disease. In: *Cholera*, pp. 11–50. Pollitzer R, Ed. Geneva: World Health Organization.

Potter C. 1998. Chronicle of influenza pandemics. In: *Textbook of Influenza*. Nicholson K, Webster R, Hay A, Eds. Oxford: Blackwell Science Ltd.

Potter C. 2001. A history of influenza. *J Appl Microbiol* 91:572–579.

Risse G. 1992. A long pull, a strong pull and all together: San Francisco and bubonic plague, 1907–1908. *Bull Hist Med* 66:260–286.

Rosenberg, C. 1987. *The Cholera Years, the United States in 1832, 1849, and 1866*, with a new afterword. Chicago: University of Chicago Press.

Schwabe C. 1985. Medical ecology. In: *Veterinary Medicine and Human Health*, 3rd ed., chapter 17. Baltimore: Williams and Wilkins.

Slack P. 1989. The black death past and present, II: Some historical problems. *Trans Roy Soc Trop Med Hyg* 83:461–463.

Snow J. 1855. *On the Mode of Communication of Cholera*, 2nd ed. London: J. Churchill.

UNAIDS. 2007. AIDS epidemic update. Joint United Nations Programme on HIV/AIDS (UNAIDS) and World Health Organization (WHO). Geneva, Switzerland, December 2007.

WHO/WER (World Health Organization/Weekly Epidemiological Record). 2006. Cholera, 2005. *Weekly Epidemiological Record* 31:297–308. http://www.who.int/wer (accessed 5 January 2008).

Wilson G. 1984. Cholera. In: *Topley and Wilson's Principles of Bacteriology, Virology, and Immunity*, 7th ed., vol. 3, pp. 446–457. Wilson G, Miles A, Parker MT, Eds. Baltimore: Williams and Wilkins.

2 The Spanish Flu of 1918

Linda M. Olson, EdD

*The important and almost incomprehensible fact about Spanish influenza
is that it killed millions upon millions of people in a year or less.*

Alfred W. Crosby

CONTENTS

2.1 THE GENESIS

2.1.1 OVERVIEW

Three major pandemics occurred during the course of the 20th century: the infamous Spanish flu of 1918, followed by two smaller flu pandemics, the Asian flu of 1957 and the Hong Kong flu of 1968. The World Health Organization describes the Spanish flu of 1918–1919 (H1N1) as "exceptional, the most deadly disease event in human history" (WHO, 2005). The Spanish flu infected an estimated 500 million people around the world and death toll estimates range from 25 to 100 million people. Most deaths occurred in a 16-week period from mid-September to mid-December of 1918 (Barry, 2004a). All modern pandemics are measured against the catastrophic 1918 Spanish flu pandemic, as the world has since not seen a virus that severe. "If the 1918 flu were to hit today in the U.S., it would kill more people than heart disease, cancers, strokes, chronic pulmonary disease, AIDS, and Alzheimer's disease combined. However, many people today are unaware that this epidemic even happened" (Kolata, 1999).

2.1.2 UNDERSTANDING WHAT HAPPENED

The origins and dynamics of the 1918 pandemic can be better understood and appreciated within the context of the wartime conditions that allowed it to originate and spread. World War I began in June 1914 after events precipitated by the assassination of Archduke Francis Ferdinand of Austria and his wife. The assassination led to a rapid escalation in the "Great War" between the Central Powers — including Germany, the Austro-Hungarian Empire, and the Ottoman Empire — versus the Allied nations of Britain, France, Italy, and Russia. The Great War was fought in Europe for nearly three years before the United States became involved. Repeated attacks on American merchant ships by German submarines forced the United States to enter the war on the side of the Allies on April 6, 1917.

The war provided perfect environmental and social conditions for spreading flu, enhancing and magnifying the flu's virulence and suffering. Soldiers and civilians were already under great strain from anxiety, depression, malnourishment, exhaustion, and physical stress. There was unprecedented overcrowding in munitions factories, bureaucratic offices, public transport, and frontline trenches (R. Brown, 2003).

Huge numbers of people were in transit throughout the war effort and the flu spread among them rapidly. However, 1918 would be a pivotal year of the war and the United States continued to ship troops to other military posts and across the Atlantic to France. As a consequence of massive human movement, in approximately one month's time the flu spread across much of the world, mostly as great numbers of people traveled by rail and sea. By the end of the pandemic, only one major region on the entire planet had not reported an outbreak: an isolated island called Marajo, located in Brazil's Amazon River delta (Rosenhek, 2005).

2.1.3 CAUSES

The epidemic occurred before scientists had an understanding or method of how to isolate an influenza virus. The germ theory of disease developed by Pasteur in the 1860s was not yet well understood, and scientists had no knowledge of the virus. Physicians'

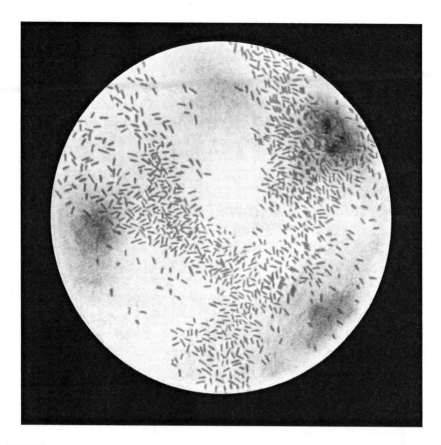

FIGURE 2.1 Photomicrograph of *Haemophilus influenzae* as seen using a Gram-stain technique. During the flu outbreak of 1918 *H. influenzae* was termed "Pfeiffer's Bacillus," where it was found in the sputum of many influenza patients, and thought to be the cause of influenza. (CDC Public Health Image Library.)

and scientists' theories of the epidemic's cause ranged from tiny plants to old dusty books to something called "cosmic influence." Electron microscopes had not yet been invented and viruses were too miniscule to be seen with ordinary microscopes. DNA and RNA, the genetic material of viruses and the clues to their destructiveness, had not yet been discovered (Kolata, 1999). It was not until 1933 that a British research team finally isolated and identified the influenza virus (Garrett, 2005). (See Figure 2.1.)

2.1.4 THE SITE OF ORIGIN

What was soon to become known as the Spanish influenza first appeared in Haskell County, Kansas, in January 1918. Both contemporary epidemiological studies and lay histories of the pandemic have identified that the first known outbreak of epidemic influenza occurred at Camp Funston, now Fort Riley, in Kansas, a large cantonment constructed just months before and where over 50,000 troops were training (Barry, 2004a). A virulent new kind of influenza killed dozens of people in the sparsely populated Haskell County, Kansas, laying 300 miles to the west of Camp Funston.

There a Kansan farm boy, who was recorded cleaning pigpens prior to his infection, was serving in the U.S. Army. This "Patient Zero" was Private Albert Gitchell, a mess cook, who complained of a sore throat and aching as he reported to sick call at Camp Funston (Hollenbeck, 2005).

> A few hours after the cook was admitted, Corporal Lee Drake came in with almost identical symptoms. One by one, men with fevers of 104°F, blue faces and horrendous coughs made their way to the infirmary. By midday, Camp Funston had 107 cases of the flu. (Rosenhek, 2005, 2)

Jessie Lee Brown Foveaux of Manhattan was 18 years old and working in the quartermaster laundry at Fort Riley when the flu struck:

> People were dying so fast. One day you would be working with a friend, the next day they didn't come to work, and the next report said they were dead.... The soldiers were dying so fast ... we heard that the bodies were being kept in a warehouse. We were all so frightened, wondering who would be next. (Foveaux, 1997, 145)

2.2 THE FIRST WAVE

In the early months of 1918, the final year of World War I, soldiers around the European front were becoming ill. The first wave was relatively mild, as the symptoms could incapacitate a person but exhibited relatively low associated mortality. It is referred to in some accounts as the three-day fever (Barry, 2004a).

Dr. Herbert French reported to the British Ministry of Health:

> In the midst of perfect health, in a circumscribed community ... the first case of influenza would occur, and then within the next few hours or days a large proportion — and occasionally every single individual of that community — would be stricken down with the same type of febrile illness, the rate of spread from one to another being remarkable.... Barrack rooms which the day before had been full of bustle and life, would now be converted wholesale into one great sick room, the number of sick developing so rapidly that hospitals were within a day or two so overfull that fresh admissions were impossible. (Hoehling, 1961, 18)

With the increasing war effort and millions of men being mobilized, the flu quickly spread to other army camps and then to cities and communities around America. The influenza hit so swiftly that it might have gone unnoticed until it had already passed. War news dominated the headlines and after a few weeks, the flu epidemic abated and most Americans believed the worst was over.

March 1918

On March 30, 1918, the occurrence of eighteen cases of influenza of severe type, from which three deaths resulted was reported at Haskell, Kansas. (Public Health Reports, March 1918. Byerly, 2005, 70, U.S. Health and Human Services, updated Crosby 2003, 18).

From April to August 1918 thousands of infected American troops traveled to exit ports on the East Coast and departed over the Atlantic to Europe. After their landing in

France, the virus spread across the continent, infecting hundreds of thousands. In France the loss of life was estimated between 125,000 and 250,000 civilians and 30,000 soldiers (Guénel, 2004). The highest mortality was in persons 25 to 30 years old. In the latter part of August 1918 in western France, the virus became highly transmissible and pathogenic. At the end of the month, the Spanish influenza virus mutated, and within the same week "epidemics of unprecedented virulence" exploded in three port cities thousands of miles apart: Freetown, Sierra Leone; Brest, France; and Boston, Massachusetts (Crosby, 2003). The virus mutated in response to increasing human antibodies.

2.3 THE SECOND WAVE

The second wave of the virus hit Europe hard, and then erupted among 1.5 million newly arrived U.S. troops. In Brest, France, which was the chief landing point for American troops, the first cases were reported on August 22, 1918. "The first case in the [pandemic's] second wave was recorded ... in Brest, a major port of incoming troops" (Gladwell, 1997). (See Figure 2.2.)

On August 31, 1918, news headlines focused on Babe Ruth as he pitched a three-hitter and banged out a long double to win the American League pennant for the Boston Red Sox (Allen, 1931, 3). On that same day, the news hardly mentioned the first recognized cases of flu among Navy personnel in Boston and that 26 sailors had died. Within two weeks, 2,000 officers and men of the First Naval District had the flu (Hoehling, 1961).

FIGURE 2.2 U.S. Army Camp Hospital No. 45, Aix-les-Bains, France. (Courtesy of National Museum of Health and Medicine, Armed Forces Institute of Pathology, Washington, D.C., H Library of Medicine.)

2.3.1 THE PROGRESSION

Ships leaving Europe bound for other ports brought the new virus with them. In Freetown, Sierra Leone, two-thirds of the native population contracted the disease; 3 percent of the entire population was dead by September. Flu raged across Europe and into Asia. Approximately 80 percent of Spain's population contracted the flu.

Because of the war, news of the outbreaks was censored for security reasons. Few people knew about the mysterious disease until the Spanish outbreaks occurred. Because Spain was a neutral country, their uncensored news of the outbreaks spread around the world. The soldiers called their illness the Spanish flu, although its origins were, and still are, unknown (Davies, 2000). (See Figure 2.3 and Figure 2.4.)

2.3.2 WORLDWIDE CAUSES AND DEATHS

The first cases of flu in the United States occurred in Boston, Massachusetts, in September 1918, brought back on the same Navy ships that had carried it to Europe. Alarming reports from Boston announced that month that thousands were coming down with the flu followed by severe pneumonia. With thousands more troops amassing at the coastline to ship off to Europe, the virus had a perfect ecological breeding environment.

The flu spread most rapidly among soldiers and sailors who were forced to live in close quarters. By September 23, approximately 20,000 U.S. soldiers were

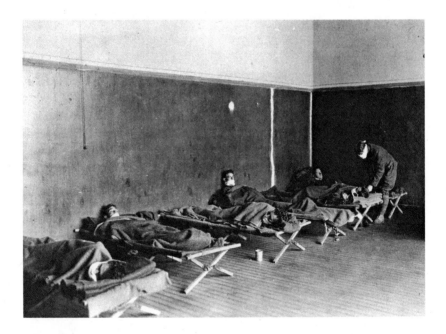

FIGURE 2.3 U.S. Army Field Hospital No. 29, Hollerich, Luxembourg, Interior View — Influenza Ward, 1918. (Courtesy of the National Museum of Health and Medicine, Armed Forces Institute of Pathology, Washington, D.C., Image Reeve 15183.)

FIGURE 2.4 A pen-and-ink cartoon, "Going Fast," shows a German military officer, possibly William II, looking at a "war map" on a table with an hour glass, "Summer of 1918," while the Grim Reaper with scythe watches. (Courtesy of National Library of Congress [CAI — Rogers, no. 242].)

infected with the new flu. By the following week nearly 31,000 American sailors were stricken. By early October, almost 2,000 U.S. sailors and 10,000 U.S. soldiers had died. Vaughn, Vaughn, and Palmer described the incidence and mortality of influenza in military personnel in 1918–1919 in detail in *Epidemiology and Public Health* (1922).

By the end of September, the flu had struck naval bases in Louisiana, Puget Sound, and San Francisco, and army camps from Massachusetts to Georgia to Washington. The U.S. government realized that regardless of what was happening in the war, they could not afford to ignore the flu. "The unthinkable was happening: something had appeared of greater priority than the war" (Crosby, 1989, 49). Recognizing the epidemic on hand, authorities suspended troop call-ups to keep the virus from spreading further. However, the containment efforts were too little, too late. The epidemic rapidly swept through the United States in September, and by early December about 20 million people were infected and 450,000 Americans were dead from the disease. "Death could come from anyone, anytime. People moved away from others on the sidewalk, avoided conversation..." (Barry, 2004a, 255).

September 1918

This epidemic started about four weeks ago, and has developed so rapidly that the camp is demoralized and all ordinary work is held up till it has passed.... These men start with what appears to be an ordinary attack of La Grippe or Influenza, and when brought to the Hosp. they very rapidly develop the most viscous type of Pneumonia that has ever been seen. Two hours after admission they have the Mahogany spots over the cheek bones, and a few hours later you can begin to see the Cyanosis extending from their ears and spreading all over the face, until it is hard to distinguish the coloured men from the white. It is only a matter of a few hours then until death comes, and it is simply a struggle for air until they suffocate. It is horrible.

One can stand it to see one, two, or twenty men die, but to see these poor devils dropping like flies sort of gets on your nerves. We have been averaging about 100 deaths per day, and still keeping it up. There is no doubt in my mind that there is a new mixed infection here, but what I don't know. (Quote from a physician stationed at Fort Devens outside Boston, late September 1918.)

The most devastating wave of the pandemic was from September to November. By September 28 approximately 31,000 American sailors were stricken. October 1918 found U.S. sailors docked in foreign harbors and infected with the virus, which then quickly spread into the continents' interiors. The United States and Europe were quickly overrun due to modern transportation systems. Public notices appeared in America, urging people to avoid contact with the sick and to wear masks. The warnings had little effect. Occupied coffins were piled on city streets for removal. Americans, being better nourished and healthier than most affected nationalities, were comparatively lucky. The virus did most of its bidding in poor and populated countries. India suffered heavily; the first cases appeared in Bombay in June 1918 followed by cases in Karachi and Madras. Many of India's doctors were away serving with the British army, so the country was unprepared and understaffed to deal with the enormous problem. In one year, 16 million Indian people died from influenza (Ramanna, 2003).

The influenza virus hit Russian shores on June 1, 1918, when infected U.S. doughboys embarked for Murmansk from England. The Michigan National Guard's 85th division totaling 5,500 men from that contingent proceeded from England and became ill with influenza while at sea, resulting in 100 deaths and 500 on sick call. They arrived on August 2, 1918, joining a coalition of forces that included British, French, Canadian, Italian, and White Russian troops involved in Allied operations against Bolsheviks (Culloton, 2005).

The pandemic seriously hindered the United States' war effort. By the fall of 1918, new troop arrivals to the western front had all but ceased. The Armed Forces suffered approximately 43,000 deaths from influenza, only 20 percent less than the number of troops killed in action (Kaplan, Webster, 1977, 88).

The pandemic caused widespread disruption throughout the world, and at its height the community life of many cities became essentially nonexistent. In the United States, there were 25 million clinical cases of influenza during the autumn and winter of 1918–1919 — nearly one-quarter of the entire population. In most major cities, theaters were closed and public gatherings prohibited. Schools closed and hospitals and morgues were overcrowded and understaffed. Despite an outpouring of volunteers, entire families became sick without anyone to care for them. Some healthy adults died within 24 hours of their first signs of illness. Countless remedies were tried, but it soon became apparent that the only effective treatment was bed rest and good nursing care (Kaplan, Webster, 1977, 88).

In September 1918, Dr. Victor Vaughn (seen in Figure 2.5), acting Surgeon General of the Army, founder of the National Board of Medical Examiners, and

FIGURE 2.5 Dr. Victor C. Vaughn, acting Surgeon General of the Army, 1918. (Courtesy of Library of Congress Reproduction Number LC-D416-600.)

a past president of the American Medical Association, responded to urgent orders to proceed to Camp Devens near Boston where 63 men had died of influenza at the camp. The following are his observations of that incident:

> ...hundreds of stalwart young men in the uniform of their country coming into the wards of the hospital in groups of ten or more. They are placed on the cots until every bed is full, yet others crowd in. Their faces soon wear a bluish cast; a distressing cough brings up the blood-stained sputum. In the morning the dead bodies are stacked about the morgue like cordwood. This picture was painted on my memory cells at the division hospital, Camp Devens, in the fall of 1918, when the deadly influenza virus demonstrated the inferiority of human inventions in the destruction of human life. (Kolata, 1999, 16)

On September 5, the Massachusetts Department of Health alerted area newspapers that an epidemic was underway. Dr. John S. Hitchcock of the state health department warned "unless precautions are taken the disease in all probability will spread to the civilian population of the city" (Public Broadcasting Service, undated). Despite the flu crisis, on September 28 over 200,000 people gathered in the streets of Philadelphia to view the kick-off of the Fourth Liberty Loan Drive. By October 4, the University of Pennsylvania's newspaper *The Daily Pennsylvanian* reported 636 new cases and 139 deaths. On that day the Board of Health closed all schools, churches, theaters, and saloons. All citizens were ordered to wear gauze masks in public (Armstrong, 2001).

The pandemic reached Camp Lewis, Washington, in mid-September after a troop ship arrived from Philadelphia with 700 cases and one death at the University of Washington Naval Training Station (Crosby, 1989). On October 29th, Seattle declared wearing gauze masks mandatory, with the rest of the state following the order the next day. Many of the schools that were closed did not open again until January or March 1919 (HHS, 2006b).

Navy nurse Josie Brown, who was stationed at Great Lakes Naval Station near Chicago, recounts her experience in an oral interview:

> The morgues were packed almost to the ceiling with bodies stacked one on top of another. The morticians worked day and night. You could never turn around without seeing a big red truck loaded with caskets for the train station so bodies could be sent home. We didn't have the time to treat them. We didn't take temperatures; we didn't even have time to take blood pressure. We would give them a little hot whisky toddy; that's about all we had time to do. They would have terrific nosebleeds with it. Sometimes the blood would just shoot across the room. You had to get out of the way or someone's nose would bleed all over you. (Brown, 1986, 18–19.)

Figure 2.6 shows the crowded sleeping area extemporized on the Drill Hall floor of the Main Barracks at the Naval Training Station near San Francisco, California, during World War I. Note the bunks arranged in columns, with alternating headings. Signs on the wall at left forbid spitting on the floor, to prevent the spread of disease.

In New York, 851 people died of the flu in a single day. But the greatest toll occurred in Philadelphia. In one week in October, the death rate there was 700

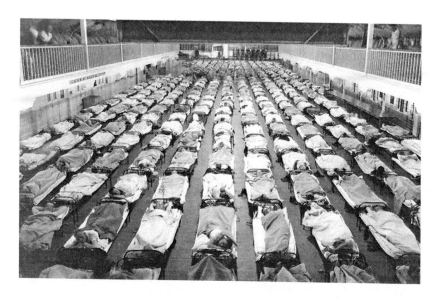

FIGURE 2.6 Naval Training Station, San Francisco, California. Crowded sleeping area extemporized on the Drill Hall floor of the Main Barracks, during World War I. Note bunks arranged in columns, with alternating headings. Signs on the wall at left forbid spitting on the floor to prevent the spread of disease. (U.S. Naval Historical Center photograph.)

times higher than normal (Public Broadcasting Service, undated) (see Figure 2.7). October 1918 was the deadliest month in our nation's history, recording the loss of 195,000 American lives to the Spanish flu. In total, the United States lost an estimated 500,000 Americans. Worldwide approximately 40 to 50 million people died from the Spanish flu (Kolata, 1999).

Historian Charles Hardy did interviews in the early 1980s for the Philadelphia radio program "The Influenza Pandemic of 1918." Louise Abruchezze, an Italian immigrant, shared her experience in Philadelphia in this excerpt from Hardy's radio program:

> …a boy about 7, 8 years old died and they used to just pick you up and wrap you up in a sheet and put you in a patrol wagon. So the mother and father were screaming, "Let me get a macaroni box." Before, macaroni, any kind of pasta, used to come in these wooden boxes about this long and that high, that 20 lbs. of macaroni fitted in the box. "Please, please, let me put him in the macaroni box. Let me put him in the box. Don't take him away like that." And that was it. (Hardy, 1986.)

Overjoyed people abandoned their concerns about the flu and celebrated the end of the war on November 11, 1918, with Armistice Day parades and large parties. A surge in influenza cases occurred in many cities following the public celebrations. Later that winter, a third wave of the flu infected millions and killed thousands (Collins, 1957).

When compared to the number of Americans killed in combat in World War I, World War II, Korea, and Vietnam combined, it is apparent that the influenza epidemic of 1918–1919 was far deadlier than the war that it accompanied

FIGURE 2.7 Mounted on a wood storage crib at the Naval Aircraft Factory, Philadelphia, Pennsylvania, on 19 October 1918. As the sign indicates, the "Spanish Influenza" was then extremely active in Philadelphia, with many victims in the Philadelphia Navy Yard and the Naval Aircraft Factory. Note the sign's emphasis on the epidemic's damage to the war effort. (U.S. Naval Historical Center photograph.)

(Crosby, 1989). The world had been exposed to epidemics in the past, but never at such a severe cost in human life. Dr. Jeffery Taubenberger and his colleagues of the Armed Forces Institute of Pathology provide a scholarly review of what they describe as the "mother of all pandemics" (Taubenberger, Morens, 2006a).

And then, as abruptly as it appeared, the Spanish flu disappeared and was put out of mind. The November 5, 1918, issue of *The New York Times* read "war had taught the people to think in terms other than the individual interest and safety, and death itself had become so familiar as to lose its grimness" (Price, 1918).

2.3.3 THE CONJUNCTION OF SOLDIERS, PIGS, AND POULTRY

In 1923, Dr. Richard E. Shope, working with the Rockefeller Institute of Comparative Anatomy, showed that swine influenza could be transmitted through filtered mucous, which implied that influenza is caused by a virus. He had observed pigs coming down with a flu-like virus in 1918 that people alive during the 1918–1919 epidemics had antibodies against, but those born after 1920 lacked such antibodies. During the 1930s, Shope reproduced the disease in healthy pigs with material taken from sick pig tissue passed through a Pasteur-Chamberland filter. This provided the first evidence that the flu virus could be transmitted by swine (Hollenbeck, 2005).

Further study of the viral strain proved its identity as an A virus. From this evidence, the possibility arose that the 1918 flu pandemic was caused by a swine zoonosis, but no evidence existed to link human flu to swine flu (Shope, 1937).

In 1933 Sir Patrick Laidlaw, Sir Christopher Andrewes, and Wilson Smith, working at the MRC National Institute for Medical Research, proved that a virus causes influenza, rather than a bacterium as had been previously believed. They discovered this while working to develop a distemper vaccine when one of their laboratory ferrets contracted influenza from a scientist in the laboratory (Smith, Andrewes, Laidlaw, 1933). Scientists were now left to wonder what other animals might carry or be susceptible to influenza.

In the 1990s, renowned flu scientist Robert Webster of St. Jude's Children's Research Hospital in Memphis formulated a new hypothesis for the spread of the 1918 flu (Russel, Webster, 2005). Webster suggested that a bird flu virus would be passed on to a pig, which at the same time would contract a human flu virus. Webster showed that inside the pig, the bird flu strain would "change in a way that would allow it to keep the bird-like features that make it so infectious and yet acquire the human flu-like properties that would allow it to grow in the lung cells of a human being" (Kolata, 1999, 223).

2.4 THE VIRUS IS RESURRECTED

In March 1997, a report appeared in the journal *Science*. In this paper, Dr. Jeffery Taubenberger and his colleagues announced that they had recovered and analyzed fragments of the RNA genome of the virus responsible for the infamous 1918 pandemic (Taubenberger et al., 1997). Taubenberger and his team had recovered 1918 viral genetic material that most scientists believed had not been isolated and preserved by extracting material from samples taken in 1918 from two U.S. soldier pandemic fatalities. The genes of the virus were retrieved from lung-tissue samples fixed by formalin, preserved in paraffin wax, and stored for the last 80 years at the National Tissue Repository located within the Walter Reed Army Medical Center in Maryland. They also obtained lung tissue from a female victim whose body was buried in permafrost in Alaska. Kolata tells the story of retired pathologist Johan Hultin, who single-handedly went to Alaska and retrieved tissue specimens from the influenza victim who had been buried in the permafrost since 1918 (Kolata, 1999, chapter 4).

Taubenberger's team reconstructed part of the genetic data (a gene sequence) of the virus and compared this with the gene sequences of other strains of influenza virus. They reported: "The 1918 case 1 HA [haemagglutinin] sequences appear to be most closely related to early swine influenza strains, corroborating the archaeserological data from the 1930s" (Taubenberger et al., 1997).

2.4.1 THE SECRETS REMAIN ELUSIVE

In 2001, Dr. Mark Gibbs, John Armstrong, and Professor Adrian Gibbs at the Australian National University's School of Botany and Zoology discovered that one of the 1918 flu genes was a hybrid produced from parts of two other influenza viruses in a process called "recombination." Their study indicated that "gene splicing" occurred just before the 1918 pandemic and one of the two progenitors of the 1918 virus was an influenza strain that probably infected pigs. The results suggest that the outbreak was triggered by this recombination, as it was within the gene that codes for the haemagglutinin (HA) protein of the virus. Changes in this protein are known to increase the virulence of the influenza (Gibbs, Armstrong, Gibbs, 2001).

In February 2004, James Stevens, Ian Wilson, and Adam Corper of the Scripps Research Institute in La Jolla, California, and their research collaborators Jeffery K. Taubenberger (Armed Forces Institute of Pathology in Washington, D.C.) and Christopher F. Basler and Peter Palese of Mount Sinai Institute of Medicine in New York described the structure of HA protein from the 1918 flu virus. This surface antigen was the first structure of this extinct virus to be characterized. By using fragments of the viral genome and assembled genes from the 1918 flu virus, the research team cloned, expressed, and crystallized the viral protein HA and used macromolecular crystallography beam lines to produce an image of the intricate coils, stalks, and heads that make up HA's structure. The structure elucidated the virulent nature of the 1918 flu virus. HA was found to be the most abundant protein on the virus's surface and that it is the primary target for the immune system's defense against infection. HA is also very critical for the virus because it binds to human lung cells and enables the virus to internalize in the cell. Once inside the cell, HA changes shape to help the viral membrane fuse to the vesicle membrane allowing for the infection process. The 1918 HA structural analysis shows that it is closely related to avian (bird) forms (Stevens et al., 2004). This may explain why the 1918 strain was so deadly: because humans are not normally infected with avian influenza strains, the world population at that time was universally vulnerable to that strain.

Tissue samples of the 1918 flu epidemic are shown in Figure 2.8. The sample blocks containing lung and brain tissue came from victims of the 1918 Spanish flu pandemic. A list of child victims is also seen. Researchers at St. Bartholomew's Hospital, London, led by Professor John Oxford, used this wax-mounted tissue to study the nature and cause of the pandemic. Using molecular biology, they isolated flu virus genetic material from these clinical samples. This research was to show whether a particularly virulent flu virus caused the pandemic, or environmental factors such as the first world war were to blame, in hopes of helping predict future pandemics.

In October 2005, Terrence Tumpey, of the U.S. Centers for Disease Control and Prevention, and his colleagues recreated the 1918 Spanish flu virus. They used an approach called reverse genetics to create the virus. Reverse genetics involves transferring gene sequences of viral RNA into bacteria and then inserting combinations of the genes into cell lines, where they combine to form a virus. Tumpey was able to generate an influenza virus bearing all eight gene segments of the pandemic virus to study the properties associated with its extraordinary virulence. He found that the 1918 flu virus had the ability to replicate in the absence of trypsin, to cause death in mice and embryonated chicken eggs, and to display a high-growth phenotype in human bronchial epithelial cells. This gives hope of designing antivirals or other interventions that would work against virulent pandemic or epidemic influenza viruses (Tumpey et al., 2005).

FIGURE 2.8 Tissue samples and victim list of 1918 flu epidemic. Sample blocks containing lung and brain tissue from victims of the 1918 Spanish flu pandemic. A list of child victims is also seen. (James King-Holmes/Courtesy Science Photo Library.)

The *New England Journal of Medicine* stated in November 2005:

> The startling observation of Taubenberger et al. was that the 1918 virus did not origi-
> nate through a reassortment event involving a human influenza virus: all eight genes
> of the H1N1 virus are more closely related to avian influenza viruses than to influenza
> from any other species, indicating that an avian virus must have infected humans and
> adapted to them in order to spread from person to person. (Belshe, 2005.)

However, analysis did not fully explain what triggered the pandemic or the cause of its severity. Even after genetic sequencing and comparison with other historical and cir-culating influenza viruses, the 1918 pandemic virus remains a mystery today. "Though clearly descended from an avian virus, the 1918 strain is genetically unlike any other influenza virus examined over the past 88 years, which indicates that its immediate origin before the pandemic is an unknown source" (Taubenberger, Morens, 2006b).

2.4.2 THE PROGRESSION

The number of deaths from influenza and pneumonia by age in registration states in 1917, 1918, and 1919 are shown in Table 2.1 (Collins, 1957). In 1918, the death rate for males was 669.0 per 100,000 population; for females, 507.5. At ages 25 to 34, the

TABLE 2.1
Influenza and Pneumonia Mortality by Age: Death-Registration States, 1917–1919

Age	1917	1918	1919
	Number of Deaths		
All ages	115,526	464,959	185,440
Under 1 year	22,207	38,428	27,736
1–4 years	12,859	49,699	21,133
5–14 years	3,319	28,054	10,598
15–24 years	4,861	78,158	20,381
25–34 years	6,915	126,792	32,159
35–44 years	9,387	60,902	20,690
45–54 years	10,652	28,596	14,043
55–64 years	12,571	19,632	12,530
65–74 years	14,771	17,643	13,065
75–84 years	13,224	11,829	9,548
85 years and over	4,600	3,680	3,173
Not stated	160	1,546	384
	Rate Per 100,000 Population		
All ages[a]	164.5	588.5	223.0
Under 1 year	1,474.5	2,273.3	1,594.2
1–4 years	211.5	718.0	293.9
5–14 years	24.0	176.2	63.3
15–24 years	38.9	580.5	141.4
25–34 years	59.3	992.6	235.9
35–44 years	98.1	554.8	181.0
45–54 years	148.8	347.8	163.9
55–64 years	281.4	381.9	233.2
65–74 years	614.6	646.3	459.6
75–84 years	1,503.0	1,179.0	913.9
85 years and over	3,187.4	2,230.6	1,842.2

Note: For 1917, area includes 27 states and the District of Columbia; for 1918, 30 states and the District of Columbia; and for 1919, 33 states and the District of Columbia.

[a] Includes deaths at ages not stated.

Source: Dauer CC. 1957. "The Pandemic of Influenza in 1918–19." Washington, D.C.: Public Health Service, National Office of Vital Statistics, 19 July 1957. (Document provided courtesy of the Office of Public Health Service Historian, 695 Parklawn Building, 5600 Fishers Land, Rockville, MD 20857.)

rate was 1,216.6 for males and 781.4 for females. These excessively high mortality rates reduced the estimated average length of life calculated for the year 1918. It was reduced 24 percent from 1917 to 1918 for males and 22 percent for females. These estimated average lengths of life in years returned to their previous trends in 1920.

2.4.3 THE AGE PATTERN OF MORTALITY

The influenza virus was exceptionally severe, with unusually high death rates among young, healthy adults. One of the most noted traits of the 1918 pandemic was the unusual age distribution of its victims. Infectious disease experts believe young adults' robust immune response may have made that group more susceptible during the 1918 pandemic. Generally a flu mortality chart shows peaks in mortality for young children and the elderly, the left and right ends of the age spectrum. The chart line is "U-shaped" as the normal distribution. When the total mortality rates for the 1918 pandemic are plotted against age, a "W-shaped" mortality curve is seen, with a disproportionate increase in the mortality rate for individuals aged 20 to 40 years. Looking at a mortality chart for the 1918 pandemic, there are three peaks — one for the very young, one for the elderly, and one for young adults (Luk, Gross, Thompson, 2001). The U.S. Department of Health, Education, and Welfare mortality chart (Figure 2.9) shows this comparison. The death curve of this pandemic peaked for babies and children under age 5, the elderly, and people ages 25 to 34. The middle curve shows the influenza-pneumonia mortality for September–October 1918, a two-month segment of the pandemic. The unusual middle peak, centered on the 20 to 29 age group, forms a W-shape curve. So many died, in fact, that the average life span in the United States fell by twelve years in 1918 (Kolata, 1999, 7).

2.4.4 FATAL IMMUNITY, PATTERNS OF FATALITY

Another oddity of the 1918 flu was that the outbreak struck hardest in summer and fall in the Northern Hemisphere. People without symptoms could be struck suddenly and within hours were unable to walk. Many died within 24 hours of becoming ill.

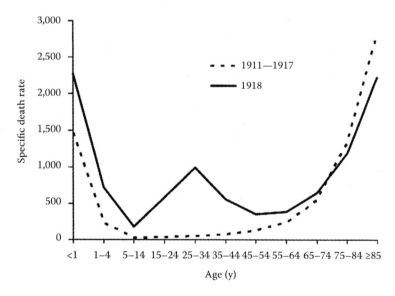

FIGURE 2.9 Male age-specific death rates in the United States per 100,000 from influenza and pneumonia, 1917 and 1918. (U.S. Department of Health, Education, and Welfare, 1959.)

Symptoms included a blue tint to the face, severe obstruction of the lungs, and coughing up blood. In some cases, an uncontrollable hemorrhaging filled the lungs and patients virtually suffocated in their own body fluids. Nurses often looked at the patients' feet first when triaging numerous new patients, and deemed those with black feet to be beyond help. Mortality was attributed to pneumonia in fast-progressing cases. A secondary bacterial pneumonia was attributed to deaths or long recuperation periods in slower-progressing cases. It is believed that there may have been neural involvement leading to mental disorders in the aftermath (Barry, 2004a).

Other deaths were the result of malnourishment and the inability to provide routine health care to individuals. Crosby details the desperation: "Many families, especially in the slums, had no adult well enough to prepare food and in some cases had no food at all because the breadwinner was sick or dead" (Crosby, 2003, 80).There was a severe lack of health care workers to tend to the sick, and no able-bodies to dig graves. Mass graves were dug and bodies buried without coffins in many places. Public buildings were put to use as temporary hospitals. (See Figure 2.10.)

The aggressiveness of an infected individual's immune response to the 1918 strain may have caused a significant impact on the fatality of the disease. It was hypothesized that the virus caused the immune system to go on a rampage by unleashing

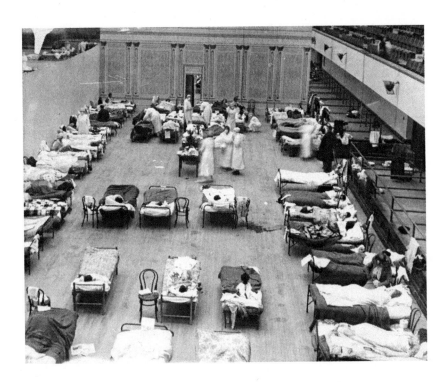

FIGURE 2.10 Volunteer nurses from the American Red Cross tending influenza sufferers in the Oakland Auditorium, in use as a temporary hospital during the influenza pandemic of 1918. (From the Joseph R. Knowland collection at the Oakland History Room, Oakland Public Library. Number in collection: 277. Creator/contributor: Edward A. Rogers.)

a cytokine storm. The healthier the immune system, the more massive the cytokine storm, which caused generalized, unchecked inflammation and consequent destruction of tissues and blood vessels (Loo, Gale, 2007). Researchers at the University of Washington and other institutions studied the response of lung cells in mice infected with the virus and found that the 1918 virus triggers a hyperactive immune response that might contribute to the virus's lethality (Kash et al., 2004). They believe that the host's inflammatory response is highly activated by the virus, and that response makes the virus much more damaging to the host. The host's immune system may overreact and kill off too many cells, and that may be a key contributor to what makes this virus more pathogenic.

While disproportionate numbers of young adults suffered more than other age groups, others were not spared, particularly very young children and pregnant women who left their orphaned children behind. Higher rates of spontaneous abortion, still-births, and premature births were reported (Woolston, Conley, 1918). In 1919, Harris reported that in a series of more than 1,300 cases of pandemic influenza in pregnancy, roughly 50 percent developed pneumonia, and of these 50 percent died. These numbers were substantially greater than nonpregnant women and men of the same age. Pregnant women critically ill with pneumonia experienced a very high pre-term delivery and fetal wastage rates (more than double the baseline rate) (Harris, 1919).

2.5   THE UNFORGETTABLE OUTCOME

2.5.1   THE IMPACT

Much of the burden of caring for the sick fell on volunteer caregivers, especially women. At Camp Dodge, Iowa, 245 nurses were on duty on October 10, 1918. Six days later, the number of nurses had increased to 598 (Red Cross, undated). Mass deployment of nurses was repeated throughout the military and civilian communities during the crisis. Crosby described the horrors facing nurses, some just recently out of school and with little practical experience:

> Visiting nurses often walked into scenes resembling those of the plague years of the fourteenth century.... One nurse found a husband dead in the same room where his wife lay with newly born twins. It had been twenty-four hours since the death and the births, and the wife had had no food but an apple which happened to lie within reach. (Crosby, 1989, 76)

Nursing shortages created an even more desperate situation. Because there was no known cure for the flu, all that the medical community could do for the flu patients was provide basic nursing care. Many people died due to the lack of nurses. People became ill faster than the nurses could be found to take care of them, and often died from dehydration, starvation, and poor care.

Since the medical practitioners were away with the troops, medical students were deputized to care for the sick in the wards. Third- and fourth-year classes were closed and the students were assigned jobs as interns or nurses (Starr, 1976). The American Red Cross recruited volunteers to contribute to the cause of fighting the influenza epidemic. The Red Cross coordinated a national response through the creation of

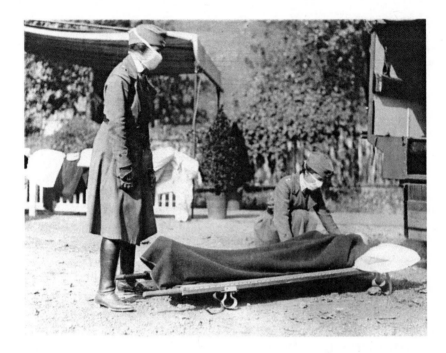

FIGURE 2.11 Demonstration at the Red Cross Emergency Ambulance Station in Washington, D.C., during the influenza pandemic of 1918. (Courtesy of Library of Congress LC-USZ62-126995.)

a National Committee on Influenza. The committee was involved in both military and civilian sectors to mobilize all forces to fight the Spanish flu. From September 14 to November 7, 1918, the Red Cross recruited a total of 15,000 women, including regularly enrolled nurses, student nurses, practical nurses, nurses' aides, and other women who had taken the Red Cross Home Hygiene course (see Figure 2.11). They served in military camps and hospitals, troop ships, civilian hospitals, and the homes of infected civilians in cities, towns, and rural areas. A total of 223 nurses and five dieticians died providing humanitarian services to flu victims (Red Cross, undated). The American Red Cross membership drive poster (Figure 2.12) shows a Red Cross nurse holding a large red cross.

Red Cross influenza nurse Denio from Oregon wrote in a 1918 letter:

> I am writing by fits and starts, as I can snatch a minute off to jot down our needs, hoping that the situation might be clear to you, and that you will be able to get us some supplies before we get snowed in for the winter. Our greatest need (next to fruit and malted milk) is feeding cups and drinking tubes, which we can't get at Winnemucca (the nearest town). We also need lots of gauze or cheese cloth and cotton for pneumonia jackets; also rubber sheeting, and quantities of old rags to be used and burned, also gallons of formaldehyde if we are to stamp out the disease as everything is thrown on the ground, and will thaw out next spring and release all these germs again. (Red Cross, undated)

FIGURE 2.12 American Red Cross membership drive poster showing a Red Cross nurse holding a large red cross. (Courtesy of Library of Congress LC-USZC4-7763.)

Cities' morgues overflowed. In Philadelphia, one of the hardest-hit cities, the morgue was built to handle 36 bodies, but overflowed with more than 500. Rotting bodies accumulated in the morgue's hallways. Convicts were recruited to dig graves. There were not enough coffins, and people were found stealing them from undertakers. Crosby described how overburdened undertakers were:

> In some cases the dead were left in their homes for days. Private undertaking houses were overwhelmed, and some were taking advantage of the situation by hiking prices as much as 600 percent. Complaints were made that cemetery officials were charging fifteen dollar burial fees and then making the bereaved dig the graves for their dead themselves. (Crosby, 1989, 77)

2.5.2 PUBLIC HEALTH'S FIGHT

Schools, theaters, churches, and dance halls in cities across the country were closed. Kansas City banned weddings and funerals if more than 20 people were to be in attendance. New York mandated staggered shifts at factories to reduce rush-hour commuter traffic. Seattle's mayor ordered his constituents to wear face masks. The U.S. Public Health Service (USPHS) played an important role in safeguarding the nation's health. Surgeon General Rupert Blue (Figure 2.13) expanded many of USPHS's responsibilities and duties. These responsibilities included safeguarding the health of personnel at military camps, improving the working conditions for industrial workers, and initiating a vigorous anti-venereal disease campaign at home and abroad. Blue issued a series of precautions to safeguard against the flu on September 13, declaring that "in most cases, a person taken with 'Spanish influenza' feels sick rather suddenly. He feels weak, has pains in his eyes, head, or back, abdomen, etc., and may be sore all over" (Blue, 1918).

State and municipal public health departments were urged to report weekly, if not daily, on their local conditions. Six million pamphlets warning people of the "Spanish Influenza," the "Three Day Fever," and "The Flu" were produced and circulated through local health departments. Widely distributed posters and public notices sought to educate the general public and medical community of the dangers of influenza. Figure 2.14 shows a newspaper clipping from the Allentown *Morning Call,* October 5, 1918, at Camp Crane, Allentown, Virginia, which told of health precautions. Camp Crane implemented a number of precautions, such as random inspection of men, isolation of cases, ventilation of barracks, cots placed in same direction with canopies used, throat and nose swabs taken to identify cases, men prohibited from entering places of public amusement in Allentown, and civilians prohibited from entering camp. The USPHS distributed a poster (Figure 2.15) warning that influenza was spread by droplets sprayed from nose and throat. It taught to cover each cough and sneeze with handkerchief, to avoid spread by contact, and to avoid crowds. It encouraged walking to work. The poster also warned not to spit on floors.

An influenza director was appointed to each state to coordinate local disbursement of funds. In most states the chief health officer directed the movement of physicians and nurses to more severely affected areas. Surgeon General Blue recruited more than 600 physicians willing to do influenza work who became Acting Assistant

FIGURE 2.13 Dr. Rupert Blue, United States Surgeon General, 1912 to 1920 (Courtesy of Library of Congress LC-DIG-ggbain-02560.)

Surgeons with a monthly stipend of $200, plus $4 per diem (Annual Report of the Surgeon General of the Public Health Service of the United States, 1919).

As the death toll increased throughout October, Blue established a network of emergency hospitals and a national system of emergency soup kitchens. Throughout the pandemic, the USPHS appointed 64 commissioned officers solely for influenza duty and employed 1,085 doctors and 703 nurses (Gernhart, 1999). The USPHS also conducted experiments in vaccine development. Incarcerated soldiers quarantined at Boston and San Francisco readily volunteered as subjects. The volunteers were repeatedly exposed to sputum and coughs of hospital patients exhibiting

DOZEN GOOD RULES TO PREVENT INFLUENZA

Through K. H. Owens, captain of the sanitary corps, U. S. A., located at Camp Crane, the Morning Call is able to present to its readers 12 rules on "How to Strengthen Our Personal Defence Against Spanish Influenza", prepared by Charles Richards, brigadier-general in the medical corps, acting surgeon-general of the U. S. Army. Copies of the rules have been sent to all camps and training stations in the country and this paper is asked to print them for the benefit of the public. They follow:

1.—Avoid needless crowding—influenza is a crowd disease.

2.—Smother your coughs and sneezes—others do not want the germs which you throw away.

3.—Your nose, not your mouth, was made to breathe through—get the habit.

4.—Remember the three Cs—a clean mouth, clean skin and clean clothes.

5.—Try to keep cool when you walk, and warm when you ride and sleep.

6.—Open the windows—always at home at night; at the office when practicable.

7.—Food will win the war if you give it a chance—help by choosing and chewing your food well.

8.—Poor fate may be in your own hands—wash your hands before eating.

9.—Don't let the waste products of digestion accumulate—drink a glass or two of water after getting up.

10.—Don't use a napkin, towel, fork, spoon, glass or cup which has been used by another person and not washed.

11.—Avoid tight clothes, tight shoes, tight gloves,—seek to make nature your ally, not your prisoner.

12.—When the air is pure breathe all of it you can—breathe deeply.

There are no cases of contagious diseases at Camp Crane at the present time, with the exception of one recovering case of typhoid fever, and, this soldier was ill when he reported for duty. Only eight cases of influenza developed at the camp, five of them developing within a few hours after arriving in Allentown. All of the cases are practically well, and are ready for discharge and no new cases have been reported.

FIGURE 2.14 Newspaper clipping from *The Allentown Morning Call*, at Camp Crane, Allentown, Virginia, October 5, 1918. (Found at www.med.umich.edu/medschool/chm/influenza/wpib.htm. All the original documents are on the site and are freely available to the public for research or educational purposes and are made available by the Center for the History of Medicine at the University of Michigan Medical School as part of a project conducted for the Defense Threat Reduction Agency.)

influenza-like symptoms in an attempt to make them contract the disease. Although the experiments failed to develop influenza in the volunteers, they all received full pardons in recognition of their participation (Kolata, 1999, chapter 3).

2.5.3 THE EFFECT OF PUBLIC HEALTH MEASURES IN U.S. CITIES

Hatchett, Mecher, and Lipsitch (2007) tested the hypothesis that in influenza pandemics early implementation of multiple interventions was associated with reduced disease transmission They reported that early implementation of certain

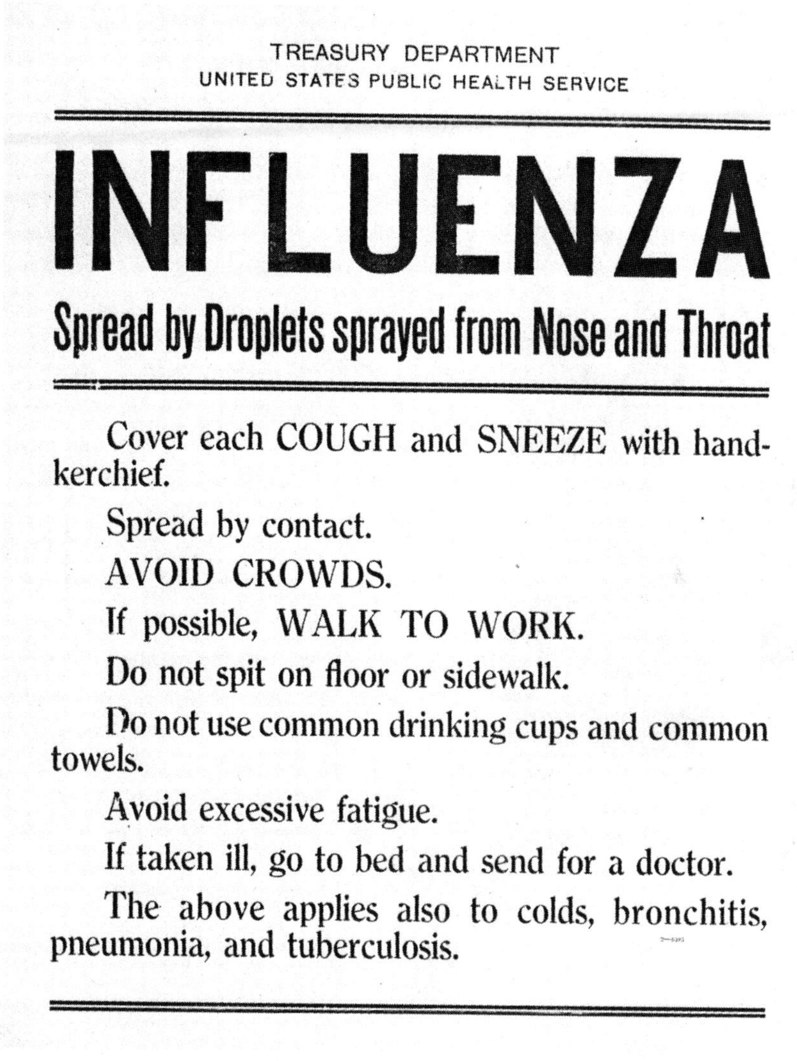

TREASURY DEPARTMENT
UNITED STATES PUBLIC HEALTH SERVICE

INFLUENZA

Spread by Droplets sprayed from Nose and Throat

Cover each COUGH and SNEEZE with hand-kerchief.

Spread by contact.

AVOID CROWDS.

If possible, WALK TO WORK.

Do not spit on floor or sidewalk.

Do not use common drinking cups and common towels.

Avoid excessive fatigue.

If taken ill, go to bed and send for a doctor.

The above applies also to colds, bronchitis, pneumonia, and tuberculosis.

FIGURE 2.15 Treasury Department, U.S. Public Health Service influenza advice, 1918. (From Library of Congress, Rare Book and Special Collections Division. Library of Congress, American Memory, http://memory.loc.gov/ammem, accessed [28 September 2007]. Printed Ephemera Collection; Portfolio 241, Folder 19, digital ID rbpe 24101900 http://hdl.loc.gov/loc.rbc/rbpe.24101900.)

nonpharmaceutical interventions (NPIs), including closure of schools, churches, and theaters, was associated with lower peak death rates; but no single intervention showed an association with improved aggregate outcomes for the 1918 phase of the pandemic. Their findings support the hypothesis that rapid implementation of multiple NPIs can significantly reduce influenza transmission, but that viral spread will be renewed upon relaxation of such measures (Hatchett, Mecher, Lipsitch, 2007).

Lipsitch, professor of epidemiology at the Harvard School of Public Health, said in an interview:

> Looking back at the comparison between cities in 1918, there were enormous variations in the severity of the pandemic in different cities and those variations seem to be closely tied to the aggressiveness and promptness with which different cities put in place a set of interventions to try to block transmission.... This gives support to the notion, which is now federal policy, that when facing the next pandemic, communities should try as early as possible to implement a set of measures similar to this if the pandemic is severe. (White Coat Notes, 2007)

2.5.4 POLITICAL, MEDICAL, AND SOCIAL ASPECTS

Many countries reported that mandatory case reporting and isolating patients during the 1918 influenza pandemic did not stop virus transmission, were impractical, and were often ridiculed by the public. According to the World Health Organization (WHO), social-distancing measures did not appear to reduce dramatically or stop transmission, but research studies that might assess partial effectiveness are apparently unavailable. In the United States, a comprehensive report on the 1918 pandemic concluded that closing schools, churches, and theaters was not demonstrably effective in urban areas, but might be effective in smaller towns and rural districts, where group contacts are less numerous (Jordan, 1927). Lessons learned from the 1918 influenza pandemic, and our knowledge base for developing guidance for nonpharmaceutical interventions for pandemic influenza remain limited. What was learned from the 1918 pandemic consists primarily of historical and contemporary observations, supplemented by mathematical models, rather than controlled studies evaluating interventions. WHO writers stated in 2006:

> The need is urgent for additional research on transmission characteristics of influenza viruses and the effectiveness of nonpharmaceutical public health interventions. Such research should include epidemiologic and virologic studies and field assessments of effectiveness and cost, supplemented by modeling studies and historical inquiry. Such research could be undertaken during epidemics of seasonal influenza, and some research investment now being devoted to influenza should be dedicated to this end. Research needs include evaluating the effectiveness of mask use and cough etiquette and evaluating interventions in terms of cases detected and prevented, cost, and effectiveness in alleviating public concerns. Research is also needed to identify ways to make quarantine and other restrictions more focused and less burdensome for individual persons and societies and to assess how "leaky" restrictions can be and still be effective. Improved methods are also needed to communicate with essential partners and the public. Finally, improved informatics capabilities would allow outbreaks to be monitored and interventions to be assessed in real time to meet the needs of all who will help control future pandemics. (World Health Organization Writing Group, 2006)

2.5.5 INTEGRATING HISTORY AND BIOLOGY: HOW DOES IT COMPARE TO H5N1?

By studying parallels between the 1918 flu virus and the current H5N1 avian virus, there is increased concern about the potential effect of another global flu pandemic. However, this new knowledge, and the modern ability to test the pathogenicity of different experimentally created viral mutants, helps target different treatment and vaccination options. The 1918 virus contains several amino acid changes that also are present in the current highly pathogenic H5N1 avian virus that has killed humans in the past nine years (Taubenberger et al., 2005). Compared with contemporary human flu viruses, the 1918 virus produced nearly 40,000 times more viral particles in lung tissue. It caused severe bronchiolitis and alveolitis, pulmonary edema, and alveolar hemorrhage — just as it had in human lungs in 1918 (Tumpey et al., 2005). More recently, Taubenberger and Morens reported: "The H5N1 influenza A virus is an avian strain as was the 1918 virus.... The 1918 pandemic strain adapted to human cell receptor binding leading to efficient human-to-human transmission. The mechanism by which this property was acquired is unknown" (Taubenberger, Morens, 2006).

2.5.6 YESTERDAY'S LESSONS INFORM TODAY'S PREPAREDNESS

If we translate the rate of death associated with the 1918 influenza virus to that in the current population, there could be 1.7 million deaths in the United States and 180 million to 360 million deaths globally (Osterholm, 2005). If this mortality were concentrated in a single year, it would increase global mortality by 114 percent. The vast majority of deaths (96 percent) would have occurred in poor countries where "scarce health resources are already stretched by existing health priorities" (Murray, 2006).

2.5.7 INSIGHTS FOR THE 21ST CENTURY

The timing and severity of a 21st century pandemic cannot be predicted, but, for the first time in history, the world has the advantage of advance warning that a pandemic may be near. This advantage must be fully exploited to enhance global preparedness. The current international awareness, leadership, and support are unparalleled. The global community has demonstrated unprecedented levels of co-operation and collective action in dealing with SARS, influenza, and other threats to bio-security. The human and technology infrastructure, including research and development of vaccines and rapid tools for diagnosis, can serve to protect people against all infectious disease threats.

If faced with a pandemic today, we would likely rely on many nonpharmaceutical interventions to attempt to mitigate the spread of the infection until pharmacological supplies of vaccine and antiviral agents were available (Ferguson, 2006; Longini et al., 2005). Today's world is much different than it was in 1918, with a larger, more mobile, and more complex technological society. Although scientific evidence is inconclusive that isolation or quarantine helped to contain the virus, it stands to reason that in the event of another influenza pandemic, many specific sub-communities (e.g., military installations, college and university campuses, childcare centers, nursing homes) may wish to consider protective sequestration measures as potential means to prevent or delay the onset of epidemic influenza in their populations (Markel, 2006). There was no advance warning for the three pandemics of the previous century, but today we have the means to monitor changes in the pattern of human flu cases. We are better geared to detect human-to-human transmission at the earliest stage possible. This includes improved surveillance for disease in animals and humans, field investigations, diagnostic support, and methods for people to report. The importance of international collaboration and global health awareness may be the most significant lesson learned from the Spanish flu of 1918.

REFERENCES

Allen F. 1931. *Only Yesterday.* New York: Harper & Row.

Annual Report of the Surgeon General of the Public Health Service of the United States. 1919. Washington, D.C.: Government Printing Office.

Armstrong JF. 2001. Philadelphia, nurses, and the Spanish influenza pandemic of 1918. *Navy Medicine* 92(2):16–20.

Barry J. 2004a. *The Great Influenza: The Epic Story of the Deadliest Plague in History.* Viking.

Barry JM. 2004b. The site of origin of the 1918 influenza pandemic and its public health implications. *J Transl Med* 2:3. Published online 2004 January 20. doi: 10.1186/1479-5876-2-3.

Belshe RB. 2005. The origins of pandemic influenza — Lessons from the 1918 virus. *New Engl J Med* 353(21):2209–2211.

Blue R. 1918. Epidemic influenza. *Memphis Medical Monthly* 39:170–171.

Brown J. 1986. A winding sheet and a wooden box. *Navy Med* 77(3):18–19. Available from http://www.history.navy.mil/library/online/influenza%20wind.htm.

Brown R. 2003. The Great War and the great flu pandemic of 1918. *Wellcome History* Oct, 24.

Byerly, C. 2005. *Fever of War: The Influenza Epidemic in the U.S. Army During World War I.* New York, NY: New York University Press, p. 70.

Collins SD. 1957. Influenza in the United States, 1887–1956. Washington, D.C.: U.S. Department of Health, Education, and Welfare, Public Health Service. [Extracted from "Review and Study of Illness and Medical Care With Special Reference to Long-term Trends," Public Health Monograph No. 48, 1957, also known as Public Health Service Publication No. 544].

Crosby A. 1989. *America's Forgotten Pandemic: The Influenza of 1918.* New York: Cambridge University Press

Crosby, A. 2003. *America's Forgotten Pandemic: The Influenza of 1918.* 2nd edition. New York, NY: Cambridge University Press, p.18.

Culloton J. 2005. American Troops in Northern Russia and Siberia, World War I, 1918–1920. Available from http://www.militaria.com/8th/WW1/siberia.html.

Dauer CC. 1957. The Pandemic of Influenza in 1918–19. Washington, D.C.: Public Health Service, National Office of Vital Statistics.

Davies P. 2000. *The Devil's Flu.* New York: Henry Holt and Company.

Ferguson NM, Cummings DA, Fraser C, Cajka CJ, Cooley PC, Burke DS. 2006. Strategies for mitigating an influenza pandemic. *Nature* 442:448–452.

Foveaux, JLB. 1997. *Any Given Day: The Life and Times of Jessie Lee Brown Foveaux.* Warner Books.

Garrett L. 2005. The next pandemic? *Foreign Affairs* (July/August). Available from www.foreignaffairs.org.

Gernhart G. 1999. A Forgotten Enemy: PHS's Fight Against the 1918 Influenza Pandemic. *Public Health Reports* 114:559–561.

Gibbs MJ, Armstrong JS, Gibbs AJ. 2001. The haemagglutinin gene, but not the neuraminidase gene, of 'Spanish flu' was a recombinant. *Philos Trans R Soc Lond B Biol Sci* 356(1416):1845–1855.

Gladwell M. 1997. "The Dead Zone." *The New Yorker*, Sept. 29.

Guénel J. 2004. Spanish influenza in France from 1918–1919. *Hist Sci Med* 38(2):165–175.

Hardy C. 1984. Interview done for WHYY-FM (Philadelphia) radio program "The Influenza Pandemic of 1918." Courtesy of Charles Hardy, West Chester University. Transcript published online: http://historymatters.gmu.edu/d/13.

Harris JW. 1919. Influenza occurring in pregnant women: a statistical study of thirteen hundred and fifty cases. *JAMA* 72:978–980.

Hatchett RJ, Mecher CE, Lipsitch M. 2007. Public health interventions and epidemic intensity during the 1918 influenza pandemic. *Proc Natl Acad Sci USA* 104(18):7582–7587. Epub 2007 Apr 6. PMID: 17416679 [PubMed — indexed for MEDLINE].

HHS (U.S. Department of Health and Human Services). 2006(a). The Great Pandemic of 1918: State by State. Pennsylvania. www.pandemicflu.gov.

HHS (U.S. Department of Health and Human Services). 2006(b). The Great Pandemic of 1918: State by State. Washington. www.pandemicflu.gov.

HHS (U.S. Department of Health and Human Services). n.d. "Voices of the Pandemic, The Great Pandemic: The United States in 1918-19." http://1918.pandemicflu.gov/the_pandemic/02.htm.

Hoehling AA. 1961. *The Great Epidemic*. Boston: Little Brown & Co.

Hollenbeck JE. 2005. An avian connection as a catalyst to the 1918-1919 influenza pandemic. *Int J Med Sci* 2(2):87–90.

Jordan EO. 1927. *Epidemic Influenza: A Survey*. Chicago: American Medical Association.

Kaplan M, Webster R. 1977. The epidemiology of influenza. *Scientific American*.

Kash C, Basler CF, García-Sastre A, Carter V, Billharz R, Swayne DE, Przygodzki RM, Taubenberger JK, Katze, MG, Tumpey TM. 2004. Global host immune response: pathogenesis and transcriptional profiling of type A influenza viruses expressing the hemagglutinin and neuraminidase genes from the 1918 pandemic virus. *J Virol* 78(17):9499–9511.

Kolata G. 1999. *Flu: The Story of the Great Influenza Pandemic of 1918 and the Search for the Virus That Caused It*. New York: Farrar, Straus, and Giroux.

Longini IM, Nizam A, Xu S, Ungchusak K, Hanshaoworakul W, Cummings DA, et al. 2005. Containing pandemic influenza at the source. *Science* 309:1083–1087.

Loo Y-M, Gale M. 2007. Influenza: fatal immunity and the 1918 virus. *Nature* 445:267–268. Published online 17 January 2007.

Luk J, Gross P, Thompson WW. 2001. Observations on mortality during the 1918 influenza pandemic. *Clin Infect Dis* 33(8):1375–1378. Epub 17 Sep. 2001.

Markel H, Stern AM, Navarro JA, Michalsen JR, Monto AS, DiGiovanni C Jr. 2006. Non-pharmaceutical influenza mitigation strategies, US communities, 1918–1920 pandemic. *Emerg Infect Dis* 12(12):1961–1964.

Military.com. World War I. The War to End All Wars. Available from www.military.com/Resources/HistorySubmittedFileView?file=history_worldwari.htm

Murray CL, Alan D, Lopez B, Chin B, Feehan D, Hill K. 2006. Estimation of potential global pandemic influenza mortality on the basis of vital registry data from the 1918–1920 pandemic: a quantitative analysis. *Lancet* 368(9554):2211–2218.

Osterholm MPH. 2005. Preparing for the next pandemic. *New Engl J Med* 352(18): 1839–1842.

Price A. 1918. "After-War Public Health Problems." *The New York Times,* November 5, sec. 1, p. 22.

Public Broadcasting Service. The American Experience: Influenza 1918. Program transcript available from www.pbs.org/wgbh/amex/influenza/filmmore/transcript/transcript1.html.

Ramanna M. 2003. Coping with the influenza pandemic: the Bombay experience. In: *The Spanish Influenza Pandemic of 1918–1919: New Perspectives,* pp. 86–98. Phillips H, Killingray D, Eds. London: Routledge.

Red Cross. Undated. Reference material and collections found at the Hazel Braugh Records Center and Archives, the official repository of the American Red Cross national headquarters.

Rosenhek J. 2005. The so-called "Spanish" flu: did a cook from a U.S. military training base cause the great flu pandemic of 1918? *Doctors Rev Med* 23(11).

Russel CJ, Webster RG. 2005. The genesis of a pandemic influenza virus. *Cell* 122:368–371.

Shope RE. 1937. The influenzas of swine and man. *The Harvey Lectures,* 1935–1936, pp. 183–213. New York: The Harvey Society.

Smith W, Andrewes CH, Laidlaw PP. 1933. A virus obtained from influenza patients. *Lancet* 2:66–68.

Starr I. 1976. Influenza in 1918: recollections of the epidemic in Philadelphia. *Ann Int Med* 85:516–518.

Stevens J, Corper AL, Basler CF, Taubenberger JK, Palese P, Wilson IA. 2004. Structure of the uncleaved human H1 hemagglutinin from the extinct 1918 influenza virus. *Science* 303(5665):1866–1870. Epub 5 Feb 2004.

Taubenberger JK, Morens DM. 2006(a). 1918 Influenza: the mother of all pandemics. *Emerg Infect Dis* 12(1):15–22.

Taubenberger JK, Morens DM. 2006(b). Influenza revisited. *Emerg Infect Dis* 12(1), available from http://www.cdc.gov/ncidod/EID/vol12no01/05-1442.htm.

Taubenberger JK, Reid AH, Krafft AE, Bijwaard KE, Fanning TG. 1997. Initial genetic characterization of the 1918 "Spanish" influenza virus. *Science* 275(5307):1793–1796.

Taubenberger JK, Reid AH, Lourens RM, Wang R, Jin G, Fanning TG. 2005. Characterization of the 1918 influenza virus polymerase genes. *Nature* 437:889–893.

Tumpey TM, et al. 2005. Characterization of the reconstructed 1918 Spanish influenza pandemic virus. *Science* 7:77–80.

Vaughn VC, Vaughn HF, Palmer GT. 1922. *Epidemiology and Public Health; A Text and Reference Book for Physicians, Medical Students and Health Workers.* St. Louis: CV Mosby Co.

White Coat Notes. 2007. Public health measures slowed 1918 flu pandemic, study finds. News from the Boston area medical community. Available from www.boston.com/yourlife/health/blog/2007/04/public_health_m_1.html.

WHO (World Health Organization). 2005. Avian Flu vs. Pandemic Flu. Available from www.wvdhhr.org/healthprep/common/Avian_vs_Pandemic_Flu.pdf.

Woolston WJ, Conley DO. 1918. Epidemic pneumonia (Spanish influenza) in pregnancy: effect in one hundred and one cases. *J Am Med Assoc* 71:1898–1899.

World Health Organization Writing Group. 2006. *Emerg Infect Dis* 12(1).

Part II

Natural History of Influenza

3 Natural History of the Influenza Virus

Jeffrey R. Ryan, PhD

> *The single biggest threat to man's continued dominance on the planet is a virus.*
>
> **Dr. Joshua Lederberg**
> *Nobel Laureate*

CONTENTS

3.1   INTRODUCTION

Pandemic planners will often ask me why they need to know the many details about the biology of the influenza virus. My reply is simple: *know thy enemy!* The more one delves into the background of this problem of pandemic influenza, the more one will become overwhelmed by the tremendous amount of technical information, terms, and jargon that come along with the subject. Furthermore, we now have the technology to examine the smallest details and the means to disseminate information at remarkable speed and with saturation. Since the discovery in 1997 that the highly pathogenic strain of type A avian influenza (H5N1) jumped from poultry to humans, we have been inundated with technical details. Pandemic planners are suffering from information overload. Public health officials and medical professionals have more medical literature to review than they have time to read it. Listservs, trade journals, and electronic mail send us conflicting reports. How much of this information is relevant?

Perhaps this chapter can help you make sense of it. We all need a good foundation of knowledge on the subject to understand the threat truly before we attempt to address it. The aim of this chapter is to provide the reader with a basic understanding of the biology of influenza viruses. Technical information about the pathogen, details on the dynamics of transmission, host range, and genetic mechanisms leading to mutation of the virus will be explained. Finally, a glossary of essential terminology is provided at the end of the chapter for reference.

3.2   WHAT IS INFLUENZA AND HOW DOES IT AFFECT US?

Influenza is any illness caused by the influenza virus. Influenza viruses are highly infectious and significant human respiratory pathogens. Influenza viruses cause seasonal, endemic infections; sporadic, localized epidemics; and periodic, unpredictable pandemics (Taubenberger, Morens, 2008). As covered in chapter 2, the worst pandemic on record, the 1918 Spanish flu, killed approximately 50 million people worldwide. The layman is not likely to consider that influenza, or the flu, is actually a zoonotic disease. The recent emergence of bird flu due to the strain H5N1 out of the depths of Asia has brought that fact to the attention of the masses. Human infections caused by H5N1 highly pathogenic avian influenza viruses have raised concern about the emergence of another pandemic. Influenza viruses continue to be a major health threat in both endemic and pandemic forms. The rapid, continuous, and unpredictable nature of influenza viral evolution makes vaccine strategies and pandemic planning difficult.

In order for us to truly know the enemy, we must understand and appreciate the connection between highly pathogenic avian influenza (HPAI) and human health. As most of us know, disease results when a pathogen encounters a susceptible host. In the case of influenza, a zoonotic triad exists between pathogen, host, and reservoir. Chapter 5 of this book goes into sufficient detail about the avian component of this dynamic of disease. However, some of that groundwork will also be discussed here.

Mankind has always been challenged by pathogens and disease. In his thought-provoking book *Guns, Germs, and Steel*, Dr. Jared Diamond discussed the epidemiological transitions human societies have faced since their existence in family collectives: nomads or hunters and gatherers. Prior to the advent of agriculture more than 10,000 years ago, humans were affected mostly by parasitic diseases, which mostly affected individuals. Following that, human societies began to herd and domesticate animals. The development of agriculture allowed for population growth and a shift from small tribal bands to the concentration of people into villages. Larger groups of people could stand up to smaller elements, thereby enabling them to compete successfully for resources and better defend the ground that they held. However, agriculture also brought mankind some deadly gifts: animal diseases that also affected man (zoonotic diseases); outbreaks of disease due to massing of people and lack of innate immunity; and, a growing reliance on animal protein (Diamond, 1999). Influenza is one such deadly gift; quite probably the deadliest of all.

In temperate regions of the world, common or seasonal influenza transmission and rates of infection increase during winter months. The reason for this is not known exactly, although it seems intuitive that this phenomenon is likely associated with people congregating and spending more time indoors during colder periods (Lofgren et al., 2007). Also, increased virus viability and transmission of the virus has been shown to be associated with colder temperatures. Influenza virus is very efficiently spread by aerosolization of the virus during the coughing and sneezing fits of an infected host. Virus may be transmitted to uninfected individuals as they make contact with contaminated materials or surfaces, later touching their mouths, noses, and eyes. Contaminated objects (fomites) also play a role in influenza virus transmission. Consideration for these modes of transmission gives emphasis to public education campaigns, whereby we must do our best to encourage people to wash their hands frequently, avoid sick individuals, and cover their own coughs and sneezes when ill.

Primary infection from the influenza virus involves the ciliated epithelial cells of the upper respiratory tract (Taubenberger, Morens, 2008). Necrosis of these cells results in the usual symptoms of the acute respiratory infection (fever, chills, muscular aching, headache, prostration, anorexia). Normally self-limited infection will last three to seven days (Taubenberger, Morens, 2008). Death from primary influenza infection is rare and appears to be determined by host factors rather than "virulence" of the pathogen. Damage to respiratory epithelium predisposes the host to secondary bacterial infections, which accounts for most deaths (Taubenberger, Morens, 2008). The chapter that follows will explain the clinical aspects of influenza in great detail.

The CDC Web site states what has become commonly accepted and widely reported in the lay and scientific press: annually "about 36,000 [Americans] die from flu" and "influenza/pneumonia" is the seventh leading cause of death in the United States (CDC[a], 2008). Rates of infection are highest among children, but rates of serious illness and death are highest among senior citizens over the age of 65, children under the age of 2 years, and persons of any age who have medical conditions that place them at increased risk for complications from the flu (CDC[b], 2008). In normal years, serious morbidity and mortality is almost entirely among elderly people with underlying chronic disease. During influenza epidemics from 1979–1980 through 2000–2001, the estimated overall number of influenza-associated hospitalizations in the United States ranged from approximately 54,000 to 430,000 per epidemic. An average of approximately 226,000 influenza-related excess hospitalizations occurred per year, with 63 percent of all hospitalizations occurring among persons aged >65 years. The CDC acknowledges a difference between flu death and flu-associated death. yet uses the terms interchangeably. Additionally, there are significant statistical incompatibilities between official estimates and national vital statistics data (Doshi, 2005). Researchers at the National Institutes of Health (NIH) recently showed that the regional spread of annual influenza epidemics throughout the United States is more closely connected with rates of movement of people to and from work than with geographical distance or air travel. They also found that epidemics spread faster between more populous locations (NIH News, 2006). In this regard, communities that have a high degree of "connectedness" are believed to be more at risk for rapid spread of a novel influenza virus.

3.3 TYPES OF INFLUENZA VIRUS AND THEIR CHARACTERISTICS

Influenza viruses belong to the family Orthomyxoviridae (Palese, Schulman, 1976). The family Orthomyxoviridae contains four genera, as defined by the International Committee on Taxonomy of Viruses: influenza viruses A, B, and C, and thogotoviruses.

Thogotoviruses, normally transmitted by ticks, are known to infect vertebrates and invertebrates. Influenza viruses are subdivided into types A, B, and C. The host range of type A influenza virus is very broad. Influenza type A viruses can infect people, birds, pigs, horses, seals, whales, and other animals; however, wild birds are the natural hosts for these viruses (Beard, 1998). As such, type A influenza virus is viewed as an ecological generalist. Many type A influenza virus strains are known to infect man, while all known avian strains are type A. Type A influenza viruses are considered the most virulent of the three types of influenza virus. Virulence is the relative capacity to cause disease; degree or measure of pathogenicity of a pathogen. The more virulent a strain or pathogen is, the more likely it is to cause illness and death.

Type A influenza viruses are generally classified into subtypes based on two surface antigens known as hemagglutinin and neuraminidase (Palese, Schulman, 1976). The hemagglutinin and neuraminidase viral envelope proteins, as well as the M2 protein, are the most relevant antigens, because they are highly immunogenic and targeted by host antibodies. Sixteen different hemagglutinin (HA or H) subtypes and nine different neuraminidase (NA or N) subtypes have been described for influenza type A. Many different H and N combinations are possible. However, only three major influenza A subtypes (H1N1, H1N2, and H3N2) are currently circulating in the world's human population (Ma et al., 2007).

Influenza type B viruses are almost exclusively found in humans. One exception to this was reported recently where seals were found to be infected with influenza type B virus (Osterhaus et al., 2000). Influenza type B viruses are not categorized into subtypes as type A viruses are. They are quite common, but clinical disease due to infection with type B influenza virus is normally less severe than infections due to influenza type A virus. On some occasions, influenza B viruses have caused human epidemics, but they have not been determined to be a cause of any of the pandemics. Because types A and B influenza virus cause severe disease, human seasonal vaccines normally contain two strains of influenza A and one strain of B virus. Influenza C viruses, which are only found in humans and swine, cause only mild illness in humans, and do not cause epidemics or pandemics (Riedel, 2006). Their pattern of surface proteins are different from the other influenza types and, like type B, they are not categorized into subtypes.

As the epidemic spread, top physicians and scientists claimed its cause was everything from tiny plants to old, dusty books to something called "cosmic influence." It was not until 1933 that a British research team finally isolated and identified the influenza virus. (Dr. Laurie Garrett, author of *The Coming Plague.*)

In the early stages of the 1918 pandemic, many scientists theorized that the agent responsible for influenza was Pfeiffer's bacillus. Research conducted during the pandemic period ultimately led scientists to discard the theory. In late October 1918, some researchers began to argue that influenza was caused by a virus. Although, for more than two decades, scientists had understood that viruses caused disease, virology was a burgeoning science at that time. Astonishingly, it was not until 1933 that the influenza A virus, which had been the cause of so much morbidity and mortality, was finally isolated. Smith, Andrewes, and Laidlaw (1933) isolated the influenza virus in ferrets and reported their findings in *The Lancet*, a British medical journal. Seven years later, the influenza B virus was isolated and 10 years after that, influenza C virus was isolated. It is worthy of note that Dr. Robert Shope isolated the first influenza virus from pigs in 1930, and after the subsequent isolation of human influenza A viruses in 1933, ferrets were identified as an excellent laboratory model for human influenza (Shope, 1934).

Viability of the influenza virus is promoted by cold, moist conditions (Bean et al., 1982). The virus is relatively labile with a half-life of a few hours at room temperature. The virus is inactivated by detergents, acidic or basic (pH) conditions, and drying. Studies showed that the virus can retain viability for up to 48 hours when deposited on a nonporous surface (Barker, Stevens, Bloomfield, 2001). In addition, lower temperature and low to moderate relative humidity were conditions that favored transmission of influenza virus to experimental animals (Lowen et al., 2007).

3.4 INFLUENZA AT THE MOLECULAR LEVEL

Nearly 75 years of detailed scientific work has placed the human influenza A virus at the pinnacle of virological knowledge (Oxford et al., 2003). Virus particles, or virions, consist of an envelope, a matrix protein, a nucleoprotein complex, a nucleocapsid, and a polymerase complex. The influenza virus capsids, or protein coat, are enveloped in a lipid (fat) bi-layer. Virions are morphologically variable (pleomorphic). Virions are spherical or ovoid to filamentous in form. Individual virus particles measure 80 to 120 nanometers in diameter and 200 to 300 nanometers in length. There are approximately 500 surface projections, which are densely dispersed, distinctive "spikes and knobs" that cover the surface evenly. These spike- and knob-like projections are made up of hemagglutinin and neuraminidase, respectively. The projections are interspersed at a ratio of H:N of approximately 4:1. Influenza virus particles may appear as spherical/ovoid or very filamentous. See Figures 3.1 through 3.3 for electron micrographs of influenza virus.

As previously mentioned, the outer surface of the particle consists of a lipid envelope from which project prominent glycoprotein spikes hemagglutinin (HA) and neuraminidase (NA). The inner side of the envelope is lined by a matrix protein (M). The genome segments are packaged into the core of the virion. A ribonucleo-protein (RNP = RNA + nucleoprotein, N) exists in a helical form with three polymerase polypeptides associated with each segment. Refer to Table 3.1 for a summary of all antigenic components of the influenza virus.

Early studies with influenza virus led to the discovery of hemagglutinin, a vital protein and potent immunogen of the virus. This antigen's characterization comes from its haemagglutination ability, enabling the virus to bind to chicken and mammalian red blood cells. More importantly, these studies led to the development of a

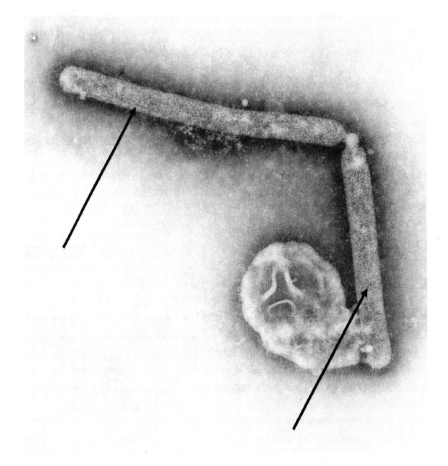

FIGURE 3.1 This transmission electron micrograph (TEM), taken at a magnification of 108,000x, revealed the ultrastructural details of two avian influenza A (H5N1) virions (as indicated by the arrows), a type of bird flu virus, which is a subtype of avian influenza A. At this magnification, one may note the stippled appearance of the roughened surface of the proteinaceous coat encasing each virion. (Photo by Cynthia Goldsmith and Jackie Katz. Image courtesy of the Centers for Disease Control and Prevention, Public Health Image Library (no. 8038).)

haemagglutination inhibition (HI) test, which, after 60 years, is still the gold standard in antigenic analysis for influenza virus strains (Hirst, 1942). The first serological studies in animal models and post-infection human sera indicated a surprising degree of antigenic change of the hemagglutinin antigen. At that time, neither the HA nor the NA spike had been visualized nor was it clear that the virus had an internal structure of nucleoprotein (NP), matrix protein (M), and polymerase proteins (PA, PB1, PB2).

Subsequent studies with type A influenza virus pointed to the importance of hemagglutinin as an antigen and showed that it was made up of two polypeptides (HA1 and HA2). These two constituents of HA were separated and studied by

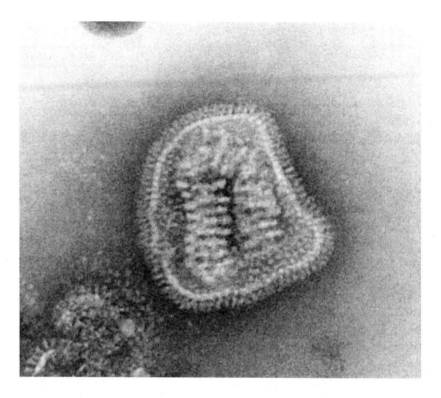

FIGURE 3.2 This negative-stained transmission electron micrograph (TEM) depicts the ultrastructural details of a number of influenza virus particles, or virions. A member of the taxonomic family Orthomyxoviridae, the influenza virus is a single-stranded RNA organism. (Photo by Cynthia Goldsmith. Image courtesy of the Centers for Disease Control and Prevention, Public Health Image Library (no. 8430).)

peptide mapping. Here, researchers discovered that antigenic change occurred almost exclusively in the HA1 component of hemagglutinin. Laver and Webster (1972) found that hemagglutinin of the different subtypes of influenza A had completely different peptide maps: each was independent and could not transform into other subtypes by mutation (Oxford et al., 2003). It was also apparent that these antigenic properties enabled type A influenza virus to take up residence in a number of different hosts.

The three viral envelope proteins of influenza A virus are the most medically relevant. The hemagglutinin (HA), neuraminidase (NA), and M2 are essential viral proteins targeted by host antibodies or the action of influenza-specific antiviral drugs (WHO, 2005). Hemagglutinin glycoproteins form spikes on the surface of virions, which mediate attachment to host cell receptors, thereby enabling the virus to gain entry through membrane fusion. Neuraminidase forms knoblike structures on the surface of the virions to catalyze their release from infected cells eventually, allowing the virus to spread and infect new host cells. The M2 antigen is a transmembrane protein that forms an ion channel required for the uncoating process that precedes viral gene expression.

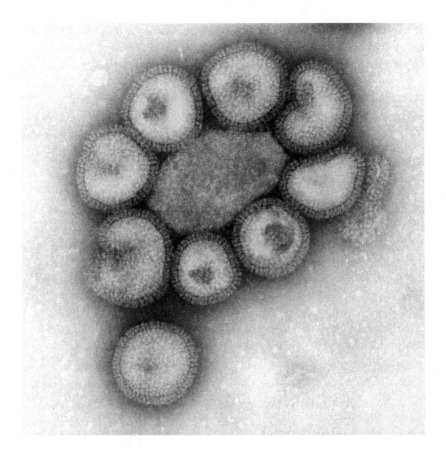

FIGURE 3.3 This negative-stained transmission electron micrograph (TEM) depicts the ultrastructural details of a number of influenza virus particles, or virions. A member of the taxonomic family Orthomyxoviridae, the influenza virus is a single-stranded RNA organism. (Photo by Cynthia Goldsmith. Image courtesy of the Centers for Disease Control and Prevention, Public Health Image Library (no. 8432).)

3.5   GENETIC MUTATION AND ANTIGENIC VARIATION

More is known about the genomic structure and genetic evolution of influenza type A virus than any other human virus. Influenza viruses contain eight genes, composed of ribonucleic acid (RNA) and packaged loosely in protective proteins. The genome of types A and B influenza viruses consist of single-stranded, missense RNA in eight segments. It is well-established that each of the eight genes contributes to the virulence of the virus (Zambon, 2001).

Difficulty in controlling illness from one flu season to the next is due to changes in virus types A and B. Both types A and B undergo constant but relatively subtle mutations (antigenic drift), accounting for the different influenza epidemiology, strains, and vaccines seen from year to year. As the virus lacks a proofreading mechanism, small errors or point mutations that occur when the virus copies itself

TABLE 3.1
Important Antigens of Influenza Type A

Antigen	Nomenclature	Function
Hemagglutinin	H or HA	Initial binding to host cell
Neuraminidase	N or NA	Release of replicated virus
Transcriptase		
	PB2	Cap binding
	PB1	Elongation
	PA	Protease activity
Nucleoprotein: RNA binding	NBP	Part of transcriptase complex; nuclear/ cytoplasmic transport of VRNA
Matrix protein	M1	Major component of virion
Integral membrane protein	M2	Ion channel
Nonstructural	NS1	Nucleus; effects on cellular RNA transport, splicing, translation; anti-interferon protein
Nonstructural	NS2	Nucleus and cytoplasm, function unknown

are left undetected and uncorrected. As a result, influenza viruses undergo constant minute changes in their genetic makeup. This strategy, known as antigenic drift, works well as a short-term survival tactic for the virus: the speed with which slight variations develop keeps host populations susceptible to infection (Brown et al., 2006). Transmission cycles and a constant viral evolution are essential to the virus's continued survival; were it to remain identical year after year, most animals would develop immunity, and the pathogen would be fended off by herd immunity. This constant mutational process explains why most humans will get influenza more than once in their lifetime and why seasonal vaccines made one year may be useless the following year (Garrett, 2005). Human influenza vaccines are formulated differently each year due to antigenic drift. Changes need to be made in order to try and match the most prevalent strain in circulation.

Influenza A and B possess two surface glycoproteins or antigens: hemagglutinin and neuraminidase. A minor change in these antigens, referred to as antigenic drift, may result in epidemics, because incomplete protection remains from past exposure to similar viruses. However, influenza A viruses reproduce sloppily: their genes readily fall apart in the host cell, with the ability to incorporate segments of RNA from different parental stains, reconstituting later in a process referred to as reassortment (Garrett, 2005). When influenza virus successfully infects a new species, the reassortant population may switch from a strain being well-adapted to avian species to one that can infect others such as mammals. When this occurs, it is referred to as antigenic shift. Antigenic shift represents a dramatic departure from the parental strain and, if the resultant progeny (reassortant population) are viable in humans, capable of causing severe illness and transmissible from human to human, the world has the makings of a pandemic strain (Garrett, 2005). One cannot emphasize enough the importance of this attribute for it is the essence of what makes type A influenza viruses such a formidable foe. Antigenic shift occurs only with influenza A viruses. It is believed that the last three pandemics (1918, 1957, and 1968) have all involved antigenic shifts. Influenza A viruses were the cause of the three pandemics in the 20th century (Hoffmann et al., 2005). Influenza pandemics occur when there is a notable genetic change in the circulating strain of influenza (Brown et al., 2006). When the next antigenic shift will occur that will lead to the next influenza pandemic is not known.

3.5.1 HOST RANGE

Type A influenza had been isolated from cats, birds (domesticated and wild), swine, dogs, cattle, horses, equines, ferrets, humans, and even whales (Woolhouse et al., 2001). This amazing host range is graphically depicted in Figure 3.4. Avian influenza viruses have been found in many bird species, but are most often found in migratory waterfowl, especially the mallard duck. Avian influenza is usually an unapparent or subclinical viral infection of wild birds. Different combinations of the two antigens appear more frequently in some groups of birds than others. In waterfowl, all nine of the neuraminidase subtypes and 14 of the 16 hemagglutinin subtypes have been found; H6 and H3 are the predominant subtypes. In shorebirds and gulls, 10 different hemagglutinin subtypes and eight neuraminidase subtypes have been found.

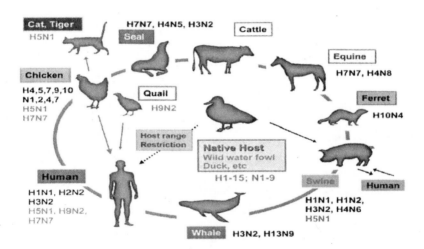

FIGURE 3.4 Schematic showing the host range of type A influenza virus. Type A influenza virus is thought of as an ecological generalist capable of infecting a multitude of hosts. Wild birds (center) are thought to be the original or natural host of the virus. Animals that share the aquatic environment with these wild birds are at risk of infection. It is unlikely that strains infecting wild birds will have the capability of directly infecting humans. However, these wild bird strains may infect other animals and subsequent passage through these secondary hosts may enable virus populations to mutate into strains that ultimately infect humans. (Image courtesy of the Centers for Disease Control and Prevention Influenza Branch.)

Many of the antigenic combinations of subtypes are unique to shorebirds; H9 and H13 are the predominate subtypes. More influenza viruses from shorebirds infect waterfowl than poultry. Hemagglutinin subtypes H5 and H7 are associated with virulence or the ability to cause severe illness and mortality in chickens and turkeys (Beard, 1998).

The only HPAI mortality event known in wild birds occurred in common terns in South Africa in 1961. This was the first documented influenza virus from marine birds; it was characterized as subtype H5N3. Other wild birds yielding influenza viruses include various species of shorebirds, gulls, quail, pheasants, and ratites (ostrich and rhea). Experimental infections of domestic birds with viruses from wildlife do not cause mortality. Likewise, virulent viruses or viruses that cause disease in domestic fowl do not cause mortality in wild waterfowl.

As previously mentioned, humans can be infected by influenza viruses of all three types, but only influenza A viruses infect birds. Most of these viruses cause no significant illness in wild birds, which are typically the natural host for all subtypes of influenza A virus. However, domestic poultry, such as chickens and turkeys, develop a severe illness and can even die from influenza. Avian influenza (H5N1) is a type A influenza virus. Many subtypes of avian influenza A have been described; some of the more recent isolates were H7 and H5 viruses. In addition, avian influenza viruses H5 and H7 can be further classified as "low pathogenicity" (LPAI) and "high pathogenicity" (HPAI) based on genetic features of the viral genome and the severity of illness they cause in poultry. HPAI is usually associated with high mortality (90 to 100 percent) in poultry, but at this time it is not clear how the distinction of high and low pathogenicity relates to human disease.

Avian influenza viruses do not normally infect humans, and all influenza viruses usually show some receptor specificity for their hosts. Receptor specificity of influenza viruses has been defined by modifications in antigenic components of the virus and specific receptors in the host cell membranes. This provides a considerable species barrier between birds and humans, which is not easily overcome. When avian influenza viruses cross species barriers and subsequently become infectious to humans, this is commonly believed to occur via an intermediate host (e.g., swine). Thusly, pigs provide an opportunity for antigenic shift. In a classic scenario involving pathogen, birds, pigs, and humans (a zoonotic tetrad), different strains of influenza virus originating from the birds and the humans in this setting co-infect a pig. The pig acts as a "mixing vessel," able to be infected by both avian and human types of virus, thus allowing the passage of avian viruses to humans (see Figure 3.5). A change in viral envelope protein structure, together with the interaction between these viral surface proteins/receptors and the cell surface receptors of mammalian cells, enables the virus to become infective for the new host. However, controversy exists within the scientific community about the existence and necessity of such an intermediate host in the transmission cycle of influenza viruses. In the past, several avian influenza viruses have been able to infect humans directly but only on a very limited basis. The human infections caused by the avian influenza H5N1 subtype in Hong Kong in 1997 represents one of the few examples of a strain capable of human infection without passing through an intermediate host.

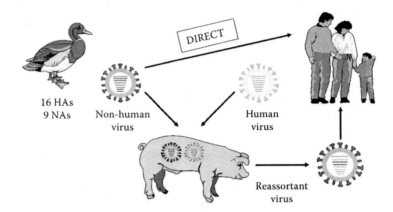

FIGURE 3.5 This is the classic "mixing vessel" scenario where two different strains of type A influenza virus, one from a wild bird and one from a human source, co-infect a host cell within a pig. The pig acts as a "mixing vessel," giving rise to a reassortant virus population that is a combination of the two parent strains. If this reassortant population is capable of causing severe disease in humans and fully transmissible from human to human, the new strain has the potential of sparking a pandemic. (Image courtesy of the Centers for Disease Control and Prevention Influenza Branch.)

3.6 PANDEMIC POTENTIALITIES

From what we know now, influenza type A viruses are the ones with true pandemic potential. In general, influenza type A virus has a very broad host range. Some would say that it is the ultimate zoonotic pathogen. Specific strains of influenza type A virus have a narrow host range, but antigenic or genetic shift through an intermediate host enables the virus to jump species. That said, we should now explore two host-specific settings where influenza in animals has implications for human health (swine and poultry).

3.6.1 SWINE FLU

Swine flu is a respiratory disease of pigs caused by type A influenza virus. Although swine influenza virus circulates throughout the year, outbreaks of swine flu occur during the late fall and winter months. Swine flu viruses cause high levels of illness and low death rates among pigs. The classical swine flu virus (type A H1N1 influenza virus) was first isolated from a pig in 1930 (Shope, 1930). H1N1 and H3N2 swine flu viruses are endemic among pig populations in the United States and are a problem that pork producers deal with routinely. Outbreaks among pigs normally occur with the introduction of new pigs into susceptible herds. Studies have shown that the swine flu H1N1 is common throughout pig populations worldwide, with 25 percent of animals showing antibody evidence of infection. In the United States, studies have shown that 30 percent of the pig population has antibody evidence of having had an infection with H1N1. More specifically, 51 percent of pigs in the north-central United States have been shown to have antibody evidence of infection with swine H1N1.

Human infections with swine flu H1N1 viruses are rare. Although H1N1 swine viruses have been known to circulate among pig populations since at least 1930, H3N2 influenza viruses did not begin circulating among pigs in the United States until 1998. The H3N2 viruses initially were introduced into the pig population from humans (Ma et al., 2007). The current swine flu H3N2 viruses are closely related to human H3N2 viruses.

Although viruses of each of the 16 type A influenza virus hemagglutinin subtypes are potential human pathogens, only viruses of the H1, H2, and H3 subtype are known to have been successfully established in humans. However, H2 influenza viruses have been absent from human circulation since 1968. As such, they pose a substantial human pandemic risk. Recently, one group of researchers isolated and characterized avian/swine virus reassortant H2N3 influenza A viruses isolated from diseased swine from two farms in the United States. The H2N3 viral isolates taken from these pigs were able to cause disease in experimentally infected swine and mice without prior adaptation. In addition, the swine H2N3 virus was infectious and highly transmissible in swine and ferrets. These findings indicate that the H2N3 virus has undergone some adaptation to the mammalian host and that their spread should be very closely monitored (Ma et al., 2007). Indeed, while the world's attention is focused on our next topic, the next pandemic strain may be brewing in pigs!

3.6.2 BIRD FLU

There has been recent concern that bird flu (which merely refers to influenza in birds or avian influenza) could cause human disease in some situations. Avian influenza has been recognized as a highly lethal, generalized viral disease of poultry since 1901. It has since been found that avian influenza viruses cause a wide range of disease syndromes — ranging from severe to mild — in domestic poultry. Highly pathogenic avian influenza (HPAI) due to H5N1 originated in 1997 in Southeast Asia, but in recent years has spread to much of Asia, parts of Europe, and Africa. Direct avian-to-human influenza transmission was unknown before 1997. Genetic studies confirm that H5N1, like other influenza viruses, is continuing to change and evolve. The avian H5N1 virus is becoming more deadly in a growing number of bird species and mammals. When compared with H5N1 viruses from 1997 and early 2004, H5N1 viruses now circulating are more lethal to experimentally infected mice and ferrets (Garrett, 2005).

There is continuing concern that migrating wild birds may further spread HPAI. Wild birds and domestic ducks may be infected asymptomatically, providing a reservoir for infection of other domestic poultry species (Beard, 1998). The virus is able to transmit directly from birds to some mammals and, in some circumstances, to people. There is sporadic spread directly from animals to humans with suspected human-to-human transmission in rare instances. The transmission of avian H5N1 and H9N2 viruses directly to humans during the late 1990s showed that land-based poultry also can serve as intermediate hosts of influenza viruses between aquatic birds and humans. That these transmission events took place in Hong Kong and China adds further support to the hypothesis that Asia is an epicenter for influenza and stresses the importance of surveillance of pigs and live-bird markets in this area.

Although H5N1 is the greatest current pandemic threat, other avian influenza subtypes have also infected people in recent years. In 1999, H9N2 infections were identified in Hong Kong; in 2003, H7N7 infections occurred in the Netherlands; and in 2004, H7N3 infections occurred in Canada. Such outbreaks have the potential to give rise to the next pandemic, reinforcing the need for continued surveillance and ongoing vaccine development efforts against these strains.

Infected birds shed flu virus in their saliva, nasal secretions, and feces. Susceptible birds become infected when they have contact with contaminated excretions or surfaces that are contaminated with excretions. It is believed that most cases of bird flu infection in humans have resulted from contact with infected poultry or contaminated surfaces. The main route of human infection is direct contact with infected poultry or surfaces and objects contaminated with their feces or blood. To date, most human cases have occurred in rural and periurban areas where households keep small poultry flocks that roam freely, often entering homes and sharing children's outdoor play areas. Millions of virus particles are excreted in the feces of infected birds. In countries where poultry is relied upon for income and food, families are known to slaughter and consume birds that are ill. Exposure occurs during slaughtering, defeathering, butchering, and preparation of poultry for cooking. Infection in humans occurs with consumption of inadequately cooked poultry or raw poultry products such as ducks' blood. There is no evidence that properly cooked poultry or eggs are a source of infection. It is not understood why some people but not others become infected with similar exposures.

With the H5N1 strain now endemic in birds in large parts of Asia, the probability that this potential for a pandemic will be realized has increased. The world has never before seen outbreaks of avian influenza on the scale of those that have swept through large parts of Asia, including densely populated China (Weir, 2005). The relatively low frequencies of influenza A (H5N1) illness in humans, despite widespread exposure to infected poultry, indicate that the species barrier to acquisition of this avian virus is substantial (Horimoto. Kawaoka, 2001).

According to the World Health Organization (WHO), no virus of the H5 subtype has probably ever circulated among humans, and certainly not within the lifetime of today's world population. Population vulnerability to an H5N1-like pandemic virus would be universal.

The argument that a highly lethal virus will not become easily transmissible assumes that the highly lethal virus incapacitates its victim before the victim can infect potential new hosts. However, H5N1 case patients (like other flu viruses) have a few days of asymptomatic viral shedding before they become incapacitated. Human cases of bird flu in Vietnam exhibited a latency period of two to four days, with an average of three. There does not appear to be the emergence of a milder or more transmissible form of H5N1.

No one can know how the pandemic virus that emerges will behave. It is possible that it will be less deadly than the current H5N1, less transmissible than typical flu, or perhaps both. Those infected with influenza are contagious both before they become symptomatic and after they feel well again, making it extremely difficult — if not impossible — to stop the spread of the virus across the globe. The speed and range of international travel makes spread of the pathogen a significant global threat should it become more adapted to humans.

As pointed out in chapter 1, a pandemic occurs when three conditions have been met: a new influenza virus subtype emerges; it infects humans, causing serious illness; and it spreads easily and is sustainable among humans. The H5N1 virus meets the first two conditions. The risk that it will acquire the ability to have efficient and sustained human-to-human transmission is present as long as opportunities for human infections occur. These opportunities will persist as long as the virus continues to circulate in domestic birds, perhaps for years to come.

3.7 CONCLUSION

Influenza viruses are significant human respiratory pathogens that cause both seasonal, endemic infections and periodic, unpredictable pandemics. There are three types of influenza viruses: A, B, and C. Humans can be infected with all three types. Generally, type A is the most serious, and type C is benign. Type A influenza can infect a multitude of hosts. Influenza A viruses have been isolated from avian and mammalian hosts, although the primary reservoirs are the aquatic bird populations of the world. In the aquatic birds, influenza is asymptomatic, and the viruses are in evolutionary stasis. The aquatic bird viruses do not replicate well in humans, and these viruses need to reassort or adapt in an intermediate host before they emerge in human populations. Pigs can serve as a host for avian and human viruses and are logical candidates for the role of intermediate host. This ability is often what gives rise to unique strains of type A influenza virus as the virus mutates readily to give it adaptive advantage in new hosts. These mechanisms are either referred to as genetic shift or genetic drift. Genetic shift results in the most virulent strains of influenza type A virus. In fact, previous epidemics and pandemics were sparked by such an event. Avian influenza concerns infection of birds with type A influenza virus. This can be very devastating to the health of a flock. Outbreaks of HPAI have cost the poultry industry billions of dollars in lost revenue over the past decade.

The worst pandemic on record, in 1918, killed approximately 50 million people worldwide. Human infections caused by H5N1 highly pathogenic avian influenza viruses have raised concern about the emergence of another pandemic. Currently, the global health community and the numerous national governments are concerned about the pandemic potential of H5N1. Officials from the World Health Organization and numerous federal organizations are conducting surveillance activities constantly to assess the status of the H5N1 strain. Should that strain develop the ability for sustained human-to-human transmission, another pandemic is likely. Influenza viruses continue to be a major health threat in both endemic and pandemic forms. The rapid, continuous, and unpredictable nature of influenza viral evolution makes vaccine strategies and pandemic planning difficult.

ESSENTIAL TERMINOLOGY

Antibody: A large Y-shaped protein used by the immune system to identify and neutralize foreign objects like bacteria and viruses. Each antibody recognizes a specific antigen unique to its target. This is because at the two tips of its "Y," it has structures akin to locks. Every lock only has one key, in this case, its own antigen. When the key is inserted into the lock, the antibody activates, tagging or neutralizing its target.

Antigen: Any foreign substance that elicits an antibody response from the host's immune system.

Avian influenza: Respiratory illness that occurs among wild birds and poultry; it is caused by type A influenza virus. Occasionally, some strains of this virus may infect humans.

Common (seasonal) flu: Influenza that occurs commonly from year to year.

Endemic: Common diseases that occur at a constant but relatively high rate in the population.

Epidemic: A disease that appears as new cases in a given human population, during a given period, at a rate that substantially exceeds what is "expected," based on recent experience (the number of new cases in the population during a specified period of time is called the "incidence rate").

Fomites: Inanimate objects or substances capable of transmitting infectious organisms from one individual to another.

Genetic drift: The ability of a virus to mutate naturally; the term is used in population genetics to refer to the statistical drift over time of allele frequencies in a finite population due to random sampling effects in the formation of successive generations.

Genetic shift: Occurs when the genetic material of a virus is fragmented and a cell is infected by two different but related viruses. The virus progeny can inherit fragments coming from both parent viruses (genetic reassortment). Influenza virus genome consists of eight RNA molecules. If a cell is simultaneously infected by a human and an avian virus, a combination of their RNA molecules in a progeny virus may result in a progeny virus with novel properties. This is also referred to as an antigenic shift, which may lead to a pandemic.

Hemagglutinin: An antigenic glycoprotein found on the surface of the influenza viruses (as well as many bacteria and other viruses). It is responsible for binding the virus to the cell that is being infected.

Immunogenic: Something that is capable of inducing an immune response.

Influenza: Illness caused by the influenza virus.

Neuraminidase: An antigenic glycoprotein enzyme found on the surface of the influenza virus.

Orthomyxoviridae: A family of RNA viruses that includes four genera: influenzavirus A, influenzavirus B, influenzavirus C, and thogotovirus.

Pandemic: A widespread epidemic caused by a highly virulent pathogen.

Pathogenesis: The development of disease; specifically the cellular events and reactions and mechanisms occurring in the development of disease.

Pathogenicity: The ability of a pathogen to inflict damage on a host.

Reassortment: The rearrangement of genes from two distinct influenza strains to produce a novel viral strain.

Virion: A single virus particle.

Virulence: The relative infectiousness of a micro-organism causing disease. The more virulent the pathogen, the more likely it is to cause illness and death.

Zoonotic disease: Any infectious disease that may be transmitted from other animals, both wild and domestic, to humans.

REFERENCES

Andrewes CH, Laidlaw PP, Smith W. 1934. The susceptibility of mice to the viruses of human and swine influenza. *J Exp Med* 224:859–862.

Barker J, Stevens D, Bloomfield S. 2001. Spread and prevention of some common viral infections in community facilities and domestic homes. *J Appl Microbiol* 91:7–21.

Bean B, Moore BM, Sterner B, Peterson LR, Gerding DN, Balfour HH Jr. 1982. Survival of influenza viruses on environmental surfaces. *J Infect Dis* 146:47–51.

Beard CW. 1998. Avian influenza (fowl plague). In: *Foreign Animal Diseases: The Gray Book,* 6th ed. U.S. Animal Health Association, Committee on Foreign Animal Disease.

Brown N, Wickham M, Coombes B, Finlay B. 2006. Crossing the line: selection and evolution of virulence traits. *PLoS Pathogen* 2(5):42.

CDC (U.S. Department of Health and Human Services, Centers for Disease Control and Prevention). [a] National Center for Health Statistics. Fast Facts A to Z. Available from http://www.cdc.gov/nchs/fastats/lcod.htm. [b] Influenza: The Disease. Available from http://www.cdc.gov/flu/about/disease.htm. [c] Influenza Branch. Weekly Flu Activity Statistics and Cumulative Data. Available from http://www.cdc.gov/flu/weekly/fluactivity.htm. All sources accessed 1 January 2008.

Diamond J. 1999. *Guns, Germs and Steel: The Fates of Human Societies.* WW Norton & Company.

Doshi P. 2005. Are US flu death figures more PR than science? BMJ 331:1412.

Ferguson N, Cummings D, Cauchemez S, Fraser C, Riley S, Meeyai A, Iamsirithaworn S, Burke D. 2005. Strategies for containing an emerging influenza pandemic in Southeast Asia. *Nature* "On Line" 10.1038/nature04017.

Garrett L. 2005. The next pandemic? *Foreign Affairs* (Jul/Aug).

Garrett L. 1995. The Coming Plague: Newly Emerging Diseases in a World Out of Balance. New York: Penguin Books.

Hirst G. 1942. The quantitative determination of influenza virus and antibodies by means of red cell agglutination. *J Exp Med* 75:47–64.

Hoffmann E, Lipatov AS, Webby RJ, Govorkova EA, Webster RG. 2005. Role of specific hemagglutinin amino acids in the immunogenicity and protection of H5N1 influenza virus vaccines. *Proc Natl Acad Sci USA* 102(36):12915–12920.

Horimoto T, Kawaoka Y. 2001. Pandemic threat posed by avian influenza A viruses. *Clin Microbiol Rev* 14(1):129–149.

International Committee on Taxonomy of Viruses. Available from http://www.ncbi.nlm.nih.gov/ICTVdb/Images/index.htm. Accessed 1 January 2008.

Laver WG, Webster RG. 1972. *Virology* 48:445–450.

Lofgren E, Fefferman N, Naumov Y, Gorski J, Naumova E. 2007. Minireview: Influenza seasonality: underlying causes and modeling theories. *J Virol* 81:5429–5436.

Lowen AC, Mubareka S, Steel J, Palese P. 2007. Influenza virus transmission is dependent on relative humidity and temperature. *PLoS Pathogen* 3(10):e151 doi:10.1371/journal. ppat.0030151. Accessed 2 January 2008.

Ma W, Vincent A, Gramer M, Brockwell C, Lager K, Janke B, Gauger P, Patnayak D, Webby R, Richt J. 2007. Identification of H2N3 influenza A viruses from swine in the United States. *Proc Natl Acad Sci USA* 104(52): 20949–20954.

NIH News. April 2006. Interregional Spread of Influenza through United States Described by Virus Type, Size of Population and Commuting Rates and Distance. National Institutes of Health (NIH), Press release. http://www.nih.gov/news/pr/apr2006/fic-19.htm.

Osterhaus A, Rimmelzwaan G, Martina B, Bestebroer T, Fouchier R. 2000. Influenza B virus in seals. *Science* 288:1051–1053.

Oxford J, Eswarasaran R, Mann A, Lambkin R. 2003. Influenza — The chameleon virus. In: *Antigenic Variation*. Craig A, Scherf A, Eds. Burlington, MA: Academic Press.

Palese P, Schulman J. 1976. Mapping of the influenza virus genome: identification of the hemagglutinin and the neuraminidase genes. *Proc Natl Acad Sci USA* 73(6):2142–2146.

Riedel S. 2006. Crossing the species barrier: The threat of an avian influenza pandemic. *Proc Baylor Univ Med Cent* 19(1):16–20.

Shope RE. 1931. Swine influenza. I. Experimental transmission and pathology. *J Exp Med* 54:349–59.

Shope RE. 1934. The infection of ferrets with swine influenza virus. *J Exp Med* 60:49–61.

Smith W, Andrewes C, Laidlaw P. 1933. A virus obtained from influenza patients. *Lancet* 2:66–68.

Taubenberger J, Morens D. 2006. 1918 influenza: the mother of all pandemics. *Emerg Infect Dis* 12:15–22.

Taubenberger J, Morens D. 2008. The pathology of influenza virus infections. *Annu Rev Pathol Mech Dis* 3:499–522.

Weir E. 2005. The changing ecology of avian flu. *Canadian Med Assoc J* 173(8):869–870.

WHO (World Health Organization, Global Influenza Program Surveillance Network). 2005. Evolution of H5N1 avian influenza viruses in Asia. *Emerg Infect Dis* available from http://www.cdc.gov/ncidod/EID/vol11no10/05-0644.htm. Accessed 1 January 2008.

Woolhouse M, Taylor L, Haydon D. 2001. Population biology of multihost pathogens. *Science* 292(5519):1109–1112.

Zambon MC. 2001. The pathogenesis of influenza in humans. *Rev Med Virol* 11:227–241.

4 Clinical Aspects of Influenza

Allen W. Kirchner, MD

An infection is an act of violence; it is an invasion, ...
and the body reacts violently.

John M. Barry

CONTENTS

4.1 INTRODUCTION

Influenza virus is one of the most efficient and infectious pathogens known. The symptoms that the virus elicits in the human respiratory tract are ideally suited for the promulgation and propagation of the disease that it causes. Influenza viruses have the ability to cause infection on a global scale in all age groups (Woodson, 2005). In addition to the highly transmissible nature of influenza, the virus can change its antigenic structure, resulting in novel subtypes that have never circulated in the human population. The emergence of a novel influenza viral subtype is one of the factors necessary for the development of an influenza pandemic. The extreme mutability of the RNA-based influenza virus makes the emergence of a novel strain much more likely than with other disease-causing organisms, such as bacteria or even DNA-based viruses. The three pandemics of the 20th century were associated with high rates of morbidity, mortality, and social disruption (Kilbourne, 2006; Osterholm, 2005).

Influenza is a respiratory disease that can be caused by three different types of influenza viruses (A, B, and C). Type A and type B influenza viruses are the cause of epidemics, and type A is generally more virulent than type B. Type C rarely causes clinically significant illness in humans. Historically, human type A influenza has been caused by viruses belonging to three hemagglutinin subtypes (H1, H2, and H3), and two neuraminidase subtypes (N1 and N2). The most common circulating type A influenza virus is, and has been for some years, H1N1, followed closely by H3N2 (CDC, 2007). With two notable exceptions, namely the highly pathogenic H1N1 strain of the 1918 pandemic and the current strains of HPAI H5N1, all of the influenza A subtypes that affect humans cause a similar array of relatively nonspecific signs and symptoms.

Other respiratory diseases, such as the common cold and some bacterial infections, may cause physical findings and symptoms similar to those of influenza. Often, the initial onsets of many different disease processes are characterized as being associated with "flu-like symptoms": fever, malaise, myalgia, headache, sore throat, and cough. Because of these similarities, early and accurate clinical diagnosis of influenza can be elusive. As discussed in more detail later, early diagnosis would be critical to the efficacious implementation of certain mitigation strategies for pandemic influenza.

Influenza viruses are spread among humans primarily via the respiratory route (Jordan, 1961), through the sneezing and coughing of infected persons (Alford et al., 1966). The majority of this viral release is in the form of large droplets containing millions of virions (Tellier, 2006). There is also evidence of pure aerosolization of virus particles during forceful expirations (Bridges, Kuehnert, Hall, 2003). In addition, the influenza virus may survive on nonporous surfaces for about 48 hours and perhaps up to 72 hours depending on ambient temperature (Bean et al., 1982). Although the direct spread of virus by coughing or sneezing may be the most common, one might protect himself from an infected person by removing himself from the immediate vicinity (>3 ft distance) of the coughing or sneezing patient or otherwise screening himself from the potential impact of the spewed infectious material. In contrast, it may be very difficult to protect oneself from contamination by virus that is invisibly deposited on contact surfaces, perhaps two days before.

Neither the large particle droplets, nor pure aerosolized virions appear to be transmissible over long distances, such as through air handling systems (Bridges, Kuehnert, Hall, 2003).

4.2   UNCOMPLICATED SEASONAL INFLUENZA

In a large percentage of cases of influenza each year, no definitive diagnosis is ever made because of the relatively mild nature of the disease in many patients. Often, patients may confuse their symptoms with those of a common cold, or if the patient self-diagnoses influenza, he or she may never seek medical attention because of the minimal intensity of the disease. Many of those patients who do seek medical care for suspected influenza do not receive confirmatory laboratory testing because the results of that testing are not likely to affect the choice of therapy or its outcome. Despite the fact that the diagnosis of influenza based solely on clinical signs and symptoms may be difficult, and that the disease is often mild in intensity, one should not overlook the reality that influenza virus infections continue to cause substantial morbidity and mortality with a worldwide economic and social impact. It is estimated that up to 36,000 Americans die each year from complications of seasonal influenza (CDC, 2003). Most of these deaths are at the extremes of age, the very young and the very old, and in those patients with confounding medical problems. Much of our understanding of the epidemiology of "seasonal" influenza is based on the knowledge of the manner in which influenza behaves in temperate climates, and may not necessarily apply to those areas of the world which maintain a relatively constant tropical (Park, Glass, 2007) or arctic climate.

Uncomplicated influenza is characterized by the abrupt onset of respiratory and constitutional signs and symptoms including fever, nonproductive cough, malaise, myalgia, headache, sore throat, and rhinitis. Gastrointestinal symptoms as well as otitis media may also be present, particularly in children.

The incubation period for most human influenza has been reported to range from one to four days, with two days being the average (Kamps, 2006). The incubation period for human cases of H5N1 infection seems to be considerably longer, with up to nine days being reported (Chotpitayasunondh et al., 2005). Of particular importance to the control of influenza epidemics is the issue of asymptomatic viral shedding by infected patients. As shown in Figure 4.1, adult patients may shed infectious viral particles at least one day before any clinical signs or symptoms of infection may

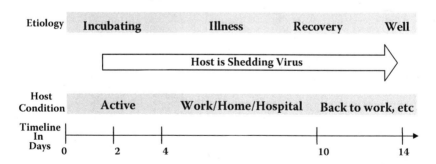

FIGURE 4.1 Timeline showing a 14-day period when someone is exposed to the influenza virus, incubates, begins to feel ill, becomes symptomatic, incapacitated, and eventually recovers and goes back to work. Note that the host is shedding virions while incubating and before feeling ill. The host continues to shed virions while ill and does so well into the recovery period. This chart illustrates the danger from an infected host who is obviously exposing others to the virus long before they know they are sick and well into the recovery period when they believe they are no longer infectious. The short incubation period for influenza and the long recovery period make containment of this contagion nearly impossible.

TABLE 4.1
Physical Signs in Uncomplicated Influenza

Area of the Body Affected	Description of Condition
Fever	38–40°C (100.4–104°F), up to 41°C (105°F) in children. Peaks rapidly, usually lasts 3 days but may persist for 4–8 days, then gradually diminishing. Secondary temperature elevations are rare.
Face	Flushed
Skin	Hot and moist
Eyes	Watery and reddened
Nasal passages	Discharge
Ear drums	Inflamed
Mucous membranes	Reddened and engorged
Cervical lymph nodes	Enlarged (especially in children)

be obvious, and may continue to shed virus for a few days after all symptoms have resolved. Children may shed virus even longer than adults, beginning several days before the onset of illness and continuing for several more days after apparent wellness returns. Immune-compromised individuals may excrete virus for weeks or months. Control and containment of an infectious disease in which the patient is contagious (i.e., shedding virus) during periods when the patient is unaware of his illness is very problematic. The potential impact of this aspect of the virology of influenza on containment measures is more thoroughly addressed elsewhere in this work.

The first signs of an influenza infection may be the abrupt onset of fever, with temperature ranging from 100 to 104°F (37.7 to 40.0°C), and a dry cough. Fever gradually diminishes over the course of the illness and secondary fever spikes are uncommon. A secondary temperature elevation may indicate the development of complications. Additional physical findings include flushing of the face, hot and moist skin, watery and reddened eyes, nasal discharge, hyperemic (engorged) mucous membranes, inflammation of the ears (otitis), and enlarged cervical lymph nodes. Table 4.1 summarizes these physical signs.

In addition to feverishness, symptoms may include headache, nasal discharge, and myalgia of the extremities and long muscles of the back, eye muscles, and calves. As systemic symptoms diminish, hoarseness and dry or sore throat may appear. In more severe influenza cases, malaise may progress to prostration. Elderly patients may experience lethargy and confusion. Children with influenza may develop croup, a condition characterized by a loud cough that resembles the barking of a seal, difficulty breathing, and a grunting noise or wheezing during breathing. Young children with influenza may show initial symptoms that are indistinguishable from bacterial sepsis, with very high fever and even febrile seizures. Table 4.2 summarizes the common symptoms of influenza.

TABLE 4.2
Symptoms of Uncomplicated Influenza

Abrupt Onset of Symptoms	
General	Feverishness, headache, malaise, myalgia (esp. extremities, back, eye muscles), prostration
Respiratory	Dry cough, runny nose, sore throat, hoarseness, croup in children

For most patients, the illness of influenza gradually diminishes and resolves in three to seven days. Some individuals may report persistent cough and malaise for up to two weeks, and influenza can exacerbate underlying medical conditions, such as cardiac or pulmonary disease. For the most part, however, in most patients, it is a self-limited disease with no long-term sequelae (Figure 4.2).

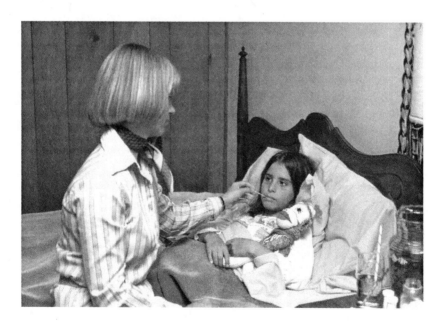

FIGURE 4.2 This photograph shows a mother caring for her child who is in bed suffering from a cold. Even though there are many similarities between influenza and the common cold, colds generally do not result in serious health problems, such as pneumonia, bacterial infections, or hospitalizations. In the midst of a pandemic, we will have to be certain that information campaigns stress the differences between the two conditions. (Image courtesy of the Public Health Image Library, Department of Health and Human Services, Centers for Disease Control and Prevention (PHIL Image No. 5703).)

4.3 DIFFERENTIAL DIAGNOSIS

Appropriate treatment of patients with respiratory illness depends on accurate and timely diagnosis. Such accuracy and timeliness remains elusive in the case of influenza. Without the ability to quickly confirm the diagnosis of a pandemic strain, our ability to react appropriately is severely compromised. To date, the tests available in the clinical setting for the rapid confirmation of the diagnosis of influenza will only tell us if the organism in the specimen is influenza A, and will not provide any information on the H/N typing of the virus in question. In February 2006, the Food and Drug Administration announced the approval of the Influenza A/H5 (Asian Lineage) Virus Real-Time Reverse Transcription-Polymerase Chain Reaction (RT-PCR) Primer and Probe set along with the inactivated virus as a positive control for the *in vitro* detection of HPAI H5N1 in humans. The availability of this test, including reagents and protocols, is controlled by the CDC and is limited to the reference laboratories in the national Laboratory Response Network (LRN). It took nearly nine years from the first identification of the H5N1 virus in humans to perfect this diagnostic test. Although the H5N1 RT-PCR test is highly accurate, it cannot be considered to be rapid and timely, at least not in the context of affecting patient care and case outcomes. If the pandemic strain of the future happens not to be H5N1 or is a subtype of that strain that is sufficiently antigenically unique, the currently available test will not be suitable, and the appropriate test could take months or even years to develop. An energetic effort is underway in this country and abroad to develop a rapid and reliable "Point of Care" (POC) diagnostic test for H5N1 that could be used in clinics, doctors' offices, hospitals, nursing homes, ports of entry, and in mass prophylaxis efforts. Until such a diagnostic tool is available, we must rely heavily on the case definition for our intervention and mitigation efforts. The case definition of H5N1 infection in humans is certainly not specific, but rather offers a series of compounding indices of suspicion (see Figure 4.3).

An additional problematic issue with diagnostic testing is the quality of the sample and the appropriate transport of that sample. Bringing a poor sample to a good test is no better than bringing a good sample to a poor test. Without the ability to identify the true nature of a clinical problem rapidly, our ability to intervene appropriately and in a timely manner is severely compromised.

The nonspecific nature of the signs and symptoms of influenza, coupled with the lack of a rapid confirmatory test, can make accurate early diagnosis problematic, and may lead to the inappropriate use of antibiotics. However, because certain bacterial infections can produce symptoms similar to influenza, bacterial infections should be considered and appropriately treated, if suspected. In addition, bacterial infections can occur as a complication of influenza.

Furthermore, the use of antiviral medications for the amelioration of influenza requires the initiation of this therapy within 48 hours of the onset of symptoms, during a time when signs and symptoms are very nonspecific and possibly confusing. In a pandemic situation, one would not want to commit to the use of antiviral medications, which may be in short supply, for a respiratory illness that may turn out

World Health Organization Case definitions for H5N1 (Human infections with influenza A)

Person under investigation: A person whom public health authorities have decided to investigate for possible H5N1 infection.

<u>Suspected</u> **H5N1 case**: A person presenting with unexplained acute lower respiratory illness with fever (>38 °C) and cough, shortness of breath or difficulty breathing.

AND

One or more of the following exposures in the 7 days prior to symptom onset:

a. Close contact (within 1 meter) with a person (e.g. caring for, speaking with, or touching) who is a suspected, probable, or confirmed H5N1 case;

b. Exposure to poultry or wild birds or their remains or to environments contaminated by their feces in an area where H5N1 infections in animals or humans have been suspected or confirmed in the last month;

c. Consumption of raw or undercooked poultry products in an area where H5N1 infections in animals or humans have been suspected or confirmed in the last month;

d. Close contact with a confirmed H5N1 infected animal other than poultry or wild birds (e.g. cat or pig);

e. Handling samples (animal or human) suspected of containing H5N1 virus in a laboratory or other setting.

<u>Probable</u> H5N1 case:

Probable definition 1: A person meeting the criteria for a suspected case

AND one of the following additional criteria:

a. infiltrates or evidence of an acute pneumonia on chest radiograph plus evidence of respiratory failure (hypoxemia, severe tachypnea) OR

b. positive laboratory confirmation of an influenza A infection but insufficient laboratory evidence for H5N1 infection.

Probable definition 2: A person dying of an unexplained acute respiratory illness who is considered to be epidemiologically linked by time, place, and exposure to a probable or confirmed H5N1 case.

FIGURE 4.3 World Health Organization Case Definitions for H5N1 (bird flu). (Taken from the WHO Web site, available at http://www.who.int/csr/disease/avian_influenza/guidelines/case_definition2006_08_29/en/. WHO Epidemic and Pandemic Alert and Response (EPR), 29 August 2006; accessed on 16 November 2007.)

Confirmed H5N1 case: A person meeting the criteria for a suspected or probable case

AND <u>one</u> of the following positive results conducted in a national, regional or international influenza laboratory whose H5N1 test results are accepted by WHO as confirmatory:

a. Isolation of an H5N1 virus;

b. Positive H5 PCR results from tests using two different PCR targets, e.g. primers specific for influenza A and H5 HA;

c. A fourfold or greater rise in neutralization antibody titer for H5N1 based on testing of an acute serum specimen (collected 7 days or less after symptom onset) and a convalescent serum specimen. The convalescent neutralizing antibody titer must also be 1:80 or higher;

d. An antibody titer for H5N1 of 1:80 or greater in a single serum specimen collected at day 14 or later after symptom onset and a positive result using a different serological assay, for example, a horse red blood cell haemagglutination inhibition titer of 1:160 or greater or an H5-specific western blot positive result.

Application of the H5N1 case definitions

The case definitions apply to the current phase of pandemic alert (phase 3) and may change as new information about the disease or its epidemiology becomes available. National authorities should formally notify only probable and confirmed H5N1 cases to WHO. The case definitions for persons under investigation and suspected cases have been developed to help national authorities in classifying and tracking cases. The case definitions are not intended to provide complete descriptions of disease in patients but rather to standardize reporting of cases. In clinical situations requiring decisions concerning treatment, care or triage of persons who may have H5N1 infection, those decisions should be based on clinical judgment and epidemiological reasoning, and not on adherence to the case definitions. While most patients with H5N1 infection have presented with fever and lower respiratory complaints, the clinical spectrum is broad.

Taken from the WHO Web site. WHO Epidemic and Pandemic Alert and Response (EPR) 29 August 2006; accessed on 16 November 2007.

FIGURE 4.3 (Continued).

to be a common cold. However, to wait for a definitive diagnosis of influenza before committing those antiviral resources may render that treatment useless.

Often, particularly during nonepidemic periods, respiratory symptoms caused by influenza may be difficult to distinguish from symptoms caused by other respiratory pathogens, such as the common cold. However, the sudden onset of the disease, the high fever, malaise, and severe fatigue are characteristically different from the common cold. Table 4.3 compares the signs and symptoms of influenza with those of the common cold.

TABLE 4.3
Differentiating Influenza from the Common Cold

Symptoms	Influenza	Cold
Fever	High, lasting 3–4 days	Unusual
Headache	Yes	Unusual
Fatigue/weakness	Lasts 2–3 weeks	Mild
Aches and pains	Common and severe	Slight
Exhaustion	Early and severe	Rare
Stuffy nose	Sometimes	Common
Sore throat	Sometimes	Common
Cough	Yes	Unusual
Chest discomfort	Common and severe	Mild to moderate
Complications	Bronchitis or pneumonia	Unusual

4.4 COMMON COMPLICATIONS OF INFLUENZA

The most commonly seen complication of influenza is pneumonia. This can occur as a primary viral pneumonia or as a secondary bacterial pneumonia. In rare cases, both viral and bacterial pneumonias may occur in the same patient. Although severe viral pneumonia may occur at any time, it is seen most often during pandemic periods. Most influenza deaths during seasonal influenza outbreaks, as well as during the "lesser pandemics," are due to secondary bacterial pneumonia, rather than to primary viral pneumonia.

Viral pneumonia in otherwise healthy adults can be a somewhat mild, self-limiting disease process. In some circumstances, however, particularly during pandemic periods, viral pneumonia can be a life-threatening or fatal complication of influenza.

Clinically, severe primary viral pneumonia may present as an acute influenza episode that does not resolve spontaneously. The clinical situation worsens with persistent fever, dyspnea, and cyanosis. Initially, physical findings may be unimpressive, but the patient's condition deteriorates rapidly. X-ray findings are consistent with acute respiratory distress syndrome (ARDS) and are associated with markedly reduced oxygen saturations (hypoxia). Viral concentrations are high in specimen cultures of respiratory secretions or lung tissue. Primary influenza pneumonia with pulmonary hemorrhages was a prominent feature of the 1918 pandemic, resulting in the rapid demise of affected patients (Barry, 2004).

Secondary bacterial pneumonia is most commonly caused by *Streptococcus*, *Staphylococcus*, and *Haemophilus influenzae*. It is an interesting historical side note that in 1918 a unique bacterium was frequently associated with severe and often fatal influenza pneumonia. Because viruses had not yet been identified, it was assumed that this bacterium was the cause of the 1918 influenza pandemic. It was named *Haemophilus influenzae*, and an effective vaccine for it was rapidly developed and distributed nationwide. Unfortunately, *H. influenzae* was not the cause of the pandemic, and the vaccine did little to mitigate the effects of the pandemic.

Typically, when secondary bacterial pneumonia becomes a complication, patients may initially recover from the acute influenza illness over two to three days before having rising temperatures again. Clinical signs and symptoms are consistent with classical bacterial pneumonia: cough, purulent sputum, and physical and x-ray signs of pulmonary consolidation. Chronic cardiac and pulmonary disease may predispose the patient to secondary bacterial pneumonia, as does older age. Initiation of an appropriate antibiotic regimen is usually sufficient for a prompt treatment response.

Mixed influenza pneumonia has clinical features of both primary viral and secondary bacterial pneumonia. It most often occurs in patients with underlying chronic pulmonary or cardiovascular diseases. Some patients have a slowly progressive course; others may show a transient improvement in their condition, followed by clinical exacerbation. Treatment aims at eradicating the bacterial pathogens involved through antibiotic therapy, and supportive therapy for the viral component.

4.4.1 Less Common Complications of Influenza

Influenza may exacerbate cardiac and pulmonary diseases and other chronic conditions. Influenza infection has also been associated with myocarditis, pericarditis, myositis, encephalopathy, transverse myelitis, and Reye's syndrome. In patients with chronic bronchitis, asthma, and other chronic respiratory conditions, influenza infection may lead to a permanent additional compromise of pulmonary function. Cardiac complications are rare, but myocarditis (Greaves et al., 2003), inflammation of the cardiac muscle, and pericarditis have been reported. These are more of a problem in elderly patients with a history of cardiac disease, but can occur in younger patients with no pre-existing cardiac compromise, and can, in fact, occur after any viral illness. Myositis, a nonspecific inflammation of the muscles, is also a rare complication, but more common than myocarditis. It occurs most often in the calf muscles of children. Encephalopathy is an alteration of brain function or even of brain structure, and may be due to the presence of the virus in the cerebro-spinal fluid; the effects are usually transient.

Transverse myelitis is a serious neurological disorder associated with the loss of the myelin encasing the spinal cord. It is the primary pathologic process in the progression of multiple sclerosis (MS), but it can also occur in rare cases following vaccinations or viral infections, including influenza. The onset may be sudden and rapidly progressive in hours and days, and the neurologic damage is usually permanent.

Reye's syndrome is a nonspecific clinical entity characterized by the combination of liver disease and encephalopathy. It is usually associated with previous viral infections, such as influenza, cold, or chickenpox, especially in children. There is a strong link between the administration of aspirin and the development of Reye's syndrome.

4.5 AVIAN INFLUENZA INFECTION IN HUMANS: IMPLICATIONS FOR THE COMING PANDEMIC

There are several strains of avian influenza (AI) virus that have been shown to cause disease in humans. Among the recent ones are the H9N2 strain from Hong Kong in 1999 and the H7N7 from the Netherlands in 2003. In most of these cases, the clinical manifestations in humans were mild. The only avian influenza strain that has repeatedly caused severe disease in humans is the H5N1 strain, which was first identified in 1997 from a child in Hong Kong who died of the disease.

The clinical manifestations of influenza H5N1 infection in humans are not well-defined as current knowledge is based on the description of a relatively few hospitalized patients. Fortunately, the number of human cases worldwide has been low: approximately 328 cases as of September 2007, according to the World Health Organization (WHO). However, the case fatality rate has been extraordinarily high. Of the 381 confirmed cases, over 60 percent of the patients (n = 40) have died. This is at least 25 times the case fatality rate of the 1918 pandemic, which killed approximately 100 million people when that avian virus developed the capacity for sustained human-to-human transmission.

As in all influenza, the clinical course of H5N1 ranges, at least theoretically, from asymptomatic infection to rapidly developing fatal pneumonia and multiple organ failure. Previously, experts in the field have believed that the alarmingly high case fatality rate seen to date from H5N1 infection in humans has been artifactually inflated because only the most severe cases had been hospitalized and those patients had experienced significant delays in diagnosis and initiation of treatment. Surely, there would be evidence of large numbers of individuals who had experienced mild cases of H5N1 infection that were either clinically unrecognized or that resolved on their own. This is a common phenomenon in seasonal influenza. Approximately 30 percent of the population may be infected annually, but only 5 to 20 percent of the population show signs and symptoms recognizable as influenza (Woodson, 2005). Most have asymptomatic infections or mild disease that is confused with a common cold or some other mild respiratory problem, and thus not reported nor included in morbidity and mortality statistics.

Alarmingly, this may not be the case with H5N1 infection in humans. Several groups have looked at the serology of close contacts, family members or health care workers involved with cases of severe or fatal H5N1 infections, as well as in the poultry workers and veterinarians who participated in the depopulation of infected bird populations (Buxton Bridges et al., 2000). Some have concluded that mild or asymptomatic infections do not occur (Katz et al., 1999). Patients either get the disease or they don't, and most that get it die.

Prajitno and colleagues (2007) conducted a serological survey of 1,000 veterinarians and other workers involved in the culling and composting of millions of H5N1-infected birds in Indonesia in 2005 and 2006. Surprisingly, only two workers showed serologic evidence of H5N1 infection.

Vong et al. reported in 2006 that testing of members of 42 households in southern Cambodia who experienced H5N1 outbreaks in their poultry flocks revealed no evidence of asymptomatic or mild infection in those humans who were in close contact with the sick birds. In contrast, surveillance in northern Vietnam has identified possible less-severe cases. Perhaps some local strains are becoming better adapted to humans (WHO, 2005).

Contrary to what might seem intuitively correct, the presence of mild cases may be an ominous sign from a pandemic epidemiological perspective. A lethal virus that is not well adapted to the human host may kill that host before that human has had an opportunity to further disseminate the disease. This is not a favorable situation for the evolutionary potential of the virus. As the virus mutates to forms better adapted to humans, its lethality must decrease in order to allow the host to remain alive long enough to transmit the disease. A similar situation exists with certain highly lethal forms of viral hemorrhagic fever, such as with the Ebola virus. Although the disease is almost uniformly fatal, the host or cluster of hosts die, off too rapidly to be able to transmit the disease outside of the immediate locale. So, although the present case fatality rate of H5N1 in humans of over 60 percent is tragic for those infected, it may be acting to protect the rest of the world population from the pandemic potential of the virus. We must be very vigilant for significant numbers of mild cases or serologic evidence of asymptomatic infection of H5N1 in humans, a trend that would indicate the virus is becoming better adapted to the human host. Given this logic, we should be very concerned when the case fatality rate of H5N1 in humans begins to decrease.

4.5.1 CLINICAL PRESENTATION OF H5N1 IN HUMANS

Initial symptoms of H5N1 influenza may include low-grade fever, headache, malaise, muscle aches, sore throat, cough, runny nose (although upper respiratory symptoms may be absent), gastrointestinal upset, and eye inflammation. All these symptoms are nonspecific and may also be associated with the currently circulating human seasonal influenza virus subtypes. At the early stage of the illness, it is difficult to predict which patients will progress to severe disease. The commonly reported laboratory findings of abnormal liver function tests, prolonged clotting time and renal impairment, are simply signs of the rapid onset of multiorgan failure rather than any laboratory data specific to H5N1. One finding that is noteworthy is the early onset of panleucopenia, the early decrease in all measured white blood cell components. Of those patients tested, all of the fatal cases and none of the less-severe cases showed this early depression of white blood cell counts (Tumpey et al., 2000).

The progression of the clinical course in severe H5N1 infection seems to be distinct from that of severe diseases observed during influenza pandemics that occurred before the 1997 outbreak of H5N1 in Hong Kong. None of the patients with severe cases of H5N1 infection had evidence of secondary bacterial pneumonia (Chotpitayasunondh et al., 2004), which was the prevailing cause of death in influenza pandemics after 1918. In addition, cases of H5N1 infection were characterized by rapid clinical progression, with evidence of lower respiratory tract involvement on hospital admission and progression to a disease stage at which the patient required ventilatory support within a few days after admission. The mean duration of illness from symptom onset to death was nine days. The median age of patients with fatal cases has been 18 years, and 90 percent of the fatalities have occurred in patients below the age of 40 (CIDRAP, 2007).

There is conflicting information regarding the risk factors associated with severe disease and fatal outcome, most likely due to the evolving nature of the virus, and the very small number of cases studied to date. In the 1997 outbreak in Hong Kong, the factors associated with severe disease included older age, delay in hospitalization, lower respiratory tract involvement, and a low total white-blood cell count. In 1997, patients below six years old usually had a self-limiting, acute respiratory disease with fever, runny nose, and sore throat. In contrast, recent avian H5N1 infections have caused higher rates of death among infants and young children, as well as in otherwise healthy young adults (Yuen et al., 1998). The numbers reported are too small to understand all of the contributing factors. We should be aware that as H5N1 strains continue to evolve, as they have over the past 10 years, clinical features of avian influenza infection in humans may well have different characteristics over time (Hien et al., 2004). What has been consistent among the fatal cases of H5N1 infection is that most of the victims died of an overwhelming primary viral pneumonia, a feature alarmingly reminiscent of the 1918 pandemic (Crosby, 2003).

The reason for the severity of human H5N1 infection remains unclear. In the 1957 and 1968 influenza pandemics, most patients with primary influenza pneumonia had active cardiovascular, pulmonary, or renal diseases; alcoholism; or were pregnant. In contrast, underlying medical illness seems not to be a necessary risk factor for severe H5N1 infection. Among the patients with fatal cases, remarkably few could be said to have underlying severe medical conditions. The intrinsically high virulence of the H5N1 virus seems to be the key determinant of the high fatality rate among infected humans.

Dr. Menno de Jong of the Oxford University Clinical Research Unit in Vietnam has developed data to support the theory of the "cytokine storm" as the cause of the unusually high fatality rate among otherwise healthy adults (de Jong et al., 2006). Cytokines and chemokines are proteins in the human immune system that concentrate in infected tissues to help the body fight off the bacterial or viral invaders. The amount of cytokines released seems to be proportional to the numbers of infecting organisms. Very high levels of cytokines can actually be dangerous and damaging to the organs of the host itself, particularly to the lung. The H5N1 virus seems to replicate far more aggressively in humans than do common influenza viruses, rapidly resulting in an unusually high viral load. In otherwise healthy adults with vigorous immune systems, when infected with the H5N1 influenza virus, abnormally large quantities of cytokines are released into the lungs, causing pulmonary edema, pulmonary hemorrhages, respiratory failure, and death. Indeed, it is the young patient's own healthy immune system that actually kills him. From all clinical descriptions available relating to the 1918 pandemic, this also seems to have been the mechanism of death in that outbreak. This is but another in a series of alarming similarities between the 1918 pandemic virus and what may be evolving with H5N1. For the first time in history, we may have the opportunity to study the evolution of an influenza pandemic from start to finish. Although the cytokine storm theory has been disputed by many, it does, however, offer possible insight into the pathogenesis of the ARDS often associated with human H5N1 infection (Kobasa, 2004; Salomon, Hoffman, Webster, 2007).

4.6 PREVENTION OF INFLUENZA

4.6.1 NONMEDICAL STRATEGIES

Nonpharmaceutical community mitigations strategies are thoroughly addressed elsewhere in this work (WHO, 2006). A few simple personal measures are worth exploring at this point. By the basic definition of a pandemic event, all are susceptible and no one is immune. Not everyone, however, will contract the disease. Projections have been made that suggest that perhaps 50 percent of the world population may become ill with the pandemic strain of influenza (Osterholm, 2005). Only a small percentage will actually show the full life-threatening syndrome, and a much larger group will likely have a milder form of the disease. It is anticipated that serologic testing after the pandemic would reveal many of the 50 percent who did not become ill have significant antibodies to the pandemic strain, indicating that they were, in fact, infected but asymptomatic. That having been said, the influenza virus cannot make an individual ill if the virus cannot enter that individual's body. The primary routes of entry into the human body for all harmful substances, including bacteria and viruses are inhalation, ingestion, absorption, and injection. For the influenza virus, we are primarily concerned with inhalation into the respiratory tract and absorption through the mucous membranes of the mouth, nose, and eyes. We have the ability through very simple measures to block completely the entry of the virus into the body by protecting the respiratory tract and mucous membranes. Unfortunately, the consistent application of these protective measures could become quite problematic.

Good personal hygiene, frequent hand washing, avoiding contact with possibly contaminated objects or surfaces, avoiding the rubbing of the eyes, and the placing of objects in the mouth will help reduce the likelihood of viral entry. One should avoid large crowds and gatherings and insist that those coughing or sneezing employ proper cough etiquette. Coughing or sneezing into a tissue or upper sleeve, followed by prompt hand washing and proper disposal of the tissue will help prevent the short-range dissemination of the virus (Ryan, Christian, Wohlrabe, 2001).

The proper use of a high-efficiency particulate air (HEPA) mask, gloves, and eye goggles will dramatically limit the ability of the virus to enter the body (Lawrence et al., 2006). Readily available HEPA masks include N95 and N100 respirators. If properly fit and worn, these respirators are capable of preventing entry of the virus into the respiratory tract. Simple surgical masks may also provide some protective benefits. It should be noted that surgical masks are designed to prevent the wearer from shedding infective material into the environment, and HEPA respirators are meant to protect the wearer from hazardous or infective particles present in the environment. Nonetheless, using an aerosol of particles sized to simulate virions, Y. Li and colleagues of the Hong Kong Polytechnic Institute showed that standard surgical masks were only 2 percent less effective than N95 masks in filtering out the test aerosol when spayed on subjects from 1 meter away (Li et al., 2004).

4.6.2 MEDICAL STRATEGIES: VACCINATION

Inoculation with a vaccine proven to be effective against the viral strain in circulation is the most effective means of preventing influenza. From a public health perspective, the best method of preventing or reducing the severity of a pandemic is the timely development, distribution, and administration of the appropriate influenza vaccine. However, such a vaccine is unlikely to be available in time or in sufficient quantities for use during the initial wave of a pandemic. U.S. Department of Health and Human Services (HHS) Secretary Michael Leavitt has cautioned us that it might take six months after identification and isolation of a novel pandemic virus to ramp up the nation's vaccine production to a rate of 5 million doses per week. The goal would be to have sufficient vaccine to vaccinate everyone in the United States, upward of 300 million people. Even during nonpandemic periods, there are often shortages of vaccine, and universal vaccination of the entire population has never been recommended in nonpandemic periods. Only once in history, in 1976, has such a universal vaccination program been attempted, and those results were far from encouraging (Silverstein, 1981).

Current influenza vaccine production in the United States is based on growing the virus in chicken eggs. It may require two chicken eggs to produce one dose of vaccine. In the case of a vaccine produced to counter the threat of H5N1 in humans, a plan is obviously flawed if it depends on a production method requiring chicken eggs when the avian virus may kill much of the domestic poultry in the world. The H5N1 vaccine produced so far has been poorly antigenic, producing immunity in less than half of those vaccinated despite using six times the amount of antigenic material usually employed in seasonal flu vaccines (Poland, 2006).

Under a best-case scenario, using the current chicken-egg-based technology for influenza vaccine production, only 5 million doses of vaccine could be produced per week by U.S. facilities after a six-month start-up time. The U.S. health care system relies heavily on vaccine production overseas during nonpandemic periods. However, it is unlikely that a foreign-produced vaccine would be available to the United States during a worldwide pandemic (Fedson, 2003).

Cell culture manufacturing technology has been in use for years for the production of most viral vaccines, such as polio, measles–mumps–rubella, and chickenpox vaccines in the United States and for influenza vaccines produced overseas. This technology does not require chicken eggs and can be more rapidly adjusted to meet demand. HHS is currently supporting a number of U.S. vaccine manufacturers in the advanced development of cell-based influenza vaccines.

Despite the shortcomings of the currently available H5N1 vaccine, HHS has contracted for the production of approximately 5 million doses of the Clade 2.2 A: H5N1 vaccine for the stockpile. There are clearly some genetic changes that must occur in the current strains of H5N1 to enable that virus to adapt fully to human-to-human transmission, and for its pandemic potential to be realized. If those changes are significant enough to alter the antigenic nature of the virus sufficiently, those H5N1 vaccines produced today may be ineffective against the pandemic strain. Of additional concern is the previously mentioned fact that the current variants of the available H5N1 vaccines are relatively inefficient in inducing an adequate antibody response in a significant percentage of the population. In one study of the Sanofi Pasteur H5N1 vaccine, only 54 percent of the test subjects showed an adequate antibody response after two doses (Treanor et al., 2001). Other vaccine producers, such as GlaxoSmithKline, have added adjuvants to their versions of the H5N1 vaccine, which have improved the antibody response considerably (Nicolson et al., 2001).

Much work is being done on various antigen-sparing techniques of vaccine production, which may be used to increase herd immunity by administering much smaller doses of antigen to a much-larger segment of the population. At the Centre for Vaccinology, Ghent University and Hospital, Belgium, Professor Leroux-Roels and colleagues (2007) reported on an "antigen sparing adjuvant strategy," which, by combining the vaccine with an oil-in-water emulsion "adjuvant," allows the body to produce up to six times the influenza virus antibody as it would with a neat (no adjuvant) vaccine with the same dose of antigen.

Despite the problems associated with the current available variants of H5N1 vaccine, some research has suggested that the administration of these vaccines to a high-risk population, such as health care workers, during the pre-pandemic period may produce "immunologic priming" in those vaccinated individuals (Stephenson et al., 2005). If such a strategy were effective, it is possible that a single dose of the actual pandemic strain vaccine, once it is identified and produced, would elicit an adequate antibody response to the pandemic strain with a single additional vaccine dose, despite subtle antigenic differences between the original H5N1 virus and the subsequent pandemic strain.

Sandbulte and colleagues (2007) have reported the likelihood of some cross-protection between the N1 antigen in seasonal influenza vaccines and H5N1. Commonality of the neuraminidase antigens in different influenza strains may reduce the severity of the disease in those vaccinated with the seasonal vaccine containing an N1 strain. The hemagglutinin antigen in the vaccine is necessary for prevention of the disease, but neuraminidase antibodies may ameliorate the disease by improving the host's response to subsequent infection with a strain containing the same neuraminidase antigen. Because H1N1 has been a component of every seasonal influenza vaccine for many years, universal vaccination with the seasonal flu vaccine may to some extent mitigate the consequences of a pandemic, if the pandemic strain is, in fact, H5N1 or another N1-containing influenza virus. If for no other reason, universal seasonal flu vaccination will reduce the overall morbidity of a community and ease the strain on medical resources (Gillim-Ross, 2007).

Vaccines against various strains differ in their ability to produce antibodies to neutralize the virus, and each person's immune system may respond somewhat differently. Limited studies have shown that when the vaccine provides a good antibody response to the virus, approximately 70 to 90 percent of healthy young adults may be protected from influenza (Stepanova, 2002). This protection drops to about 30 to 40 percent for the elderly and those suffering from chronic illness or disease. It is, however, precisely this segment of the population that is generally targeted by seasonal flu vaccine programs. The goal of influenza vaccination during interpandemic years is to lessen the overall burden of influenza-like illness (ILI) in the general population and to reduce deaths and disease in the at-risk population. This at-risk population includes the elderly, those with chronic diseases and depressed immune systems, as well as health care workers. Children would also be included depending on the age range for which the specific vaccine is approved. However, except for the health care workers, these are the segments of the population least likely to benefit from vaccination because of their overall poor immunologic response to the vaccine.

Optimal vaccination strategy depends on the transmission rate of the involved virus. With a highly transmissible virus such as influenza, a strategy that aims at producing herd immunity by targeting school children and teachers may be more effective than directly targeting the at-risk population, namely the elderly and infirm. Herd immunity is reached when the level of immunity in a population is sufficient to limit the spread of a disease or prevent an epidemic. The Japanese showed rather conclusively that if you wish to reduce influenza illness and death in the elderly, you should vaccinate the children. The dramatic improvement in a population's herd immunity that is produced by universal vaccination of school children does more to protect the elderly than does direct vaccination of the elderly. From 1962 to 1987, nearly all school children in Japan were vaccinated against influenza. Very few of the sick and elderly were vaccinated during that time. In 1987, the requirements for mandatory vaccination were relaxed, and repealed completely in 1994. From the mid-1970s to the late 1980s, the morbidity and mortality from influenza in the elderly dropped significantly. When the school vaccine program was curtailed in 1987, the influenza morbidity and mortality in the elderly began to rise. When the school program was abandoned completely in 1994, the illness and death from influenza in the elderly returned to pre-1962 levels. It is estimated that vaccinating Japanese school children prevented 37,000 to 49,000 deaths per year in the elderly population while the school vaccination program was in place (Reichert, 2001).

The transmissibility or transmission rate of a virus is expressed as its reproductive number or basic reproductive rate (RO). The RO relates to the average number of secondary cases of disease generated by a typical primary case in a susceptible population, and is a measure of the potential for a contagious disease to spread from person to person in a population. The higher the RO, the less likely would be the possibility of containing the disease. If the RO is less than 1, it is generally considered that an epidemic would not be sustainable, but an RO of 2 or higher might indicate an uncontrollable outbreak. The transmission rate of influenza virus is variable and difficult to predict, and the transmissibility of influenza can accelerate rapidly as the virus better adapts to the human population (Giesecke, 2002).

4.6.3 MEDICAL STRATEGIES: ANTIVIRAL DRUGS

Antiviral chemoprophylaxis is another effective method that can be used to prevent influenza or reduce the severity of influenza illness. Four antiviral drugs, amantadine (Symmetrel®), rimantidine (Flumadine®), oseltamivir (Tamiflu®), and zanamivir (Relenza®), are approved and commercially available for use in the treatment and prevention of influenza. The first three drugs are oral medications taken in tablet or capsule form, and zanamivir is inhaled in a powder form. An injectable form of zanamivir and a new injectable drug, peramivir, are under development at the time of this writing. All of these are prescription drugs. Antibiotics are ineffective against viruses, including influenza virus. Amantadine and rimantidine are classified as M2 inhibitors, and oseltamivir and zanamivir are neuraminidase inhibitors. These classifications are based on the mode of action of the drugs, specifically with respect to how they interfere with viral invasion and replication (Cooper et al., 2003).

Some strains of influenza A, including the current H5N1 strain posing a potential pandemic risk, are resistant to the M2 inhibitors, and recent reports from Asia and Africa indicate that some strains of H5N1 may be at least partially resistant to the neuraminidase inhibitors as well. Nevertheless, antiviral drugs are a key component of the HHS pandemic response plan and of the plans of most states as well (McKimm-Breschkin et al., 2007).

The resistance to the neuraminidase inhibitors seems to be due to isolated mutations in the H5N1 virus rather to repeated exposure of the virus to the drug. The resistance to the M2 blockers, on the other hand, was probably produced by the injudicious exposure of the virus to the M2 blockers very early in the emergence of the H5N1 strains (Cheung, 2006).

There are many other issues surrounding the use of antiviral medications, not the least of which is the relatively limited worldwide supply of the drugs and the anticipated extraordinary demand that might arise in a pandemic situation. Difficult decisions have to be made with regard to the allocation of limited supplies between treatment and prophylactic uses. If prophylactic use is chosen as an option, there will be ethical and practical issues involved in determining who should receive the preventative medications. The U.S. government, in cooperation with state governments, has undertaken an ambitious program to purchase enough antiviral medications to treat approximately 25 percent of the population of the country (CIDRAP 2005; HHS 2005). *The recent federal doctrine that limited the use of the antiviral stockpile to treatment rather than prophylaxis is changing rapidly. It is likely that once the federal stockpile is deployed, its use will be determined by the state and local jurisdictions that receive these assets.* The World Health Organizations rapid response stockpile of approximately 60,000,000 doses of oseltamivir (Tamiflu), however, is planned to be used solely for a ring prophylaxis strategy.

To be effective for prophylaxis, antiviral medications must be administered at or immediately after exposure to the flu. In the case of oseltamivir (Tamiflu), the drug must then be taken daily in a dose of 75 mg until the risk of infection is over. In simplest terms, the drug would need to be taken daily until the pandemic is past. The cost of this mode of use could be prohibitive and might not be an efficient use of the limited supplies of the drug. Most plans that allocate a portion of the antiviral supply to prophylaxis designate a 45-day course for prevention of infection. This is, of course, an arbitrary number based on a scenario of a six-week pandemic duration in any one locale. Epidemiologists remind us that while antiviral medications may be beneficial to some individuals in terms of averting infection or reducing complications, they may not be able to alter the course of a pandemic markedly at a population level. Another possible prophylactic use of antiviral medications would be to protect individuals in quarantine after possible exposure to an infected person for the duration of the incubation period of influenza. In this situation, a 10-day "prophylactic" course would be protective for that one exposure, but would not be sufficient to protect against subsequent exposures once the quarantine were lifted.

4.7 TREATMENT OF INFLUENZA

Typically, little needs to be done to treat uncomplicated influenza in most people. Home therapy is adequate for the vast number of otherwise healthy people who contract influenza. Rest, symptomatic treatment, and prevention of dehydration are usually all that is needed in most cases. Rest and hydration are the most important aspects of care. Bed rest is preferred, but any limitation of activity is helpful. Dehydration due to fever is a very real potential hazard and must be avoided. Dehydration can be fatal to a patient who would otherwise survive, and prevention of dehydration in flu patients will save more lives than all other treatments combined. Hydration with eight ounces of fluid every hour during febrile episodes will prevent this complication. Fluids may be in the form of water, soup, fruit juice, sports drinks (e.g., Gatorade®), or an oral rehydration solution. Exclusive administration of water or sports drinks should be avoided. Most sports drinks are too hypertonic. Water is too hypotonic, and can lead to water intoxication. Sports drinks can be diluted 50 percent with water, or a simple oral rehydration solution may be prepared mixing four cups of clean water with three tablespoons of sugar or honey, and one-quarter teaspoon of salt.

Symptomatic treatment of fever, headache, muscle aches, and cough can be accomplished with acetaminophen (Tylenol®), naproxen (Aleve® and Naprosyn®), ibuprofen (Advil®), and cough suppressants. Aspirin should not be used to treat fever in children because of its association with Reye's syndrome.

Intervention by a health professional may be needed if the patient's fever remains over 102°F, the fever persists for over three days, a productive cough develops, or any respiratory distress develops. If the patient seems to improve, but then suffers a relapse, he may be at risk for developing a secondary bacterial pneumonia or one of the less-common complications previously mentioned.

Antiviral drugs are effective when used for treatment of influenza, but should be administered within 24 to 48 hours of the onset of symptoms in order to have a significant effect on the duration and severity of the illness. This early in the clinical course, symptoms are nonspecific and diagnosis may be erroneous. It may be difficult to determine when to commit the limited resources of an antiviral stockpile to a treatment program when definitive diagnosis is elusive. If the available stock is less than the clinical attack rate, it may be necessary to limit treatment to priority groups. There will be significant ethical issues in determining who will comprise these priority groups. The stock available for use in treatment will also depend on how much, if any, of the antiviral supply is used for prophylaxis.

The normal course of therapy for the treatment of influenza with oseltamivir (Tamiflu) is 150 mg per day for five days. Some researchers have suggested that due to declining susceptibility of some strains of H5N1 to oseltamivir in some parts of the world, a 10-day course of therapy may be needed (Yen, 2005). Laboratory testing of the H5N1 viruses from Indonesia show that the virus is now 20 to 30 times less susceptible to oseltamivir as compared to the H5N1 viruses that circulated in Cambodia over the last few years (McKimm-Breschkin et al., 2007). If this declining susceptibility were to be seen worldwide, the implications for the world supply of antiviral drugs are obvious.

Recent research has shown some positive results with the use of powdered IgG antibodies that can be inhaled to help ward off influenza infection or reduce its severity (Simmons et al., 2007). This technology, if perfected, could significantly add to our response armamentarium in a pandemic. It was found in 1918 that if patients with severe influenza were transfused with the serum of victims who had recovered, the fatality rate in the transfused patients declined by 22 percent (Luke et al., 2006). They were, in fact, simply administering influenza-specific antibodies.

There is no doubt that folk medicines and herbal remedies can have significant therapeutic effects in many diseases. The same holds true with influenza. There is adequate substantiation for the claim that Sambucol™ is effective in reducing the symptoms and duration of influenza A and B. Sambucol is based on a standardized black elderberry extract and has antiviral properties, especially against various strains of influenza virus. Sambucol has been shown to be effective against 10 strains of influenza virus and can reduce the duration of flu symptoms significantly. Higher serum antibody levels to influenza virus are found in patients treated with Sambucol, which seems to activate the healthy immune system. That having been said, one must be aware that the postulated cause of death from the primary viral pneumonia seen in some influenza cases is due to a cytokine storm, thought to be due to the patient's overactive immune system. It may be imprudent to use a drug that stimulates the immune system in a disease in which the vigorous immune system may be the lethal link.

Although there have been great advances in critical care and in antiviral therapy, results have been disappointing in treating cases of severe influenza infection. There is no cure for influenza and the treatment of the severe primary viral pneumonia that has been seen in pandemic situations is still only supportive and empirical. It could be said that we are no better at treating this rapidly progressive and often fatal complication than Hippocrates was when he first described an influenza pandemic in 412 BC. Treatment today is limited to respiratory support, hydration, and symptomatic treatment. There are fewer than 120,000 mechanical ventilators in the United States today, and 85 percent of those are currently in use. Conservative estimates suggest that nearly 1 million ventilators may be needed if a severe pandemic affects the United States (HHS Pandemic Predictions).

Source: U.S. Government, Department of Health and Human Services, a Pandemic Influenza Preparedness and Response Plan, Part 1: Strategic Plan.

4.8   CONCLUSION

In summary, vaccines and antiviral drugs are the two most important medical interventions for reducing morbidity and mortality during a pandemic, but they will not be available in adequate supplies. Vaccines are universally considered the first line of defense, but it is unlikely that an effective vaccine will be available in the early stages of a pandemic. It is assumed that the supply of antiviral drugs may be inadequate in every country in the world. Authorities in all countries will need to make the most of nonpharmaceutical measures to reduce morbidity, mortality, and social disruption. The problems of inadequate supplies of vaccine and antiviral drugs, and inequitable access to them, need to be addressed with particular urgency. Citizens should be instructed in home-care remedies and therapies that would be useful if hospital-based and traditional medical-based care is unavailable.

The major treatment considerations in a pandemic are associated with the vastly larger number of patients and the inevitable shortage of vaccine, antiviral medications, and health care resources in general. A larger percentage of the population will become ill, a larger percentage will require intensive hospital care, and a larger percentage will die. The number of hospitalizations and deaths will depend on the virulence of the pandemic virus. Estimates differ about tenfold between more- and less-severe scenarios. HHS notes that the death rate associated with the 1918 influenza applied to the current population would produce about 2 million deaths in the United States and up to 360 million deaths globally.

One does not have to presume that a pandemic will be as severe or as deadly as the 1918 event to appreciate how rapidly the health care resources in the United States, indeed throughout the world, could be overwhelmed. The issue of medical surge capability in the face of a pandemic is addressed elsewhere in this work.

As health care services in general, and hospital services in particular, become rapidly overwhelmed in the face of an evolving pandemic, many families may have to resort to home care of the sick and perhaps even of the critically ill. Family-administered supportive therapy may be the only treatment available, but it is a form of treatment that can save lives.

REFERENCES

Alford RH, Kasel JA, Gerone PJ, Knight V. 1966. Human influenza resulting from aerosol inhalation. *Proc Soc Exp Biol Med* 122:800–804.

Barry, John M. 2004. *The Great Influenza*. Penguin Books.

Bean B, Moore BM, Sterner B, Peterson LR, Gerding DN, Balfour HH Jr. 1982. Survival of influenza viruses on environmental surfaces. *J Infect Dis* 146:47–51.

Boyce JM, Pittet D. 2002. Guideline for hand hygiene in health-care settings: recommendations of the Healthcare Infection Control Practices Advisory Committee and the HICPAC/SHEA/APIC/IDSA Hand Hygiene Task Force. *Am J Infect Control* 30:S1–S46.

Bridges CB, Kuehnert MJ, Hall CB. 2003. Transmission of influenza: implications for control in health care settings. *Clin Infect Dis* 37:1094–1101.

Buxton Bridges C, Katz LM, Seto WH, et al. 2000. Risk of influenza A (H5N1) infection among health care workers exposed to patients with influenza A (H5N1), Hong Kong. *J Infect Dis* 181:344–348.

CDC (Centers for Disease Control and Prevention). 2003. CDC Finds Annual Flu Deaths Higher Than Previously Estimated. Press release.

CDC (Centers for Disease Control and Prevention). 2007. Update: Influenza Activity—United States, 1 Oct 2006–3 Feb 2007. MMWR 56:118–121.

Cheung C-L, Rayner JM, Smith GJD, et al. 2006. Distribution of amantidine-resistant H5N1 avian influenza variants in Asia. *J Infect Dis* 193(12): 1626–1629.

Chotpitayasunondh T, Ungchusak K, Hanshaoworakul W, et al. 2005. Human disease from influenza A (H5N1), Thailand, 2004. *Emerg Infect Dis* 11:201–209.

CIDRAP (Center for Infectious Disease Research and Policy, University of Minnesota). 2006. "Pandemic Influenza." Available from <http://www.cidrap.umn.edu/cidrap/content/influenza/panflu/biofacts>.

CIDRAP (Center for Infectious Disease Research and Policy, University of Minnesota). 2007. Avian Influenza: Implications for Human Disease.

Cooper NJ, Alexander JS, Abrams KR, Wailoo A, et al. 2003. Effectiveness of neuraminidase inhibitors in treatment and prevention of influenza A and B: systematic review and meta-analysis of randomized controlled trials. *BJM* 326:1235–1242.

Crosby, AW. 2003. *America's Forgotten Pandemic. The Influenza of 1918*. Cambridge University Press.

de Jong MD, Simmons CP, Thanh TT, et al. 2006. Fatal outcome of human influenza A (H5N1) is associated with high viral load and hypercytokinemia. *Nat Med* 12:1203–1207.

Fedson DS. 2003. Pandemic influenza and the global vaccine supply. *Clin Infect Dis* 36(12):1552–1561.

Giesecke J. 2002. *Modern Infectious Disease Epidemiology*, 2nd ed. London, UK: Arnold Publishing.

Gillim-Ross L, Subbarao K. 2007. Can immunity induced by the human influenza virus N1 neuraminidase provide some protection from avian influenza H5N1 viruses? PLoS Med 4(2):e91.

Greaves K, et al. 2003. The prevalence of myocarditis and skeletal muscle injury during acute viral infection in adults. *Arch Intern Med* 165–168. Available from http:archinte. ama-assn.org/cgi/content/abstract/163/2/165.

Hamburger M Jr, Robertson OH. 1948. Expulsion of Group A hemolytic streptococci in droplets and droplet nuclei by sneezing, coughing, and talking. *Am J Med* 4:690–701.

HHS (U.S. Department of Health and Human Services). November 2005. Pandemic Influenza Plan. Available from http://www.hhs.gov/pandemicflu/plan/.

Hien TT, Liem NT, Dung NT, et al. 2004. Avian influenza A(H5N1) in 10 patients in Vietnam. *N Engl J Med* 350:1179–1188.

Jordan WS Jr. 1961. The mechanism of spread of Asian influenza. *Am Rev Respir Dis* 83:29–40.

Kamps B, Hoffman C, Preiser W. 2006. Uncomplicated Human Influenza. Influenza Report. Available from http://www.influenzareport.com/ir/cp.htm.

Katz JM, Lim W, Bridges CB, et al. 1999. Antibody response in individuals infected with avian influenza A (H5N1) viruses and detection of anti-H5 antibody among household and social contacts. *J Infect Dis* 180:1763–1770.

Kilbourne E. 2006. Influenza pandemics of the 20th century. *Emerg Infect Dis* 12(1):9–14.

Kobasa D, Takada A, Shinya K, et al. 2004. Enhanced virulence of influenza A viruses with the haemagglutinin of the 1918 pandemic virus. *Nature* 431(7009).

Kolata G. 2001. *Flu: The Story of the Great Influenza Pandemic of 1918 and the Search for the Virus That Caused It.* School & Library Binding. NY: Farras, Straus, and Giroux.

Lancet (2007, August 22). Antigen Sparing Strategy Could Boost Bird Flu Vaccine Production. *Science Daily*. Retrieved April 22, 2008, from http://www.science daily.com/ releases/2007/08/070818103241.htm.

Lawrence RB, Duling MG, Calvert CA, Coffey CC. 2006. Comparison of performance of three different types of respiratory protection devices. *J Occup Environ Hyg* 3:465–474.

Leroux-Roels JM, Borkowski A, Vanwolleghem T, Dramé M, Clement F, Hons E, Devaster G. 2007. Antigen sparing and cross-reactive immunity with an adjuvanted rH5N1 prototype pandemic influenza vaccine: a randomised controlled trial. *Lancet* 370:580–589.

Li Y, Wong T, Chung J, et al. 2004. In vivo protective performance of N95 respirator and surgical facemask. *Am J Respir Crit Care Med* 169:1198–1202.

Loosli CG, Lemon HM, Robertson OH, Appel E. 1943. Experimental airborne influenza infection. I. Influence of humidity on survival of virus in air. *Proc Soc Exp Biol* 53:205–206.

Luke TC, Kilbane EM, Jackson JL, Hoffman SL. 2006. Meta-analysis: convalescent blood products for Spanish influenza pneumonia: a future H5N1 treatment? *Ann Intern Med* 145:599–609.

McKimm-Breschkin JL, Selleck PW, et al. 2007. Reduced sensitivity of influenza A (H5N1) to oseltamivir. *Emerg Infect Dis* 13(9).

Nicholson KG, Colegate AE, Podda A, et al. 2001. Safety and antigenicity of non-adjuvanted and MF59-adjuvanted influenza A/Duck/Singapore/97 (H5N3) vaccine: a randomized trial of two potential vaccines against H5N1 influenza. *Lancet* 357:1937–1943.

Osterholm M. 2005. Preparing for the next pandemic. *N Engl J Med* 352:1839–1842.

Park AW, Glass K. 2007. Dynamic patterns of avian and human influenza in east and southeast Asia. *Lancet Infec Dis* 7(8):543.

Poland, GA. 2006. Vaccines against avian influenza—A race against time. *N Engl J Med* 354:1411–1413.

Prajitno TY. Letter to international society for infectious diseases, 5 June 2007.

Reichert TA, Sugaya N, Fedson D, et al. 2001. The Japanese experience with vaccinating schoolchildren against influenza. *N Engl J Med* 344(12):889–896.

Ryan JR, Kirchner AW, Glarum JG, Davey J, et al. 2006. Training the nation's responders for pandemic influenza: a Department of Homeland Security planning and preparedness initiative. *J Emergency Mgmt* 4(6):33–40.

Ryan MA, Christian RS, Wohlrabe J. 2001. Handwashing and respiratory illness among young adults in military training. *Am J Prev Med* 21:79–83.

Salomon R, Hoffman E, Webster R. 2007. Inhibition of cytokine response does not protect against lethal H5N1 influenza infection. *Proc Natl Acad Sci* 104:12479–12481.

Sandbulte MR, Jimenez GS, et al. 2007. Cross-reactive neuraminidase antibodies afford partial protection against H5N1 in mice and are present in unexposed humans. *PLoS Med* 4(2):e59.

Schulman JL. 1968. The use of an animal model to study transmission of influenza virus infection. *Am J Public Health Nations Health* 58:2092–2096.

Silverstein AM. 1981. *Pure Politics and Impure Science: The Swine Flu Affair*. Baltimore and London: The Johns Hopkins Press.

Simmons CP, Bernasconi NL, Suguitan Jr. AL, et al. 2007. Prophylactic and therapeutic efficacy of human monoclonal antibodies against H5N1 influenza. *PLoS Med* 4(5):e178.

Stepanova L, Naykhin A, Kolmskog C, Jonson G, et al. 2002. The humoral response to live and inactivated influenza vaccines administered alone and in combination to young adults and elderly. *J Clin Virol* 24(3):193–201.

Stephenson I, Burgarini R, Nicholson KG, et al. 2005. Cross reactivity to highly pathogenic avian influenza H5N1 viruses after vaccination with nonadjuvated and MF59-adjuvanted influenza A/Duck/Singapore/97 (H5N3) vaccine: a potential priming strategy. *J Infect Dis* 191:1210–1215.

Tellier R. 2006 Nov. Review of aerosol transmission of influenza A virus. *Emerg Infect Dis* 112(11).

Treanor JJ, Wilkinson BE, Masseoud F, et al. 2001. Safety and immunogenicity of a recombinant hemagglutinin vaccine for H5 influenza in humans. *Vaccine* 19:1732–1737.

Tumpey TM, Xiuhua L, Morken T, Zaki S, et al. 2000. Depletion of lymphocytes and diminished cytokine production in mice infected with a highly virulent influenza A (H5N1) virus isolated from humans. *J Virol* 74(13):6105–6116.

Vong S, Coghlan B, Mardy S, Holl D, et al. 2006. Low frequency of poultry-to-human H5N1 virus transmission, southern Cambodia, 2005. *Emerg Infect Dis* 12(10):1542–1547.

Ward P, Small I, Smith J, Suter P, Dutkowski R. 2005. Oseltamivir (Tamiflu) and its potential for use in the event of an influenza pandemic. *J Antimicrob Chemo* 55(Suppl S1):i5–i21.

WHO (World Health Organization). 2005. WHO inter-country-consultation: influenza A/H5N1 in humans in Asia: Manila, Philippines, 6–7 May 2005.

WHO (World Health Organization). 2006. Responding to the avian influenza pandemic threat: Recommended strategic actions, 2005.

Woodson G. 2005. *Preparing for the Coming Influenza Pandemic*. Self published monograph, Druid Oaks Health Center, Decatur, GA.

World Health Organization Writing Group. 2006. Nonpharmaceutical public health interventions for pandemic influenza, national and community measures. *Emerg Infect Dis* 12:88–94.

Yang Y, Halloran ME, Sugumoto J, Longini I. 2007. Detecting human-to-human transmission of avian influenza (H5N1). *Emerg Infec Dis* Sept. 13(9).

Yen, HL, Monto AS, Webster RG, et al. 2005. Virulence may determine the necessary duration and dosage of oseltamivir treatment for highly pathogenic A/Vietnam/1203/04 influenza virus in mice. *J Infect Dis* 192(4):665–672.

Yuen KY, Chan PK, Peiris M, et al. 1988. Clinical features and rapid viral diagnosis of human disease associated with avian influenza A H5N1 virus. *Lancet* 351:467–471.

5 Avian Influenza

*James C. Wright, DVM, PhD, Kenneth
E. Nusbaum, DVM, PhD, and James
G.W. Wenzel, DVM, PhD*

Flu virus is a networked enemy. We must fight it with a networked army.

Michael O. Leavitt
Secretary, Department of Health and Human Services

CONTENTS

5.1　INTRODUCTION

Proper preparedness for pandemic influenza must include an understanding of the behavior of the virus in birds. Water birds are the natural reservoir for the virus. Domestic poultry (i.e., backyard flocks of chickens, game fowl, fighting birds, ducks, and geese) play an important role as bridges between the virus in the wild and humans. How humans associate with the birds is the key. Live-bird markets are a special concern because customers, operators, and their families are in close proximity to the birds over a long period of time. Thankfully, at this time, entry of a pandemic avian influenza virus into the United States is speculation. There are a number of different possible scenarios; however, all but one involves birds as the source.

Avian influenza is a classic emerging and re-emerging zoonosis, and prevention/control always will be a challenge. The prevention/control of this virus brings into play the entire public health community and is illustrative of the one-health, one-medicine concept for human and animal disease. The public also needs to "buy into" their need to be observant with respect to the possible presence of the virus in birds. The importance and sheer size of the poultry industry in the United States should help to emphasize every individual's responsibility in preventing the entry of highly pathogenic avian influenza (HPAI). The chain of infection for avian influenza can become catastrophic if it changes from bird–bird–bird or bird–human–bird to bird–human–human.

5.2 INFLUENZA AND ANIMAL HEALTH

5.2.1 SCOPE OF PRODUCTION

The broiler industry in the United States is highly integrated, and raising and slaughtering or processing of the birds is accomplished in units usually referred to as production complexes. A broiler production complex (concentrated animal feeding operation, CAFO; see Figure 5.1) consists of all the farms with growing houses, the breeders and hatcheries that supply them with chicks, and the feed mills that keep the breeders and the growing birds fed. Birds are produced in numbers

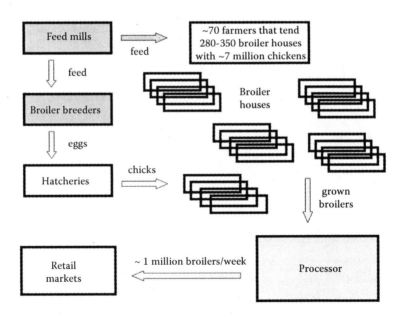

FIGURE 5.1 Schematic representation of an integrated broiler production complex.

FIGURE 5.2 Approximate weekly broiler production, in millions, by state in 2006.

sufficient to keep one processing plant supplied with sufficient numbers (about 200,000 birds daily) to meet their capacity for processing and distribution. Because growing houses usually hold 20,000 to 25,000 birds, the week's processing empties 40 to 50 houses. The distribution of the top broiler-, egg-, and turkey-producing states are represented in Figures 5.2 through 5.4, respectively.

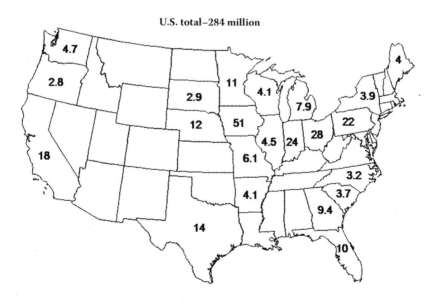

FIGURE 5.3 Approximate inventory of table-egg layers, in millions, in the top egg-producing states and the U.S. total in 2006.

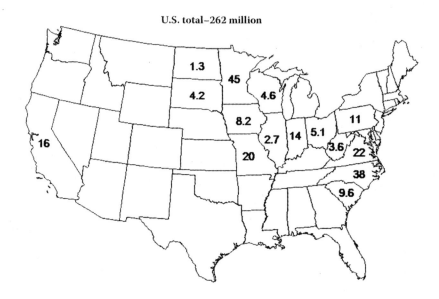

U.S. total–262 million

FIGURE 5.4 Approximate number of turkeys, in millions, raised in top turkey-producing states and the U.S. total in 2006.

However, the growing birds take about seven weeks to reach slaughter weight, so there are about 240 to 300 other growing houses with about 6 million younger birds that are also a part of the production complex. The numbers of millions of broilers slaughtered each week in 2006 in the major broiler-producing states (U.S. Poultry and Egg Association, 2006), which is also the approximate number of production complexes, are shown in Figure 5.2. Note, however, that for each of these, there are (approximately) an additional 6 million birds in the process of growing to slaughter weight. Feed sources and shipping requirements of birds may vary by region and production complex or company. The goal of the broiler industry is to produce a four-pound bird in approximately five to seven weeks.

The almost 300 million table-egg layer hens produce over 6 billion eggs each month. About half the national flock in the United States is concentrated in California, Indiana, Iowa, Ohio, and Pennsylvania. Despite the large number of birds and tremendous productivity, only about 250 companies have flocks of over 75,000 hens and control about 95 percent of the market (U.S. Poultry and Egg Association, 2006). Turkey farms function on a grand scale as well. There were over 1,500 turkey farms reported in the 2002 U.S. Census of Agriculture that produced 30,000 to 99,999 birds, and approximately 800 farms that produced over 100,000 (National Agricultural Statistics Service, 2007b). Turkey production is concentrated in California, Indiana, Minnesota, Missouri, North Carolina, and Virginia (Figure 5.4). Optimally, turkeys should reach a market weight of 30 to 40 pounds in approximately three to four months.

5.2.2 Affected Groups of Birds

Waterfowl, particularly certain ducks, are the principal reservoirs for influenza viruses, and disease rarely occurs in these birds. Certain species of waterfowl may play a role in the epidemiology of influenza by spreading the viruses through migration and transmission of influenza viruses to other species such as swine. Influenza virus rarely is found in exotic, companion, or aviary birds. Although any bird may be affected by avian influenza, it is a disease causing virus predominantly in poultry (Association of Avian Veterinarians, 2006), particularly those raised in CAFO's or sold through the live-bird market system (LBMS) (chickens and turkeys in the United States; chickens and ducks in Southeast Asia).

The virus is spread among birds by direct contact or contaminated clothing or equipment. Infected birds can shed the virus in their feces and other secretions. The disease caused by HPAI in birds may be clinically similar to exotic Newcastle disease (END), and the incubation of HPAI usually is shorter. Clinical signs in infected birds include facial edema (swollen wattles, combs, and conjunctiva), respiratory distress, diarrhea, opisthotonos (arching of the back), torticollis (twisting of the head and neck), and high mortality approaching 100 percent (Kyeema Foundation, 2004).

Riley (2007) has suggested that large-scale transmission of human influenza follows, for the most part, a spatial multigroup model. In this type of model, membership in certain groups (e.g., households, schools, workplaces) affects the probability of transmission. Avian influenza, including HPAI, likewise has a probability of transmission among birds that is affected by the groups to which the birds belong (e.g., commercial poultry, game birds). The presence or endemicity of HPAI may have far-reaching economic and ecologic consequences even before its zoonotic potential (to become more easily transmissible from birds to humans) increases. Heavy losses initially may occur in commercial flocks before a substantial increase in human cases occurs. If human surveillance is not adequate, cases of avian influenza could occur in people returning to their home country from an avian influenza epizootic region. In this event, human cases might occur either before avian cases are recognized or in the absence of avian cases.

5.2.3 Economic Impact

The value of production and sale of commercial poultry in the United States in 2004 was approximately $29 billion. The vast majority of this amount was from young meat chickens, called broilers ($20.4 billion, or about 71 percent of the total). Production of eggs by layers resulted in $5.3 billion in sales (about 18 percent), and turkeys accounted for an additional $3.1 billion (about 11 percent of total sales) (U.S. Poultry and Egg Association, 2006). Geographic areas of the United States where these types of commercial poultry production are concentrated would be most affected by an outbreak of HPAI.

With influenza widespread in poultry-rearing areas, depopulation of affected and at-risk poultry flocks is more epidemiologically sound and economically efficient than testing individual birds, treatment, vaccination, or other means of control. International trade will be affected because many countries will not accept animal products from areas where such diseases exist; therefore, rapid eradication or "stamping-out" of the disease may allow a more rapid return to the profitable export of products from the species. Diseases of poultry that trigger a rapid response and such severe control measures include HPAI and END. From the above-presented economic figures associated with poultry production in the United States, one may begin to understand their impact on the economy.

5.3   EXAMPLES THAT MATTER

5.3.1   INITIAL DETECTION OF H5N1 VIRUS

The HPAI virus (H5N1) first was detected in a farmed goose in China in 1996 (Sims et al., 2005). Human infections with this strain of influenza first were reported in 1997 (WHO, 2007). Rapid distribution of the virus occurred in 2006 as a result of movement of commercial birds and wild-bird migration and now H5N1 HPAI has been found in 64 countries (OIE, 2007). While specific disease patterns in individual countries have not been reported, there are regional differences in outbreaks of the disease. The virus primarily has affected wild birds in Western and Northern Europe and backyard and commercial poultry operations in Africa, Eastern Europe, the Indian subcontinent, and the Middle East (APHIS, 2006). Outbreaks of H5N1 in Asia from 2003 through 2005 have resulted in the death or culling of over 200 million birds throughout that region (Intervet, 2007). Presently, developing countries are paying a tremendous social and economic price to reduce the risk of transmission of H5N1 to more developed countries in Europe and North America.

Transmission of influenza H5N1 from birds to humans has occurred rarely with 328 total cases reported and 200 deaths (overall >60 percent case-fatality rate) as of September 2007 (WHO, 2007). Human-to-human transmission has only been reported rarely and close contact through occupational exposure, handling of contaminated tissues or caring for sick birds appears to be necessary (CDC, 2007). There is concern that the virus could mutate and become more efficient in human-to-human transmission. The higher fatality rate, the evidenced human-to-human transmission, combined with the absence of pre-existing natural immunity in people, makes the presence of this strain an important public health threat.

5.3.2   HIGHLY PATHOGENIC AVIAN INFLUENZA IN THE UNITED STATES

There have been several outbreaks of HPAI in the United States. In 1924, an H7 HPAI strain was found in East Coast live-bird markets. A strain of H5N2 HPAI occurred in the northeastern United States in 1983 and 1984 and resulted in the destruction of approximately 17 million chickens, turkeys, and guinea fowl (Suarez, Senne, 2000). In 2004, H5N2 HPAI was detected in chickens in Texas and a quick response limited this outbreak to a single flock (Pelzel, McCluskey, Scott, 2004). The H5N1 HPAI strain has not been detected in the United States; however, low pathogenic H5N1 was reported in mute swans in Michigan in 2006 (USDA, 2006a). Low pathogenic H5N1 primarily occurs in wild birds and seldom causes clinical disease.

5.3.3 Lessons Learned from Earlier Outbreaks

An outbreak of HPAI in Pennsylvania began in 1983, but its eradication was not complete until 1984. Over 17 million birds died from the disease or from depopulation to control its spread. The federal government spent over $63 million in the control effort for this outbreak. About $40 million of this was in the form of indemnity payments to producers, but the industry had to absorb approximately $15 million in nonindemnified losses. There was a 30 percent increase in the cost of eggs as a result of this outbreak and consumers spent an estimated $350 million in increased food costs (Swayne, Halvorson, 2003).

In October 2002, an outbreak of END began in small, backyard flocks of "game birds" (jungle fowl, fighting cocks) in Los Angeles and spread to commercial flocks and to nearby states. By the time the outbreak was declared over in September of 2003, an estimated $160 million was spent on the eradication effort, including the depopulation of over 3 million birds. The negative impact on trade was estimated to be $121 million (Center for Emerging Issues n.d.).

Important lessons for prevention and control of avian influenza in the United States can be gained from the recent Newcastle disease outbreak in California. At the height of the outbreak more than 370 government personnel were involved and many were working 12-hour days to contain the disease. The U.S. Department of Agriculture (USDA) would have been severely limited in its ability to respond to a simultaneous disease problem occurring during this outbreak. The California Pilot Project resulted from problems identified during that outbreak (Ross, 2005). This involved several agencies in California along with USDA the Animal and Plant Health Inspection Service, (APHIS, 2003). Specific project goals were (1) to develop solutions to problems of data collection; (2) to function as a surveillance and emergency taskforce system; and (3) to allow for data sharing among agencies. Additionally, Veterinary Services (VS) of the USDA established the National Animal Health Emergency Response Corps (APHIS, 2007). This is a group of private practice veterinarians and animal health technicians who are available to provide assistance during animal health emergencies such as an outbreak of avian influenza. All countries need to become better prepared to respond locally to outbreaks of avian influenza. Rapid and efficient use of personnel continues to be a challenge.

Some of the challenges for the control of avian influenza are illustrated by an outbreak of highly pathogenic avian influenza (H7N7) in the Netherlands in 2003. During this outbreak, 453 people developed conjunctivitis (77 percent) or an influenza-like illness. Influenza H7N7 was detected in 89 (20 percent) of the cases. A veterinarian who had visited several of the farms during the outbreak died of influenza (ProMED mail, 2007). Four workers from Poland and one from Belgium who had been involved in culling of the birds in the Netherlands had H7N7-confirmed conjunctivitis. While the risk for serious human disease was low, these workers may have represented a possible source for transmission of this strain of influenza into poultry in their respective countries (ProMED mail, 2003). This was further reinforced by the finding that human-to-human transmission occurred within households. This outbreak illustrates the need for strict biosecurity procedures in all avian influenza outbreaks. The risk for human-to-avian transmission needs further study.

Outbreaks of low pathogenic avian influenza (LPAI) occur more commonly in the United States. Strict control measures are instituted when the outbreak strain is H5 or H7 because these isolates have known potential for mutation to HPAI. In April 2002, an LPAI was detected in commercial poultry flocks (78 percent of these were turkey) from Virginia and West Virginia. This outbreak involved 197 premises, and approximately 4.7 million birds were depopulated at a cost of $130 million (APHIS, 2007; McQuiston et al., 2005). In this outbreak, carcass disposal was a major challenge (large size of turkey carcasses) and was resolved with on-the-farm composting. The National Incident Management System (NIMS) along with use of the Incident Command System (ICS) played an important role in the eradication effort. More recently, an H5N2 LPAI outbreak in turkeys in West Virginia in 2007 resulted in China's Ministry of Agriculture suspending imports of U.S. poultry and products from that state (Bean, Schriber, 2007). Because broiler production in West Virginia is less than 1 percent of the total U.S. output, this did not have a considerable industry impact; however, an outbreak in a major broiler-producing state would result in major losses to the industry.

5.3.4 PREVENTION THROUGH BIOSECURITY

Biosecurity, the protocols and procedures used for control of disease, has been well-described for many human institutions such as hospitals, and developed specifically for the growth of different species of farm animals (e.g., Antec® Biosentry®). Biosecurity demands control of access to agricultural premises and assurance of decontamination of materials coming onto or leaving the farm (Table 5.1). Avian influenza is moderately resistant to environmental inactivation, and therefore no extraordinary biosecurity measures are needed. However, in several recent U.S. outbreaks of avian influenza, the major source of virus has been through violations of even basic biosecurity protocols through introduction of fomite (contaminated inanimate objects) or infected birds back onto the farm. An outbreak of low-pathogenicity H7N2 avian influenza occurred in turkeys in Virginia and West Virginia in 2002. From a list of about 50 risk factors, the most likely source of infection was identified as use of

---

TABLE 5.1
Biosecurity Precautions to Prevent Introduction of Avian Influenza onto Poultry Farms

"All-in, all-out" flock management.
No contact with wild or migratory birds, including any source of water.
Farm entry to essential workers and vehicles.
Clean clothing and disinfection facilities for employees.
Clean and disinfect equipment and vehicles (including tires and undercarriage) entering and leaving the farm.
No shared equipment or vehicles from other farms.
Avoid visiting other poultry farms and farmsteads.
Do not bring birds from slaughter channels or live-bird markets back to the farm.

Source: After USDA APHIS Veterinary Services Fact Sheet, 2004, Questions and Answers: Highly Pathogenic Avian Influenza.

---

off-the-farm rendering to dispose of dead birds. Rendering trucks visited many premises without being disinfected, and thus served as fomites for the H7N2 virus (McQuiston et al., 2005). When on-farm burial was instituted, the outbreak was quickly brought under control. In 2004, some 300 undersized birds were returned to their farm of origin in Texas after being rejected from a live market. These birds apparently acquired the HPAI H5N2 virus in the market, spread the virus to the home farm and to an adjacent farm through a transfer of birds. In the United States, live markets are a consistent source of infection and impediment to the control of avian influenza (Suarez and Senne, 2000; Pelzel, McCluskey and Scott, 2004). Return of the birds to the home flock violated the protocol of quarantining animals before adding them to established flocks. The subsequent transfer of birds to another farm is also a violation of widely recognized biosecurity procedures. These reports and many out of Asia and Africa emphasize the importance of fomite sanitation and of not bringing birds of unknown provenance onto a farm (Ferguson et al., 2005, 2006).

Part of the resolution of live markets serving as distribution points for influenza is "rest days," when the markets are closed to all trade (Pelzel, McCluskey, and Scott, 2004) and cleaned and disinfected (USAHAC FAD, 2004). Another possible means of infection of commercial poultry is exposure to wildlife carriers, particularly migrating waterfowl. Some models for dispersion of H5N1 hold that birds migrating from Asia through Alaska to the West Coast flyways will bring the virus to the United States. Another important component of biosecurity, then, is separation of domestic and commercial birds from wildlife species (Weber, Stilianakis, 2007).

5.3.5 EPIDEMIC CONTROL

Although vaccination of poultry against avian influenza H5N1 is being undertaken in Asia, and alternative strategies are under consideration here, the United States still embraces a zero-tolerance policy on antibody positive birds. Thus depopulation of infected flocks is the accepted practice of control for avian influenza virus in the United States. Depopulation is distinguished from euthanasia in that depopulation refers to expedient procedures for killing animals that present a danger to other animals, or whose humane destruction would present a danger to people (AVMA, 2007). Several expedient measures in terms of speed of process and minimum human exposure include heat asphyxiation through turning off barn ventilation and raising the side curtains, or the use of Class A fire-fighting foam. The latter method, under ideal circumstances, is rapid and has a disinfection aspect in addition to adding moisture needed if the birds are to be composted in the barns or in windrows. However, details of foam depopulation have not been uniformly accepted, and communities should investigate nozzle configurations and foam base availability before declaring it the method of choice. Considerations for carcass disposal include soil and environmental conditions, land availability, and community attitudes. The two most-common disposal methods are trench burial and composting. Composting is gaining widespread acceptance as details of successful composting, moisture, temperature, additional carbon, etc., are resolved (Flory et al., 2007). Approaches at composting are part of the draft plan for response to highly pathogenic influenza developed by the USDA (USDA, 2006b).

5.4 IMPLICATIONS FOR HUMAN HEALTH

5.4.1 POTENTIAL FOR SPECIES RADIATION

The radiation of the influenza historically started with waterfowl as the original species, and subsequently infected gallinaceous birds, horses, swine, and people. Although stable for many years, swine influenza, H1N1SW, has changed recently under the influence of reassortment with a newly introduced H3N2, and perhaps the widespread use of swine influenza vaccination (Wuethrich, 2003). The disease is more severe in infected adult swine, and protection provided by maternal antibody is small and short-lived. Two shocking radiations occurred recently: tigers fed chickens that died of HPAI subsequently died of an influenza-like illness (ILI) whose pathogenicity was confirmed when the isolated virus was inoculated into domestic cats (Kuiken et al., 2004). Similarly, racing greyhounds were diagnosed with infection by equine influenza (Crawford et al., 2005). Transmission may have been by proximity, but greyhounds are fed raw horsemeat for its purported enhancement of speed in racing dogs. The distribution of dogs along the East Coast parallels the racing circuit. Recent outbreaks in animal shelters and kennels suggest that the virus may become endemic among dogs in the United States.

Between animal and human medicine, there is no dividing line — nor should there be (Rudolf Virchow, 1856).

The ability of an infectious agent to spread from an animal host to people is referred to as its zoonotic potential, a zoonosis (pl. zoonoses) being an animal disease transmissible to and affecting humans. The current epidemic of avian influenza H5N1 was first reported in Hong Kong in 1997 when six of 18 infected individuals died. In an attempt to eradicate the virus, 1.4 million chickens were killed. Reports from Southeast Asia now indicate that, as of 2007, avian influenza (AI, H5N1) still has limited zoonotic potential in that the deaths of millions of birds from AI has been accompanied by relatively few confirmed human cases and deaths. Most human cases occurred when people lived in close proximity to chickens, nursed sick poultry, or attempted to salvage dead chickens. Some exceptions occurred through exposure of people in live or "wet" poultry markets, thus hinting that the zoonotic capability of H5N1 is subject to change (Kung et al., 2002; Yu et al., 2007).

Although H5N1 influenza is predominantly a disease of wild and domestic birds, its zoonotic character, its ability to be transmitted from animals to humans, cannot be ignored. Thus, even though it has caused disease and death in relatively few humans, its potential to do so cannot be ignored or forgotten. This is due to the character of the viral genome. The eight segments of the genome are capable of rapid reassortment at any time, and the single-stranded RNA is subject to a high rate of copy errors, thus permitting essentially an infinite variety of progeny virus to emerge. However, there are significant barriers to the avian virus becoming readily adapted to human beings, the primary obstacle being the replication site of the avian virus. The surface composition of the avian respiratory tree bears different sugar-related receptors than does the mammalian respiratory tract. Although the avian virus can be mutated to recognize the mammalian receptors, this event has not occurred in observed human infections.

The H5N1 virus already carries a potent virulence factor due to a mutation at position 92 of the nonstructural gene (NS) product switching from aspartic acid to glutamic acid (E92D). This single mutation renders influenza virus resistant to innate chemical messengers or cytokines such as interferons (IFN) and tumor necrosis factor alpha by blocking several interferon activation steps including inhibition of a protein translation, gene activation, and IFN regulatory factors. Clinically, this cytokine resistance appears as higher and longer fevers and higher fatality rates. Hosts produce higher titers of virus in the presence of cytokines leading to hypercytokinemia or "cytokine storm," which contributes to severity of clinical signs (Seo, Hofmann, Webster, 2002). The E92D mutation of NS1 probably functions to bind cytokine messengers, thus preventing the release of IFN alpha/beta. The NS1 also depresses activity of the dendritic cells preventing the maturation of host cellular immune response (Fernandez-Sesma et al., 2006).

We know from history, however, that the zoonotic potential of influenza viruses can increase greatly through simultaneous infection of biologic mixing vessels such as turkeys, swine, or ducks. If a host cell is simultaneously infected with two different strains of influenza type A virus, this can result in genetic shift: a reassortment population of progeny virus with mixed genotypes usually resulting in a different dominant hemagglutinin type. However, the use of animal models, cell culture, and molecular biology has revealed the changes needed for an increase in the zoonotic potential of avian influenza H5N1. In order for a virus to escape from its natural host and radiate into a new species, the virus must first overcome virus–host barriers through mutation, then host–host barriers through contact, and finally sustain transmission in the new host (Kuiken et al., 2006; see Figure 5.5 and Figure 5.6).

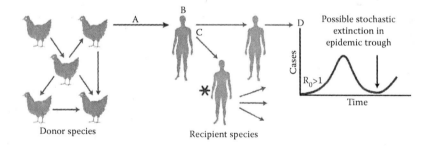

FIGURE 5.5 Schematic illustrating phases in overcoming species barriers. (A) Interspecific host–host contact must allow transmission of virus from donor species to recipient species. (B) Virus–host interactions within an individual of recipient species affect the likelihood of the virus replicating and being shed sufficiently to infect another individual of recipient species. (C) Intraspecific host–host contact in recipient species must allow viral spread (R_0 > 1) in the presence of any pre-existing immunity. Super spreader events (large asterisk) early in the transmission chain can help this process. (D) The pathogen must persist in the recipient species population even during epidemic troughs (after most susceptible individuals have had the disease) so that subsequent epidemics can be seeded. If few susceptible hosts are left, the virus may (stochastically) go extinct in epidemic troughs. Viral variation and evolution can aid invasion and persistence, particularly by affecting host–virus interactions. *Source:* Van Riel D, Munster VJ, de Wit E, Rimmelzwaan GF, Fouchier RAM, Osterhaus ADME, Kuiken T. 2006. H5N1 virus attachment to lower respiratory tract. *Science* 312:399. With permission.

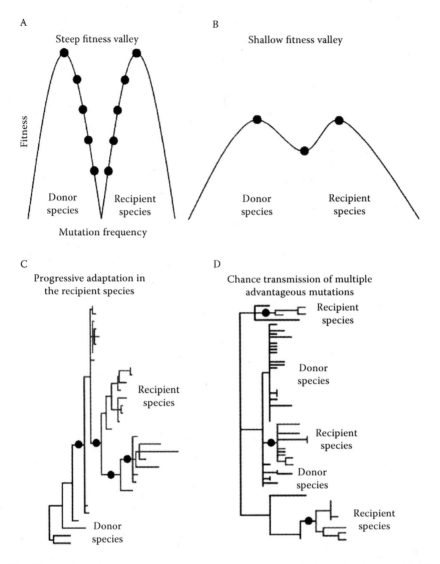

FIGURE 5.6 Evolutionary models for the cross-species transmission of pathogens. (A) The donor and recipient species represent two distinct fitness peaks separated by a steep fitness valley. Multiple adaptive mutations (solid circles) are therefore required for the virus to establish onward transmission successfully in the recipient host species. (B) The donor and recipient species are separated by a far shallower fitness valley. This facilitates successful cross-species transmission because only a small number of advantageous mutations are required. (C) When multiple mutations are required for a virus to adapt to a new host, these may evolve progressively in the recipient species. However, this necessarily requires some onward transmission. (D) It is also possible that many of the mutations required to allow adaptation to a new host species were pre-existing in the donor species and transmitted simultaneously. This will accelerate successful viral emergence. (Image reproduced with kind permission of the journal *Science*.)

A single mutation at position 92 of the NS gene, aspartic acid changes to glutamic acid (E92D), renders the virus resistant to the innate reactions of the host immune system, and permits prolonged viral replication and shedding, six days versus two days, and higher fever and greater weight loss in swine (Seo, Hofmann, Webster, 2002).

To overcome virus–host barriers, H5N1 would have to be able to replicate in the host trachea, not in the alveoli of the deep lung, which would increase the concentration of expired virus. A change in the hemagglutinin receptor site would favor attachment to human cells, especially in the trachea, and alter the action of nonstructural (NS) proteins to resist host immune reactions. Although not important for human pathogenesis, a series of polybasic amino acids in the hemagglutinin contributes to the ability of H5N1 to cause fatal disease in chickens by increasing the variety of enzymes capable of clearing and activating the hemagglutinin (Seo, Hofmann, Webster, 2002; Stevens et al., 2006).

Avian influenza viruses typically attach to ciliated epithelium via a 2-3 linked sialic acid-bearing glycolipid or glycoprotein whereas mammalian viruses typically attach to nonciliated sialyl-galactosyl cells in the trachea bearing 2-6 linked sialic acid, providing a barrier to direct avian-to-human infection (Matrosovich et al., 2004). Sufficient ciliated cells bearing 2-3 sialic acids exist to support the initial replication of avian virus in human tracheal epithelium to initiate infection. Cells bearing 2-3 linked sialic acid are found in lung parenchyma, type II pneumocytes, alveolar macrophages, and nonciliated cuboidal epithelium (Van Riel et al., 2006), thus explaining H5N1 pneumonia and, through inference, need for a heavy inoculum of inspired virus. Cell-to-cell spread has been suggested as a means of virus propagation and further adaptation. As little as two mutations in the receptor binding domain (RBD) gene can convert isolates from a specificity of alpha 2-3 sialic acid (avian) to an alpha 2-6 sialic acid (human) specificity; the reverse is also true (Stevens et al., 2006).

5.5 CONTAINING THE CONTAGION

5.5.1 COMMUNITY SUPPORT

An outbreak of HPAI is rare when compared to other more-common emergencies (i.e., HazMat spills, storms, vehicle crashes that impede traffic). Thus, there is little community motivation for preparation for a large-scale influenza epidemic among birds. The "fatigue" of preparing for a large-scale outbreak that never happens also comes into play; therefore, bottom-up preparations move slowly or not at all. However, local community response, both operative and social, is crucial for the prevention and control of avian influenza. Efficient communication between local authorities and federal agencies will help in the activation of disease control procedures to prevent further spread of the disease. This is especially important in areas with large numbers of poultry farms or live-bird markets. Effective community support

TABLE 5.2
Groups Involved in the Prevention and Control of Avian Influenza

Commercial poultry producers
Poultry workers
Owners of backyard flocks/game birds
Operators of live-bird markets
Emergency management personnel
Law enforcement
Fire departments and HazMat teams
Veterinarians
Government agencies (wildlife, agriculture)

not only involves producers but a wide array of groups including the general public (Table 5.2).

Preparedness through biosecurity procedures and response to an outbreak of avian influenza are covered in previous sections. Community support as it relates to recognition, restrictions on movement, and recovery will be addressed below. Local plans for control of an outbreak of avian influenza often are developed by federal and state government officials involved with animal disease control; however, local emergency management agencies also must be involved. Ideally these plans should be practiced through table-top exercises or full-scale emergency drills that bring together key personnel.

5.5.2 MITIGATION

As mentioned previously, effective biosecurity practices are crucial for prevention of avian influenza. Biosecurity must become a way of life for poultry producers and anyone else who has contact with poultry (backyard flocks, live-bird markets). Some procedures such as restriction of access may be viewed as inconvenient; however, they are critical measures for prevention of an avian influenza outbreak. Producers also need to be certain that all personnel working for them understand the importance of the measures instituted to prevent the entry of disease agents onto the farm. Procedures for biosecurity do not apply only to large commercial poultry operations. Owners of backyard poultry flocks and game birds must understand that their birds are at risk from avian influenza. They should purchase birds only from reputable sources and should be certain no recent disease problems have occurred in the source flock.

5.5.3 RECOGNITION

Everyone must have knowledge of who to call concerning disease problems in birds. In general, sick birds initially are reported to the local veterinarian or poultry company who will report the problem to the state veterinarian if further investigation is necessary. The state veterinarian then will notify the federal veterinarian if influenza is the diagnosis.

The timeliness of reports of disease from individuals to veterinarians or local authorities will help to reduce the number of premises affected by an outbreak of avian influenza. Producers see their birds every day and, as the first line of defense, they must be willing to report disease problems immediately and institute the necessary control procedures. Appropriate samples from sick birds should be submitted to a diagnostic laboratory. Companion animal veterinarians who do not routinely see birds need to be willing to assist bird owners and producers by directing them to the appropriate authorities for diagnosis of disease problems in their birds. This is especially important for backyard flocks and live-bird markets.

5.5.4 RESPONSE

Response to an outbreak of avian influenza would involve restricted access to individual farms and travel restrictions within the outbreak area. Local emergency management agencies may become involved in restricting access to an area. For this reason, the local emergency management agencies need to be able to apply incident scene control zones to a disease outbreak situation (Moats, 2007).

5.5.5 RECOVERY

Recovery from an outbreak of avian influenza likely will be prolonged and will involve farms and other areas affected by restrictions of movement. A major area of concern in rural areas is the psychological effect of the outbreak (Nusbaum, Wenzel, Everly, 2007).

5.5.6 PSYCHOLOGICAL FIRST AID

The psychological effects on farm and rural populations of controlling an animal disease emergency gained recognition for their impact after the massive 2001 foot and mouth disease (FMD) epidemic in the United Kingdom. These effects have been widely observed by U.S. regulatory veterinarians engaged in eradication campaigns in the United States. Impacts of flock and herd depopulation extend throughout the community, and include both economic and personal devastation of agriculture and devastation of all the collocated businesses of farm supply and rural life. Some estimates indicate that one business fails for every eight farms that go out of business (Williams, 1988). Five categories of mental health syndromes are reported after disasters: specific psychiatric illness; distress; alterations in normal health; alterations in life patterns, including income and solvency; loss or perceived loss of community (Butler, Panzer, Goldfrank, 2003). All of these signs were reported from both farmers and villagers in the FMD outbreak in 2001. UK responders were instructed in psychological first aid (PFA), and it would be appropriate for first responders including veterinarians in the United States to be instructed in PFA as well (Deaville, Jones, 2003). PFA has eight competencies (Table 5.3), the most basic being active listening, that allow the first responder to maintain self-care while recognizing the needs of afflicted individuals and advising them ("what you are feeling is perfectly normal and appropriate") or directing them to appropriate mental health or financial resources.

TABLE 5.3
Basic Competencies for Psychological First Aid

Active listening skills.
Prioritization of human needs.
Recognition of mild psychological and behavioral reactions.
Recognition of incapacitating psychological and behavioral responses.
Instruction for victims in acute stress management.
Recognition risk factors for adverse outcomes from intervention.
Distinguish between needed formal and informal interventions.
Maintenance of appropriate self-care.

REFERENCES

APHIS (Animal and Plant Health Inspection Service). 2003. National Animal Health Emergency Response Corps: You Can Make a Difference. Available from http://www.aphis.usda.gov/publications/animal_health/content/printable_version/pub_ahvsreserves.pdf. Accessed July 15, 2007.

APHIS 2006. Recent Spread of Highly Pathogenic (H5N1) Avian Influenza in Birds. Veterinary Services Info Sheet, May 22.

APHIS 2007. Low Pathogenic Avian Influenza in Virginia. http://www.aphis.usda.gov/vs. Association of Avian Veterinarians. 2006. Statement on Asian H5N1 Highly Pathogenic Avian Influenza. Available from http://www.aav.org/AAVStatementavianflu.htm. Accessed August 1, 2007.

AVMA (American Veterinary Medical Association) 2007. Poultry depopulation: More news from the boardroom. *J Am Vet Med Assoc.* 230: 173.

Bean C, Schriber J. 2007. China suspends imports of US poultry from West Virginia. USDA GAIN report: CH7034.

Butler AS, Panzer AM, Goldfrank LR. 2003. *Preparing for the Psychological Consequences of Terrorism.* Washington, D.C.: National Academies Press, pp. 40–45.

CDC (Centers for Disease Control and Prevention). 2007. Avian Influenza: Current Situation. Available from http://www.cdc.gov/flu/avian/outbreaks/current.htm. Accessed June 29, 2007.

Center for Emerging Issues, USDA-APHIS-VS Centers for Epidemiology and Animal Health. Summary of selected disease events, Summary — July to September 2003. Fort Collins, Colorado. http://www.aphis.usda.gov/vs/ceah/cei/taf/allsummary.htm. (Accessed August 28, 2007).

Crawford PC, Dubovi EJ, Castleman WL, Stephenson I, Gibbs EPJ, Chen L, Smith C, Hill RC, Ferro P, Pompey J, Bright RA, Medina MJ, Johnson CM, Olsen CW, Cox NJ, Klimov A, Katz JM, Donis R. 2005. Transmission of equine influenza virus to dogs. *Science* 310:482–485.

Deaville J, Jones I. 2003. The Impact of the Foot and Mouth Outbreak on Mental Health and Wellbeing in Wales. http://www.rural-health.ac.uk/publications/respub.php#impactfm. Accessed February 2008.

Ferguson NM, Cummings DAT, Chauchemez S, Fraser C, Riley S, Meeyai A, Iamsirithaworn S, Burke DS. 2005. Strategies for containing an emerging influenza pandemic in Southeast Asia. *Nature* 437: 209–214.

Ferguson NM, Cummings DAT, Fraser C, Cajka JC, Cooley PC, Burke DS. 2006. Strategies for mitigating an influenza pandemic. *Nature* 442:7101.

Fernandez-Sesma A, Marukian S, Ebersole BJ, Kaminski D, Park MS, Yuen T, Sealfon SC, García-Sastre S, Moran TM. 2006. Influenza virus evades innate and adaptive immunity via the NS1 protein. *J Virol* 80:6295–6304.

Flory GA, Bendfeld ES, Peer RW, Zirkle C. 2007. Guidelines for In-House Composting Poultry Mortality as a Rapid Response to Avian Influenza. Virginia Department of Environmental Quality. Available from http://www.eeq.virginia.gov.waste (accessed October 2007).

Intervet. Avian Influenza Outbreak, Asia 2003–2005. 2007. http://www.avian-influenza.com (accessed June 15, 2007).

Kuiken T, Rimmelzwaan G, van Riel D, van Amerongen G, Baars M, Fouchier R, and Osterhaus A. 2004. Avian H5N1 influenza in cats. *Science* 306:241.

Kuiken T, Holmes EC, McCauley J, Rimmelzwaan GF, Williams CS, Grenfelt BT. 2006. Host species barriers to influenza virus infections. *Science* 312:394–397.

Kung NY, Morris RS, Perkins NR, Sims LD, Ellis TM, Bissett L, Chow M, Shortridge KF, Guan Y, Peiris MJS. 2002. Risk for infection with highly pathogenic influenza A virus (H5N1) in chickens, Hong Kong. *Emerg Infect Dis* 13:412–418.

Kyeema Foundation. Diseases: Avian Influenza Characteristics. 2004. http:// www.kyeema-foundation.org/rural_poultry/Avian%20Influenza.htm (accessed August 1, 2007).

Matrosovich MN, Matrosovich TY, Gray T, Roberts NA, Klenk HD. 2004. Human and avian influenza viruses target different cell types in the cultures of human airway epithelium. *Proc Nat Acad Sci* 101:4620–4624.

McQuiston JH, Garber LP, Porter-Spalding BA, Hahn JW, Pierson FW, Wainwright SH, Senne DA, Brignole TJ, Akey BL, Holt TJ. 2005. Evaluation of risk factors for the spread of low pathogenicity H7N2 avian influenza virus among commercial poultry farms. *J Am Vet Med Assoc* 226:767–772.

Moats JB. 2007. *Agroterrorism: A Guide for First Responders*. College Station, Texas: Texas A&M University Press.

National Agricultural Statistics Service. 2006. Chickens and Eggs. Available from http://www.usda.mannlib.cornell.edu/usda/nass/ChicEggs//2000s/2006/ChicEggs-07-21-2006.txt.

National Agricultural Statistics Service. 2007a. Number of Turkeys Raised, Selected States, 2006. Available from http://www.nass.usda.gov/Charts_and_Maps/Poultry/tkymap.asp.

National Agricultural Statistics Service. 2007b. Table 27. Poultry — Inventory and Number Sold: 2002 and 1997. 2002 Census of Agriculture. http://www.nass.usda.gov/census/census02/volume1/us/index1.htm.

Nusbaum KE, Wenzel JGW, Everly GS. 2007. Psychological first aid and the veterinarian in rural communities undergoing livestock depopulation. *J Am Vet Med Assoc.* 231:1–3.

OIE (Office of International Epizootics). 2007. Avian Influenza, Facts and Figures: H5N1 Timeline. http://www.oie.int/eng/info_ev/en_factoids_H5N1_Timeline.htm (accessed August 27, 2007).

Pelzel AM, McCluskey BJ, Scott AE. 2006. Review of the highly pathogenic avian influenza outbreak in Texas, 2004. *J Am Vet Med Assoc* 228:1869–1882.

PROMED mail. 2007. Avian influenza, human (91): Veterinarians, Source: Science Daily. http://www.promedmail.org (accessed June 15, 2007).

PROMED mail. 2003. Avian influenza, human — Netherlands (13), Source: Eurosurveillance Weekly, Vol. 7, 18, 1 May 2003. http://www.promedmail.org (accessed June 15, 2007).

Riley S. 2007. Large-scale spatial-transmission models of infectious disease. *Science* 316:1298–1301.

Ross JP. 2005. The California pilot project. NAHSS Outlook, October 2005. www.aphis.usda.gov/vs/ceah/ncahs/nsu/outlook (accessed June 15, 2007).

Seo SH, Hofmann E, Webster R. 2002. Lethal H5N1 influenza viruses escape host anti-viral cytokine responses. *Nature Med* 8:950–954.

Sims LD, Domenech H, Benigno C, Kahn A, Lubroth J, Martin V, Roeder P. 2005. Origin and evolution of highly pathogenic H5N1 avian influenza in Asia. *Vet Rec* 157(6):159–164.

Stevens J, Blixt O, Tumpey TM, Taubenberger JK, Paulson JC, Wilson IA. 2006. Structure and receptor specificity of the hemagglutinin from an H5N1 influenza virus. *Science* 312:404–410.

Suarez DL, Senne DA. 2000. Sequence analysis of related low-pathogenic and highly pathogenic H5N2 avian influenza isolates from United States live bird markets and poultry farms from 1983 to 1989. *Avian Dis* 44:356–364.

Swayne DE, Halvorson DA. 2003. Influenza. In: *Diseases of Poultry*, Saif YM, Ed. Ames, IA: Iowa State University Press, pp. 135–160.

USAHAC FAD (U.S. Animal Health Association Committee on Foreign Animal Diseases). 2004. Cleaning and disinfection. In: *Foreign Animal Diseases*. Richmond, VA: United States Animal Health Association, pp. 445–448. Available online from http://www.vet.uga.edu/vpp/gray_book02/index.php.

USDA. 2006a. Confirmatory Tests Being Conducted on Michigan Wild Bird Samples. http://www.usda.gov/wps (accessed October 2007).

USDA. 2006b. Summary of the National Highly Pathogenic Avian Influenza Response Plan. http://www.aphis.usda.gov (accessed October 2007).

U.S. Poultry and Egg Association. 2006. Economic Information. http:// www.poultryegg.org/EconomicInfo/index.html.

Van Riel D, Munster VJ, de Wit E, Rimmelzwaan GF, Fouchier RAM, Osterhaus, ADME, Kuiken T. 2006. H5N1 virus attachment to lower respiratory tract. *Science* 312:399.

Weber TP, Stilianakis NI. 2007. Ecologic immunology of avian influenza (H5N1) in migratory birds. *Emerg Infec Dis* 13:1139–1143.

WHO (World Health Organization). 2007. H5N1 Avian Influenza: Timeline of Major Events. Available from http://www.who.int/csr/disease/avian_influenza/Timeline_07_Aug27.pdf.

Williams R. 1988. Farmers in distress: how veterinarians can help out. *J Am Vet Med Assoc* 193:1062–1065.

Wuethrich B. 2003 Chasing the fickle swine flu. *Science* 299:1502–1505.

Yu H, Feng Z, Zhang X, Xiang N, Huai Y, Zhou L, He J, Guan X, Yuan Z, Li Y, Xu L, Hong R, Liu X, Zhou X, Yin W, Zhang S, Shu Y, Wang M, Wang Y, Lee C-K, Uyeki TM, Yang W. 2007. Human influenza A (H5N1) cases, urban areas of People's Republic of China, 2005–2006. *Emerg Infect Dis* 13(7):1061–1067.

Part III

Defining the Response

6 Federal and International Programs and Assets

Jane Thomas Cash, PhD, and
Martha Griffith Lavender, DSN

The (1918 Spanish influenza) epidemic killed , at a very, very, conservative estimate, 550,000 Americans in ten months; that's more Americans than died in combat in all the wars of this century, and the epidemic killed at least 30 million in the world and infected the majority of the human species. As soon as the dying stopped, the forgetting began.

Alfred W. Crosby
Influenza 1918: The American Experience

CONTENTS

6.1 INTRODUCTION

The next pandemic, whether the result of a mutation of H5N1 or a different virus altogether, will likely overwhelm our nation's health and medical capabilities, resulting in millions of hospitalizations and deaths and billions of dollars in direct and indirect costs. The impact will be global in nature — one which requires pre-event collaborative planning, a coordinated response, and a commitment to recovery efforts for the betterment of humankind. The United States' approach to preparedness has been promulgated by the questions raised in the Department of Homeland Security's National Preparedness Guidelines (2007) that, if applied to a pandemic, essentially asks

1. How prepared are we for the next pandemic or worldwide outbreak of a new influenza virus?
2. How prepared do we need to be, in order to be able to protect and secure the citizens of our nation?
3. How do we close the gap in our current level of preparedness and achieve the desired capabilities to respond effectively to the next pandemic?

Although the timing and severity of the next pandemic is unknown, the threat is real and the consequences will be significant. Three pandemics occurred in the 20th century, most notably the 1918 Spanish flu, which left millions dead worldwide. But as Crosby (1989) noted, the nation and the world soon became complacent, almost forgetting the devastation of the most severe pandemic of the century. The purpose of this chapter is to describe current national and international pandemic preparedness programs and capabilities with the intent of identifying potential partnerships and collaborations that will provide an effective and efficient global response to the inevitable — a biological event of unpredictable proportions. An effective response will not only require government intervention and international partnerships, but will also depend on the actions of individual citizens of all nations.

6.2 FEDERAL PROGRAMS AND ASSETS

Recognizing the potential impact on the health care, social, and economic status of the nation, several initiatives have been directed by the Executive Branch of the federal government. In November 2005, $7.1 billion was requested from Congress to support national activities directed at pandemic preparedness; a total of $3.8 billion was appropriated to meet the requirements identified for the first year. A portion of the funding, $600 million provided targeted assistance to states and communities in their efforts to obtain supplies and resources to achieve the federal goal of stockpiling antivirals for 25 percent of the population. These measures are bold and reflect a commitment by the federal government; however, many experts advise much more aggressive and comprehensive measures (Hampton, 2007).

A pandemic event is not a singular incident, but one that is felt in waves, each lasting weeks or months. Regardless of the place of origin, a pandemic will pass through communities and nations, and migrate around the world. If the United States faces another pandemic as severe as the 1918 pandemic, it has been projected that a five percent reduction in the gross domestic product could occur over the year following the outbreak.

The Homeland Security Act of 2002 (HSA, 2002) and the Homeland Security Presidential Directive (HSPD) 5: Management of Domestic Incidents (White House, 2003) specified the development of two important and fully integrated systems to provide an all-hazards approach to emergency incident management: the National Incident Management System (NIMS) and the National Response Plan (NRP).* NIMS was created to define how to manage an emergency incident; the NRP defines what needs to be done to manage an emergency incident. These complementary documents form the basis of the federal response to any incident, including an influenza pandemic. In addition to the guidance provided by the NIMS and the NRP, states may request federal assistance to manage the excessive demands when local and state resources are depleted. The Robert T. Stafford Disaster Relief and Emergency Assistance Act of 1974 (the Stafford Act) establishes the processes and mechanisms whereby the federal government can provide assistance to state and local governments and tribal nations. The Secretary of the Department of Health and Human Services (HHS) also has authority to declare a public health emergency and institute emergency actions to address the situation. These actions include making grants, entering into contracts, conducting investigations, waiving HHS regulatory requirements, and authorizing the emergency use of unapproved products or approved products for unapproved uses (GAO, 2007). Depending on the severity of the next pandemic, it is likely that federal resources will be depleted due to competing and overwhelming demands from the impacted states.

While it is known that a pandemic influenza outbreak will not damage the physical infrastructure of the United States, it will have a devastating impact on the sustainment of the nation's infrastructure by removing the men and women who are responsible for day-to-day operation and protection of the nation's critical infrastructure, and thus potentially crippling the economy at the local, state, and national levels. Recognizing the need to be prepared and versatile, the Homeland Security Council (HSC) issued two planning documents. The first document, National Strategy for Pandemic Influenza, released in November 2005, was intended to provide a broad, strategic overview of the federal government's plan to prepare for and respond to a pandemic in the 21st century. The second document, National Strategy for Pandemic Influenza Implementation Plan (2006), was designed to provide specific guidance and describe requirements and responsibilities for federal agencies as well as nonfederal entities. The Plan includes 324 action items related to the various roles, responsibilities, and requirements. These documents, along with HHS's Pandemic Influenza Plan (2005), serve as a foundation for the nation's planning and response goals for the uncertainties associated with the next pandemic; they also serve as critical resources to guide policy decisions related to seasonal influenza.

Goals of the Federal Response

- Limit the spread of a pandemic.
- Mitigate disease, suffering, and death.
- Sustain infrastructure.
- Lessen impact of the economy and functioning of society.

---

* The NRP was superceded by the National Response Framework in 2008.

6.3 NATIONAL STRATEGY FOR PANDEMIC INFLUENZA

HSC's 2005 National Strategy for Pandemic Influenza has served as a guide for advancing the preparedness and response goals of (1) stopping, slowing, or otherwise limiting the spread of a pandemic to the United States; (2) limiting the domestic spread of a pandemic and mitigating disease, suffering, and death; and (3) sustaining infrastructure and mitigating impact to the economy and functioning of society.

The Strategy emphasizes that preparedness and response to a pandemic is a joint responsibility of all levels of government as well as all nongovernmental sectors. It is grounded in the following principles:

- All instruments of national power will be used by the federal government to address the pandemic threat.
- States and communities must have detailed and functional plans to respond to an outbreak.
- Responsibilities of the private sector must be delineated and integrated into local, state, and federal plans.
- Individual preparedness must be defined, and citizens must be educated on how to limit the spread of infection.
- Global partnerships are critical to an effective response to the pandemic threat.

The pillars of the Strategy are broad in nature and undergird the federal government's approach to a pandemic threat in every community and every nation affected by an outbreak. Table 6.1 lists the pillars and provides a brief description of each area. Each pillar is applicable to domestic and international efforts as well as animal and human efforts.

6.3.1 PREPAREDNESS AND COMMUNICATION

The starting point for an effective strategy is built on adequate preparedness planning. Both public and private sector agencies and departments from the federal, state, and local levels have been actively engaged in developing and exercising preparedness and response

---

TABLE 6.1
Pillars of the National Strategy for Pandemic Influenza

Preparedness and communication	Pre-pandemic actions that ensure preparedness as well as the communication of roles and responsibilities to all government sectors, society, and individual citizens.
Surveillance and detection	Focuses on situational awareness, both in domestic and international systems, to ensure early detection and early warning to the public and critical response elements.
Response and containment	Activities designed to limit the spread of infection and mitigate health, social, and economic impacts of a pandemic.

Source: State HSC, National Strategy for Pandemic Influenza (2005).

plans using a pandemic outbreak as the scenario event. The U.S. Congress has appropriated $600 million over the past year for preparedness planning (HSC, 2007), and such efforts as community mitigation, medical surge, and mass prophylaxis. The "meta-checklist" has been developed to provide a comprehensive measure of pandemic preparedness plans; this resource is available at <www.pandemicflu.gov> for any agency or department to use as a one-stop portal to U.S. government avian and pandemic influenza information.

Engaging the private sector is critical to an effective national response. More than 85 percent of the critical infrastructure in the United States is owned and operated by the private sector. Therefore, continuity of operations becomes of paramount importance in maintaining the flow of goods and services needed by society. Entities that provide essential services such as food, water, health care, power, and telecommunications have a special responsibility for ongoing support to the nation. Moreover, private businesses, both large and small, must address employee health and safety measures to ensure continued operations and thus limit the negative impact of a pandemic on the community, the economy, and society. Some of the specific challenges of businesses, organizations, and financial institutions associated with planning for an avian or pandemic influenza are as follows:

- Potential for significant absenteeism over an extended period; this may arise from illness or attempts to limit spread of the infection and may fluctuate with pandemic waves of attack.
- Absenteeism may become so severe that continuity of operation plans may be inadequate and succession plans are rendered insufficient.
- Widespread economic disruption may lead to increased risk and potential downturn in overall performance of the organization/institution.
- Business continuity plans must have back-up plans to maintain critical operations while ensuring that key and essential staff are relatively well protected.
- Risk assessments must address widespread economic and infrastructure disruption including lack of transportation, electricity, telecommunications, etc. (IMF, 2006).

Extensive efforts to address the preparedness of financial institutions, public health officials, and other relevant federal, state, and local entities have resulted in policies designed to minimize economic impacts while limiting disease entry and transmission. Many of the exercises conducted in this arena have been related to the resilience of the financial services sector during a pandemic.

HHS required all states to submit pandemic preparedness plans in April 2007. Through this effort, many states were able to identify shortcomings in their preparedness strategies and correct deficiencies that were not identified prior to this process. However, the level of national preparedness is still uncertain and a baseline of preparedness remains undefined. The planning process has assisted in identifying gaps in foundational preparedness. Further, it is recognized that it is imperative that the focus shift to all-hazards preparation — not just preparedness for the next pandemic, terrorist threat, or natural disaster. Although any event, whether man-made, natural, or accidental, has unique and specific aspects, emergency preparedness must evolve from a paradigm that creates a culture of preparedness — one that is built on a solid foundation of all-hazards preparedness for individuals as well as community, state, and federal officials and agencies.

Clear, effective, and coordinated risk communication is a critical element of pandemic planning. The National Strategy recognized that one of our greatest vulnerabilities during Hurricane Katrina in 2005, and even today, has been our lack of connectivity between the various response elements: communities to communities, public to private sectors, and state to federal. To ensure that the federal government speaks in one voice, a trusted voice, all pandemic-related documents have been reviewed for consistency prior to release. It is essential that citizens and nonhealth-related entities understand their roles in preparedness planning and the response to a pandemic. Self-isolation techniques and prevention of disease transmission actions must be taught to individuals during the pre-pandemic period.

The planning cycle must also address traditional public health measures, vaccines, and antiviral drugs that will form the foundation of the national infection control strategy. Vaccination is the most important element of this strategy, but antiviral prophylaxis and treatment must also be included in the plan. The deployment of the Strategic National Stockpile (SNS) as a response action must be addressed, along with distribution plans for who receives vaccination and treatment, in what priority, and in what amounts. Once federal and local authorities agree that the SNS is needed, the system is designed for immediate delivery of 12-hour push packages of antivirals and nonpharmacological countermeasures from pre-positioned, strategically located warehouses across the United States.

6.3.2 Surveillance and Detection

To manage a pandemic outbreak effectively, the national and global public health system must be prepared to monitor and report disease progression through a sophisticated and collaborative surveillance program. Once detected, rapid deployment of resources to contain the spread of the disease will result in saved lives and sufficient notification of the need to activate federal, state, and local response plans.

One of the shortfalls in this area relates to biosurveillance and the lack of available rapid diagnostic tests that can quickly discriminate pandemic influenza from noninfluenza illnesses. To advance the capability for "real-time" clinical surveillance in acute care settings, more emphasis is needed on diagnostic test development and deployment. Once disease progression is detected, the spread of infection can be controlled, even arrested, by a variety of pre-pandemic plans for travel advisories, travel restrictions, and social isolation.

How will we know when a pandemic begins? The answer to that key question has driven the search for new and better ways to scan the world for clues that a pandemic influenza virus might be emerging.

In April 2007, the National Institutes of Health (NIH) awarded $161 million to help expand surveillance programs internationally and bolster domestic influenza clinical research, along with research on how viruses cause disease and how the human immune system responds to influenza viral infections. The Centers for Disease Control and Prevention (CDC) has also invested $180 million to help high-risk countries strengthen their capacity to recognize, diagnose, and report influenza outbreaks caused by both avian influenza A (H5N1) and seasonal influenza. Diagnostic tests for a range of viruses help doctors and field epidemiologists assess patients for the presence of H5N1, other emerging influenza viruses, and the more common seasonal influenza. In November 2006, the CDC tapped four commercial companies to develop new viral diagnostic tests with quicker and more accurate results. Lab tests for use at the patient's bedside and at ports of entry and tests designed for large reference and public health laboratories are also being improved.

HHS has also supported state and local health departments as they increase the number of clinicians providing influenza viruses for testing, improve public health laboratory detections, add influenza coordinators in each jurisdiction, and encourage clinicians to test for possible influenza infections.

In January 2007, the CDC, in partnership with the Council of State and Territorial Epidemiologists (CSTE), recommended adding "novel influenza viruses" — those with the potential to cause a pandemic — to the list of diseases that states must report to the CDC each week. States and territories have now adopted this recommendation.

6.3.3 RESPONSE AND CONTAINMENT

Once human-to-human spread of a new pandemic virus has been confirmed by health care authorities, implementation of the response activities must be initiated from the site of the transmission to all locations around the globe. The most effective strategy for protecting the citizens of the United States is to contain an outbreak beyond the nation's borders. Many lives can be saved if disease progression is slowed, allowing time for full implementation of response plans. If international containment efforts fail and a pandemic reaches the United States, federal and state stockpiles contain sufficient antivirals to treat approximately 50 million people (see Figure 6.1), with

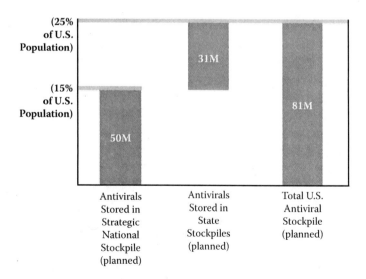

FIGURE 6.1 Proposed antiviral stockpile for the United States. (State Pandemic Toolkit. Available at http://www.statepandemictoolkit.com/tamiflu-supplyordering/tamiflu-govstockpiling. aspx.)

TABLE 6.2
Detection and Containment Strategies

Improve detection and response	Enhance global and domestic biosurveillance capability
	Coordinate international containment and rapid response
	Prepare to implement layered border measures
	Develop rapid diagnostic tests
	Create ability to care for large numbers of ill
	Stockpile critical medical materiel
	Maintain essential government services
	Sustain critical infrastructure and business continuity
	Communicate accurate and timely information to the public
Reduce disease transmission	Encourage hand hygiene and cough etiquette
	Promote use of face masks and respirators, as appropriate
	Prepare to implement community mitigation measures
	Expand vaccine production capacity and technology
	Stockpile pre-pandemic vaccine
	Develop ways to stretch our vaccine supply (adjuvants)
	Stockpile antiviral medications
	Education and inform the public about measures to reduce disease transmission

Source: HSC (Homeland Security Council), 2007, National Strategy for Pandemic Influenza: Implementation Plan One-Year Summary, p. 2.

up to 6 million courses reserved for containment efforts (HSC, 2007). To safeguard the nation's health, the government has provided resources to the state and local health departments to increase the number of providers and improve laboratory detection at public health laboratories. Specific strategies are highlighted in Table 6.2.

When appropriate, the pandemic plan will specify when nonessential travel and/or movement of people, goods, and services should be limited. Specific infection control measures should be identified and address circumstances where social distancing or quarantine may be indicated.

Attitudes toward Quarantine

The importance of containing newly emerging infectious diseases, such as a pandemic influenza, becomes a priority for public health policy planning and policy development. Wearing masks in public to prevent the spread of infection has been readily accepted, especially when people become more concerned about a health threat than a change in behavior.

Blendon et al. (2006) found that 42 percent of Americans supported compulsory quarantine, strongly favored home quarantine, and expressed concern about access to health care or prescription drugs. Additionally, 40 to 66 percent reported they would be worried about losing work/pay during the time of quarantine. The authors compared U.S. findings to other countries — Hong Kong, Singapore, and Taiwan — and concluded that the United States, the country with the least experience with quarantine, would have the highest noncompliance rate.

A pandemic outbreak will significantly challenge the existing health care system. The U.S. health care system, often touted as the best sick-care system in the world, is fragmented, privatized, competitive, and far from sufficient. Integrating a medical response with public health presented unique challenges in the current environment (Whitley et al., 2006). From a national perspective, it has been suggested that the U.S. health care system needs a 191-percent increase in hospital beds and a 461-percent increase in intensive-care beds to effectively respond to a 1918-like pandemic. For a moderate pandemic, such as the one in 1968, a 19-percent and 46-percent increase in beds will be needed (Hampton, 2007). As the pandemic waves of attack progress, the medical burden will exist for an extended period of time. Medical surge planning and the expansion of health care capacity to care for large numbers of ill patients is a major issue to be addressed. Since most hospital and emergency departments nationwide are operating at or near full capacity, medical surge planning is critical to a successful response. Expanding acute-care capacity by increasing qualified staff and the number of hospital beds will require significant and recurring investments that may not be practical in today's health care environment. Staffing shortages in hospital personnel, nurses, and laboratory personnel, as well as shortages in state and local health departments, shall be difficult to remedy with past practices. It is recognized that a pandemic outbreak will impact communities almost simultaneously and result in many times the normal demand for acute health care. Contingency planning for such situations must involve alternative strategies; it is unrealistic to conceive of a plan that increases staff and hospital beds to a level necessary for pandemic preparedness. Beds and staff are not the only resources that will be in short supply. Most hospitals now operate on an "as needed" basis with short supplies of medications and other products necessary to deliver quality patient care. It is anticipated that even basic supplies will be quickly depleted in a pandemic event.

Hospitals must be prepared to make very difficult decisions on discharging patients to make room for influenza patients, reconfiguring private rooms to semi-private rooms or wards, converting nontraditional hospital space (e.g., cafeteria or conference rooms) into treatment or patient care areas, mandating staff overtime, discontinuing or altering treatment for individuals who are consuming large amounts of resources, canceling surgeries and diagnostic tests, and using volunteer (and unlicensed) staff. Alternative care facilities should be designated in advance with specific staffing and treatment plans. Mass casualty incidents (MCIs), such as will be likely with the next pandemic, will require adaptation and modification of health care practices. To make such decisions during the event would be disastrous and chaotic. Staff must be prepared for the emotional turmoil that will result from altering traditional practices and care delivery models before those changes are instituted during an influenza pandemic (AHRQ, 2005).

Online Training for Public Health Response

To improve domestic response efforts, the Centers for Disease Control and Prevention (CDC) has released an online version of its three-day training course that provides a standardized curriculum to state and local public health responders about how to identify and control human infections and illness associated with avian influenza A H5N1.

The course, entitled "CDC/CSTE Rapid Response Training: The Role of Public Health in a Multi-Agency Response to Avian Influenza in the United States," is the result of a partnership between the CDC and the Council of State and Territorial Epidemiologists (CSTE) and is available at www.cste.org/influenza/avian.asp.

6.4 HHS PANDEMIC INFLUENZA PLAN

Recognizing the need for a comprehensive document that could guide states and communities in developing effective pandemic preparedness plans, HHS created and published the HHS Pandemic Influenza Plan (HHS, 2005). The authors of the HHS Plan emphasized the need for all plans to be viewed as living documents that should be updated periodically and exercised to identify weakness and promote effective implementation (HHS, 2005, 2). The HHS Plan supports the National Strategy for Pandemic Influenza and outlines planning assumptions and doctrine for health sector pandemic preparedness and response. The HHS Plan also provides public health guidance for state and local partners and features 11 detailed supplements to assist with pandemic planning.

The planning assumptions underpin the foundations of any national, state, or local pandemic plan and describe the expected evolution and impacts of a pandemic outbreak. The planning assumptions identified in the HHS Plan are listed in Table 6.3. It is clear that a pandemic will place overwhelming and sustained demands on public/private health care and the public health systems that are responsible for delivery of care in the United States and throughout the world.

TABLE 6.3
Pandemic Planning Assumptions

All age groups will be susceptible to the influenza virus causing the next pandemic.

A 30% attack rate in the overall population will exist with the highest rate seen in school-aged children.

At least 50% of those affected will seek outpatient medical care.

Virulence of the virus is unpredictable, requiring plans that call for hospital and death projections based both on moderate and severe health outcomes.

Risk groups cannot be predicted accurately.

A two-day incubation period from exposure to appearance of symptoms.

Viral shedding and risk for transmission will be greatest during the first two days of illness.

An average of two secondary infections will occur.

A pandemic outbreak will last about six to eight weeks with at least two waves.

Following a pandemic, a new viral subtype will evolve and contribute to seasonal influenza.

Seasonality of a pandemic cannot be predicted with accuracy.

In 2005, a vaccine prioritization plan was presented by the Advisory Committee on Immunization Practices (ACIP) and the National Vaccine Advisory Committee (NVAC) to HHS on the use of vaccine and antiviral drugs in an influenza pandemic. The plan's recommendations were based on critical assumptions related to morbidity and mortality projections, limitations in the health care system, infectious rates in the workforce, critical infrastructure, and vaccine production capacity (see Table 6.4). Since the development of the 2005 vaccine prioritization plan, the government has supported efforts to increase the production capacity of domestic influenza vaccine. Significant funding has been allocated with the intent of providing pandemic influenza vaccine for any person in the United States who wants to be vaccinated within six months of a pandemic declaration. New guidelines were disseminated for comment in October 2007.

Recommendations were also made on distribution of antiviral countermeasures considering pandemic response goals, pandemic planning assumptions, and a thorough review of past pandemics, annual influenza disease, and data on antiviral drug impacts (see Table 6.5). The ACIP and NVAC recognized that the recommendations will need to be reconsidered at the time of a pandemic when information on disease progression, transmission, available drug supply, and impact on society are known. It was assumed that antiviral treatment will be effective in reducing pneumonia, and thus decreasing mortality. It was also assumed that early treatment, within the first 48 hours, is necessary to decrease the risk of complications and shortening illness duration.

While much has been accomplished to prepare the nation for a pandemic event, there is a growing concern that policy makers and the public in general, are too complacent in their approach and dedication to preparedness planning. Due to the concern expressed by Congress, the Government Accountability Office (GAO) conducted an assessment of the federal government's readiness to lead a response to an influenza pandemic. The study methodology focused on analyzing the extent to which the National Strategy and the Implementation Plan address the six characteristics of an effective national strategy. The GAO made two recommendations to enhance federal preparedness efforts (GAO, 2007). The first recommendation emphasized the need for the HHS and DHS secretaries to work together to conduct rigorous testing and training exercises. The Strategy and the Plan clearly describe leadership roles and responsibilities that are consistent with the NRP — with the HHS secretary assuming the federal medical response and the DHS Secretary assuming the lead for domestic incident management and federal coordination. There is no clarity in the documents on how these leaders share the responsibilities in practice. In addition, recent changes in the organizational structure of the Federal Emergency Management Agency (FEMA) and the recent designation of the FEMA administrator as the principal domestic emergency management advisor to the president adds further complexity to the leadership structure in a pandemic event. Once leadership roles have been clarified, it is also required that these roles are understood by state, local, and tribal governments; the private sectors; and the international community.

The second recommendation was that the HSC establish a process and timeline for updating the Implementation Plan. It was recommended that key nonfederal

TABLE 6.4
Vaccine Priority Group Recommendations

Tier	Subtier	Population	Rationale
1	A	Vaccine and antiviral manufacturers and others essential to manufacturing and critical support (~40,000)	Need to assure maximum production of vaccine and antiviral drugs
		Medical workers and public health workers who are involved in direct patient contact, other support services essential for direct patient care, and vaccinators (8–9 million)	Health care workers are required for quality patient care delivery; there is little surge capacity among health care sector personnel to meet increased demand
	B	Persons >65 years with one or more influenza high-risk conditions, not including essential hypertension (~18.2 million)	These groups are at high risk of hospitalization and death; excludes elderly in nursing homes and those who are immunocompromised and would not likely be protected by vaccination
		Persons 6 months–64 years with two or more influenza high-risk conditions, not including essential hypertension (~6.9 million)	
		Persons 6 months or older with a history of hospitalization for pneumonia or influenza or other influenza high-risk condition in the past year (~740,000)	
	C	Pregnant women (~3 million)	In past pandemics, pregnant women have been at high risk; vaccination will also protect the infant who cannot receive vaccine
		Household contacts of severely immune-compromised persons who would not be vaccinated due to likely poor response to the vaccine (2.7 million)	Vaccination of household contact of immune-compromised and young infants will decrease risk of exposure and infection among those who cannot be protected directly by vaccination
		Household contacts of children <6 months old (5 million)	
	D	Public health emergency response workers critical to pandemic response (150,000)	Critical to implement pandemic response such as providing vaccinations and managing/monitoring response activities
		Key government leaders	Preserving decision-making capacity also critical for managing and implementing a response
2	A	Healthy 65 years and older (17.7 million)	Groups that are also at increased risk but not as high as population in Tier 1B
		6 months– 64 years with one high-risk condition (35.8 million)	
		6–23 months old, healthy (5.6 million)	

TABLE 6.4 (CONTINUED)
Vaccine Priority Group Recommendations

Tier	Subtier	Population	Rationale
	B	Other public health emergency responders (300,000)	Includes critical infrastructure groups that have impact on maintaining health (e.g., public safety or transportation of medical supplies and food); implementing a pandemic response; and on maintaining societal functions
		Public safety workers including police, fire, 911 dispatchers, and correctional facility staff (2.99 million)	
		Utility workers essential for maintenance of power, water, and sewage system functions (364,0000)	
		Transportation workers transporting fuel, water, food, and medical supplies as well as public ground public transportation (3.8 million)	
		Telecommunications/IT for essential network operations and maintenance (1.08 million)	
3		Other key government health decision makers	Other important societal groups for a pandemic response but of lower priority
4		Healthy persons 2–64 years but not included in above categories (179.3 million)	All persons not included in other groups based on objective to vaccinate all those who want protection

Source: HHS Pandemic Influenza Plan, 2005, pp. D13–D14.

stakeholders be actively involved in the process and that lessons learned from exercises and other sources be incorporated into the revision. The GAO specifically identified the following information to be included in the next plan update:

- Cost, resources, and allocations needed to complete the action items in the plan
- A process for monitoring and publicly reporting on the plan's progress
- Clearer linkages with the pandemic strategies and plans of other government agencies
- Straightforward descriptions of priorities and relationships among action items and greater use of outcome-oriented performance measures

TABLE 6.5
Antiviral Drug Priority Group Recommendations

Group	Estimated Population (millions)	Strategy	# Courses For Target Group	# Courses Cumulative	Rationale
1 Patients admitted to hospital	10.0	T[a]	7.5	7.5	Consistent with medical practice and ethics to treat those with serious illness and who are most likely to die
2 Health care workers (HCW) with direct patient contact, emergency medical service providers	9.2	T	2.4	9.9	HCW are required for quality patient care delivery; there is little surge capacity among health care sector personnel to meet increased demand
3 Highest risk outpatients: immune-compromised persons, pregnant women	2.5	T	0.7	10.6	Groups are critical risk for hospitalization and death; immune compromised cannot be protected by vaccination
4 Pandemic health responders, public safety, government decision makers	3.3	T	0.9	11.5	Groups are critical for an effective public health response to a pandemic
5 Increased risk patients: young children 12–23 months old, persons >65 yrs old, persons with underlying medical conditions	85.5	T	22.4	33.9	Groups are at high risk for hospitalization and death

TABLE 6.5 (CONTINUED)
Antiviral Drug Priority Group Recommendations

	Group	Estimated Population (millions)	Strategy	# Courses For Target Group	Cumulative	Rationale
6	Outbreak response in nursing homes and other residential settings	NA	PEP[b]	2.0	35.9	Treatment of patients and prophylaxis of contacts is effective in stopping outbreaks; vaccination priorities do not include nursing home residents
7	HCWs in emergency departments, intensive care units, dialysis centers, EMS providers	1.2	P[c]	4.8	40.7	These groups are most critical to an effective health care response and have limited surge capacity; prophylaxis will best prevent absenteeism
8	Pandemic societal responders (e.g., critical infrastructure groups as defined in the vaccine priorities), HCW without direct patient contact	10.2	T	2.7	43.4	Infrastructure groups that have impact on maintaining health, implementing a pandemic response, and maintaining societal functions
9	Other outpatients	180	T	47.3	90.7	Includes others who develop influenza and do not fall within the above groups

(*continued*)

TABLE 6.5 (CONTINUED)
Antiviral Drug Priority Group Recommendations

	Group	Estimated Population (millions)	Strategy	# Courses		Rationale
				For Target Group	Cumulative	
10	Highest risk outpatients	2.5	P	10.0	100.7	Prevents illness in the highest risk groups for hospitalization and death
11	Other HCWs with direct patient contact	8.0	P	32.0	132.7	Prevention would best reduce absenteeism and preserve optimal function

Source: HHS Pandemic Plan, 2005, p. D21.

[a] Treatment (T) = requires a total of 10 capsules and is defined as 1 course.

[b] (PEP) Post exposure prophylaxis also requires a single course.

[c] (P) Prophylaxis is assumed to require 40 capsules (4 courses) though more may be needed if community outbreak last for a longer period.

6.5   HOMELAND SECURITY PRESIDENTIAL DIRECTIVE 21

Federal guidance has evolved as more is learned about capabilities and shortcomings. Most recently, guidance on public health and medical preparedness for all disasters, including a pandemic, was provided in the HSPD 21 (White House, 2007). In this directive, preparedness was defined in terms of plans, guidance (e.g., policies and procedures), personnel training, and equipment needed to maximize an appropriate response to a catastrophic health event. The key principles applied to this directive are consistent with previous national strategy documents (e.g., National Strategy for Homeland Security, National Strategy to Combat Weapons of Mass Destruction, and Biodefense for the 21st Century) and include (1) preparedness for all potential events; (2) vertical and horizontal coordination at all levels; (3) regionalization; (4) involvement of all nongovernmental, private, and academic sectors; and (5) roles of individual citizens, families, and communities (White House, 2007, 2). The intent of the directive is to foster a timely and coordinated public health and medical response to meet the needs of the American public in the case of a catastrophic health event. Issues related to biosurveillance, countermeasure distribution, mass casualty care, and community resilience are addressed.

The shortcomings in the current health care system, such as the inability of the majority of American communities to meet the objective of dispensing counter measures to an entire community population within 48 hours after a decision is made, are clearly recognized. The directive calls for the development of four foundational elements to foster preparedness. These include the development of doctrine; establishment of innovative system designs; capacity building; and focused, coordinated training and education. The directive provides a clear road map to preparedness of the health care system while also recognizing the great strides that must be made to create a culture of preparedness that addresses and values the need for altered standards of care and modified health care practices that must be instituted during a catastrophic health event.

Lessons from the 1918 Pandemic Can Help Communities Today

Researchers studying the outcomes of the 1918 pandemic in dozens of U.S. cities have concluded that the speed of the public health response matters tremendously. Implementing multiple nonpharmaceutical interventions early in a local epidemic can save lives.

For example, there is a striking contrast between the reported mortality rates of Philadelphia and St. Louis. The first cases of disease among civilians in Philadelphia were reported on September 17, 1918, but authorities allowed large public gatherings, most notably in a citywide parade on September 18, 1918, to continue. School closures, bans on public gatherings, and other social distancing interventions that reduce contacts between people were not implemented until October 3, when disease spread had already begun to overwhelm the city. In contrast, the first cases of disease among civilians in St. Louis were reported on October 5, and authorities introduced interventions essentially identical to those introduced in Philadelphia on October 7. The difference in response times between the two cities was approximately 14 days, when measured from the first reported cases. The costs of this delay were enormous. During the fall of 1918, Philadelphia ultimately experienced a cumulative excess pneumonia and influenza death rate more than twice that of St. Louis (HSC, 2007, 18).

6.6 INTERNATIONAL PROGRAMS AND ASSETS

Because of its unique nature, responsibility for preparedness and response to a pandemic extends across all levels of government and all segments of society. No single entity alone can prevent or mitigate the impact of a pandemic. (National Strategy for Pandemic Influenza, 2005)

6.6.1 WORLD HEALTH ORGANIZATION

The World Health Organization (WHO) is the lead agency responsible for coordinating and managing the global response to human cases of H5N1 avian influenza as well as monitoring the threat of an influenza pandemic. The WHO focuses on five priority areas that are of concern to human health:

1. Reducing human exposure to the H5N1 virus
2. Strengthening the early warning system
3. Containing an emerging pandemic influenza at its source

4. Increasing the capacities of countries and the international community to prepare for and respond to a global pandemic of influenza
5. Encouraging all possible efforts into research and development of pandemic vaccines and antiviral medications and into improving global production capacity (CDC, 2006)

In 2005, the WHO secretariat updated guidance for pandemic influenza and redefined the phases of a pandemic. Table 6.6 depicts a summary of the WHO guidance to the international community and to governments on preparedness and response for pandemic threats and pandemic disease.

6.6.2 INTERNATIONAL ORGANIZATIONS: LINKAGES AND PROGRAM ASSETS

In the event of an outbreak of pandemic influenza spreading outside of the immediate vicinity and across international borders, countries will face surges on their health services that may cause high levels of mortality, morbidity, and social and economic disruption. The ability of countries and the international agencies to cope with the arrival of a pandemic and mitigate its impact will depend greatly on the precise and complete preparedness plans. Thus, the WHO is working with all countries in helping them to write and exercise their national pandemic preparedness plans in order to identify gaps in their capacities.

In September 2005, President Bush announced the International Partnership on Avian and Pandemic Influenza (IPAPI) at the U.N. General Assembly. The Partnership was developed with the WHO to ensure that nations address a series of key goals in their preparedness planning. Specific areas included elevating the issue of avian influenza on national agendas; coordinating efforts among nations; mobilizing and leveraging resources; increasing disease reporting; improving surveillance; and building local capacity to identify, contain, and respond to an influenza pandemic.

Over the past year, through the IPAPI, the United States and the international community have worked together to address the threat of an influenza pandemic at its source by containing H5N1 poultry outbreaks and rapidly identifying associated cases of human disease. Additionally, the United States is supporting efforts to improve laboratory diagnosis and early warning networks in more than 75 countries. Working with its partners to expand on-the-ground surveillance capacity, to enhance national and regional laboratories, and to improve knowledge about the movement and changes in H5N1 on a global scale, the United States is helping to ensure that countries are able to quickly confirm outbreaks in animals or people (IPAPI, 2005).

In collaboration with WHO, UNICEF, the U.N. Food and Agriculture Organization (FAO), the World Organization for Animal Health, and other partners, the United States is working on avian influenza issues in more than 100 countries. The United States is supporting communications and public education activities in more than 50 countries in order to create awareness about avian influenza and promote healthy behaviors and practices in an attempt to reduce the risk of disease transmission. To help achieve this goal, the United States has supported the training of more than 113,000 people in the delivery of avian influenza communications messages.

Additionally, the United States has sent scientists, veterinarians, public health and communications experts as well as health care workers to affected and high-risk

TABLE 6.6

Phases of Alert in the WHO Global Influenza Preparedness Plan

Period	Definition	WHO Phase	Strategic Actions
Inter-pandemic period	Low risk of human cases	Phase 1	Reduce opportunities for human infection Strengthen the early warning system
	Higher risk of human cases New virus in animals, no human cases	Phase 2	
Pandemic alert period	No or very limited human-to-human transmission	Phase 3 (emergence of a pandemic virus)	Contain or delay spread at the source
	Small cluster(s) with limited human-to-human transmission but spread is highly localized, suggesting that the virus is not well adapted to humans	Phase 4 (emergence of a pandemic virus)	Reduce morbidity, mortality, and social disruption Conduct research to guide response measures
	Larger cluster(s) but human-to-human spread is still localized, suggesting that the virus is becoming increasingly better adapted to humans but may not yet be fully transmissible (substantial pandemic risk)	Phase 5 (emergence of a pandemic virus)	
Pandemic period	Efficient and sustained human-to-human transmission	Phase 6 (Pandemic declared and spreading internationally)	

Source: http://www.hhs.gov/pandemicflu/plan/appendixc.html.

countries to assist in the development and implementation of emergency preparedness plans for response to avian and pandemic influenza. As a result of these efforts, much progress has been made across the spectrum of animal health protection, public health preparedness, information sharing, and public communication and awareness.

The U.S. Department of Defense's Global Emerging Infections Surveillance and Response System (GEIS) is supporting surveillance activities in the military health system worldwide. There are five laboratories located in Egypt, Indonesia, Kenya, Peru, and Thailand representing a global network of expertise in emerging infectious disease detection.

The United States has provided funding to enhance the WHO's Global Outbreak Alert and Response Network (GOARN). GOARN is a collaboration of existing institutions and networks that pool human and technical resources for the rapid identification, confirmation, and response to disease outbreaks of international importance (GOARN, 2000).

The United States has expanded the HHS/CDC network of Global Disease Detection (GDD) Centers, which works closely with the WHO. The CDC's Influenza Branch has expanded its role and scope to meet the demands of establishing a functional surveillance network and has been very proactive in establishing training programs and information campaigns (see Figure 6.2 and Table 6.7). This program is a network of international centers dedicated to the surveillance of emerging

FIGURE 6.2 This photograph was taken during a 2004 press conference where CDC officials made statements and answered questions about the inadvertent distribution of H2N2 influenza A virus to a number of laboratories around the world. Pictured here are Director of the CDC Julie Gerberding, M.D., M.P.H., standing at left, and virologist Dr. Nancy Cox, Chief of the Influenza Branch in the National Center for Infectious Diseases (NCID), speaking at the podium. (Photo taken by James Gathany; image courtesy of the Public Health Image Library, Department of Health and Human Services, Centers for Disease Control and Prevention (PHIL Image No. 7303).)

TABLE 6.7
CDC's Domestic and International Response to Avian Influenza

Domestic Activities	International Activities
In May 2005, CDC joined a new, inter-agency National Influenza Pandemic Preparedness Task Force organized by the U.S. Secretary of Health and Human Services. This task force is developing and refining preparedness efforts with international, state, local, and private organizational partners to help ensure the most effective response possible when the next influenza pandemic occurs. For more information about the Pandemic Influenza Preparedness Plan of the U.S. Health and Human Services Department and other aspects of this coordinated federal initiative, please visit www.pandemicflu.gov.	CDC is one of four WHO Collaborating Centers and in this capacity provides ongoing support for the global WHO surveillance network, laboratory testing, training, and other actions.
CDC developed the first test approved by FDA for the detection of the H5 viruses that first emerged in Asia in 2003.	CDC has worked collaboratively with WHO to conduct investigations of human H5N1 infections in China, Indonesia, Thailand, Turkey, and Vietnam and to provide laboratory diagnostic and training assistance.
CDC reconstructed the 1918 Spanish influenza pandemic virus to help develop strategies for early diagnosis, treatment, and prevention, if a similar pandemic virus emerged.	CDC has performed laboratory testing of H5N1 viruses from Indonesia, Thailand, and Vietnam.
CDC has collaborated with the Association of Public Health Laboratories to conduct training workshops for state laboratories on the use of molecular techniques to rapidly identify H5 viruses.	CDC is implementing a multi-million dollar initiative to improve influenza surveillance in Asia.
CDC is working collaboratively with the Council of State and Territorial Epidemiologists and other partners to assist states with pandemic planning efforts.	CDC has led or taken part in nine training sessions to enhance local capacities in Asia to conduct surveillance for possible human cases of H5 and to detect avian influenza A H5 viruses using laboratory techniques.
CDC is working with other agencies, such as the Department of Defense and the Department of Veterans Affairs, on antiviral stockpile issues.	
	CDC has developed and distributed a reagent kit for the detection of the currently circulating influenza A H5 viruses.
	CDC has worked with other international and national agencies in Asia to develop a training course for rapid response teams that will be used to help prepare the region to respond to outbreaks when they occur.
	CDC has developed an international program to support surveillance, laboratory capacity, health education, rapid response training, and other activities for avian influenza.

Source: http://www.cdc.gov/flu/avian/outbreaks/cdcresponse.htm.

infectious diseases, outbreak detection, identification, tracking, and response, as well as the provision of training programs for field epidemiology and laboratory scientists. New GDD Centers have been instituted in China, Egypt, and Guatemala, and GDD Centers in Kenya and Thailand have been enhanced and have trained rapid response teams and stockpiles of protective equipment available for deployment internationally within 24 hours. Additionally, plans are underway to establish regional rapid response teams and stockpiles at GDD Centers in China and Egypt.

Although the H5N1 avian influenza virus has not spread to North America, the United States is working closely with Canada and Mexico through the Security and Prosperity Partnership to coordinate and communicate surveillance for the early detection of the virus in wild birds migrating within and across North America. This collaboration also extends to pandemic preparedness and response activities.

By its very nature, a pandemic has no respect for borders. An outbreak of pandemic influenza anywhere in the world poses a risk to people everywhere. International efforts to contain and mitigate the effects of an outbreak of pandemic influenza are a central component of every country's pandemic strategy.

6.6.3 ETHICAL CONCERNS IN PANDEMIC PLANNING

In the beginning stages of an influenza pandemic, it is most likely that the demand for vaccines, prophylaxis, and palliative care will be far higher than the supply available at the national as well as the international level. Governments and authorities will therefore be forced to make difficult and sometimes politically unpopular decisions over asset access. In addition, some of the measures that may be needed in order to meet the needs of critical infrastructures may conflict with the rights and freedoms of individuals and communities. At the heart of many of these decision lie ethical issues and concerns, which, when identified, discussed, and agreed upon by key stakeholders prior to a pandemic, cannot only help to guide decision making, but can help to make difficult choices more understandable and palatable.

The WHO is working with ethical experts and human rights specialists to help member states identify those areas in pandemic planning and response in which ethical issues may arise and to begin the process of delineating their decisions within their own national ethical framework. When the next human influenza pandemic occurs, the international community will look to the WHO to lead countries under the International Health Regulations (IHR, 2005). As part of the implementation of the IHR, the WHO has established contact points that are available on a 24-hour basis at headquarters and in the regional offices to receive reports of any indication of possible cases of pandemic influenza. Additionally, the WHO is also strengthening its own systems of alert and response. A new event management system (EMS) is being established that will be the official repository of all information relevant to any event that may constitute a public health emergency of international concern, including an outbreak of pandemic influenza. The EMS will coordinate global communications and updates on the outbreak and the evolving pandemic within the WHO and with all key partners and member states. The EMS will increase the efficiency, timeliness, and inclusiveness of the WHO's decision-making process and maintain a record of operational activities and decisions.

6.6.4 Preparedness Planning with Nongovernmental Sectors

While the primary responsibility for pandemic planning lies with governments and health authorities, there is a wide range of nongovernmental sectors who hold responsibility for the health and well-being of groups of people within their care, or who could have a significant role in preventing the spread of the virus during a pandemic. The global nature of an influenza pandemic will require that all stakeholders, some of which may be beyond the scope of the WHO's traditional partners, are identified and brought into preparedness planning at an early stage. For example, international and regional banks have essential roles in helping resource-stretched countries finance their pandemic response activities. The Asian Development Bank has become a major partner of the WHO in providing financial assistance to support its activities. The WHO has also been working closely with the humanitarian community to address pandemic influenza control measures. Nongovernmental organizations (NGOs) are frequently the principal health care providers in humanitarian emergencies. Other key partners include U.N. agencies, such as the Office of the U.N. High Commissioner for Refugees (UNHCR) and UNICEF, as well as leading humanitarian NGOs and other international organizations such as the International Organization for Migration and the International Committee of the Red Cross.

6.6.5 Continuity Planning: A Global Perspective

The WHO is working with international organizations that are developing plans for business continuity and the health and safety of employees who would be required to work during a pandemic. In the development of these plans there are multiple issues to consider. Examples include travel policies, international meetings, preventive measures, scaling down of nonessential functions, increases in teleworking, and possible in-office quarantine measures for essential staff during a phase 6 pandemic situation.

6.7 GLOBAL PREPAREDNESS AND RESPONSE

6.7.1 Investigating Outbreaks and Assessing Risk

The WHO's operational activity in investigating outbreaks and assessing risk is focused on responding to and investigating actual instances of human infection with the H5N1 virus. In the event of human infection with this virus, multi-disciplinary international teams are deployed as rapidly as possible to areas in which cases have been reported. Although human cases of avian influenza remain sporadic, the disease is severe and the case fatality rate is high (HHS, 2005).

6.7.2 Surveillance and Diagnosis

Early warning of the emergence of a pandemic influenza virus is essential in order to mobilize all efforts to contain its spread. Countries affected by outbreaks must be able to detect and manage cases quickly, while the WHO and the international community must obtain the epidemiological data and clinical specimens needed in order to determine the level of pandemic alert and to develop pandemic influenza vaccines. This requires strong and effective surveillance and reporting systems at the national and international level. Unfortunately, existing surveillance systems in many countries on the frontline of avian influenza remain inadequate, particularly in areas where many cases have occurred. This limitation jeopardizes the accuracy of risk assessment and leads to gaps in the epidemiological understanding of the evolution of the virus.

The International Health Regulations are designed to provide a standardized way for the global community to detect, report, and respond to signs that a public health emergency of international importance may be developing. As countries work toward improving their own capacities that will be needed under these regulations, the international health community will have a clearer early warning should pandemic influenza appear.

The National Influenza Centers (NIC) at the country level are frequently the first stage in the global process of collection and sampling of influenza viruses. They play a crucial role in ensuring that influenza virus strains collected from patients together with analytical information on their genetic structure are provided to vaccine producers. The WHO diagnostic kits for seasonal influenza have been updated and distributed to all National Influenza Centers.

In addition to strong surveillance systems, reliable global telecommunications connectivity is needed to ensure rapid reporting and exchange of information. This will be particularly important in the early stages of a pandemic when existing channels are likely to become overloaded rapidly. The WHO is establishing connections for its country offices based on a global private network that will be able to continue to operate when external communication systems may be compromised.

Epidemiological data and operational information about outbreaks is not static and changes rapidly. The WHO has developed a comprehensive event management system that will manage critical information about outbreaks and ensure accurate and timely communications. Features of the event management system include:

- Comprehensive databases on epidemic intelligence, verification status, laboratory investigation, and operational information
- Tracking and recording outbreak history, critical decisions, important actions by the WHO and partners and key documents
- Management of logistic support and specialized response equipment, materials, and supplies
- Integrated database on the skills, experience, and availability of international experts for response teams
- Profiling of technical institutions in the GOARN concentrating on readiness and capacity to support international outbreak response
- Standardized information products for member states, public health officials, media, and the public
- Communications with the GOARN to enhance operational readiness (GOARN, 2000)

6.7.3 VACCINE DEVELOPMENT AND PRODUCTION

In many countries, vaccine production capacity cannot meet the needs of its citizens. To help extend protections to global partners, HHS provided $10 million to the WHO, which then awarded that sum to six key developing countries in April 2007.

This money was used to expand their local infrastructure and produce safe, effective seasonal influenza vaccines as well as to help fill their own (and possibly regional) needs in the event of a pandemic.

The challenge of producing enough pandemic vaccine for the U.S. population is significant. However, an even greater challenge is producing and providing world-wide access to pandemic vaccine. The global capacity for influenza vaccine production is approximately 350 million doses per year but could be scaled up to 500 million doses per year in an emergency such as a pandemic. Unfortunately, even with the current investments in expanded capacity, global vaccine production will remain well below projected demand during a pandemic. The United States is working in collaboration with the WHO and international partners to enhance surveillance and pandemic preparedness as well as increasing vaccine development and vaccine access. Four tenets guide this international effort: (1) transparency; (2) rapid reporting; (3) sharing of data; and (4) scientific cooperation. Withholding influenza viruses from the Global Influenza Surveillance Network would greatly threaten global public health and is not consistent with the spirit of the legal obligations member nations have in adhering to the International Health Regulations.

Recently, the World Health Assembly adopted a resolution on pandemic influenza preparedness. This resolution emphasized the need for increased vaccine access. The United States has invested more than $1 billion toward the development of new vaccine technologies that will benefit the international community. Additionally, the United States has supported and financed the WHO's efforts to meet the long-term global need for an influenza vaccine through the Global Pandemic Influenza Action Plan to Increase Vaccine Supply.

The WHO's strategic approach in vaccine development and production must focus on several concurrent activities. First, any outbreak of avian influenza in humans demands an immediate response to investigate its source in order to minimize the risk of others being infected. Collecting evidence from actual events of the transmission from birds to humans can provide valuable information to reduce human exposure.

This information is also necessary for the development of policies related to public education on the health risks associated with close contact with poultry and how to protect themselves. Additionally, there is a need to understand how to protect particular groups that could be most at risk, such as poultry workers, laboratory workers, or health care providers.

6.7.4 RESPONSE AND CONTAINMENT

The WHO has established an antiviral stockpile with Hoffman LaRoche, producers of the antiviral drug oseltamivir, which is marketed under the name Tamiflu®. This company donated 3 million courses of oseltamivir specifically for the use of the WHO in the event of a launch of a rapid containment operation. In addition, Hoffman LaRoche donated 2 million additional courses of oseltamivir for stockpiling at the national level to assist countries in their efforts to respond to local outbreaks of avian influenza as they occur.

Recent studies suggest that an initial outbreak caused by an emerging pandemic virus might be contained provided several demanding conditions were met within a very short time frame. Mass administration of antiviral drugs within the outbreak zone was the foundation of the containment strategy, followed by additional non-pharmaceutical measures, such as area quarantine and social distancing. The studies further concluded that, should the containment strategy fail to prevent the emergence of a fully transmissible pandemic virus, it could nonetheless delay international spread.

Once the potential start of an influenza pandemic is suspected, authorities should immediately notify the WHO in order to assess all relevant technical, operational, logistical, and political factors. At this juncture, the WHO would consult with external experts about the situation and provide input and relevant advice to national authorities. If the information is insufficient to make a decision, additional field assessment (with the WHO and international support as needed) would be initiated. Although there would be joint discussions, the ultimate decision to initiate a containment operation would require the full agreement of the national authorities, who would be responsible for leading and managing the national activities related to the containment operation.

In the assessment process preceding the decision about whether to proceed, there are two critical and central questions to address:

1. Is there compelling evidence to suggest that a novel influenza virus has gained the ability to transmit easily enough from person to person to initiate and sustain outbreaks, especially community level outbreaks?
2. If so, are there any compelling reasons why a containment operation should be deferred?

If a decision is made to proceed with a containment operation, the WHO will also request and coordinate assistance from international agencies and partners to support the containment operation. Such support could include personnel (e.g., epidemiologists, logisticians, lab technicians, and communications and social mobilization experts), supplies (e.g., personal protective equipment and antivirals), and other essential requirements.

It is highly unlikely that any single country, no matter how well prepared and resourced, would be able to initiate and manage containment without assistance from the global community. Preventing the emergence of a fully transmissible pandemic virus will require a global response characterized by unprecedented international coordination and the necessary human, financial, technical, and logistical resources.

In summary, it seems that there are two principal tasks facing the international community: (1) reduce the opportunities for the H5N1 virus to reach its pandemic potential, and (2) be prepared for a pandemic should these efforts fail.

6.8 SUMMARY

Constant vigilance is the key to combating avian influenza and preventing pandemic influenza. By detecting avian influenza outbreaks early and with improved surveillance and laboratory diagnostic capacity, the United States and the world community have the opportunity to contain outbreaks in birds and intensify surveillance for human H5N1 cases that may accompany those outbreaks. All governmental sectors and individual citizens share the responsibility to remain vigilant and committed to pandemic preparedness.

6.9 USEFUL INTERNET RESOURCES

Visit www.pandemicflu.gov for one-stop access to United States and international avian and pandemic flu information.

6.9.1 NONGOVERNMENTAL ORGANIZATIONS

Association of State and Territorial Health Officials (ASTHO) — www.astho.org
Infectious Disease Society of America — www.idsociety.org
Institute of Medicine (IOM) — www.iom.edu
National Foundation for Infectious Diseases — www.nfid.org
World Health Organization (WHO) — www.who.org

6.9.2 INFLUENZA BACKGROUND INFORMATION

CDC (www.cdc.gov/flu): Presents information on the symptoms, treatment, and complications of the disease, prevention and control, the types of influenza viruses, questions and answers on symptoms, vaccination, and myths.

National Vaccine Program Office (www.hhs.gov/nvpo/pandemics): Presents a historical overview of pandemics that occurred throughout the past century (Spanish flu, Asian flu, Hong Kong flu), and three influenza scares (swine flu, Russian flu, and avian flu).

World Health Organization (www.who.int/csr/disease/influenza/pandemic/en): Defines an influenza pandemic, explains how a new influenza virus can cause a pandemic, presents the consequences of an influenza pandemic, explains the global surveillance systems, and provides links to other pandemic plans from other nations.

6.9.3 ADDITIONAL RESPONSE RESOURCES

CDC Cooperative Agreements on Public Health Preparedness (www.bt.cdc.gov/planning/continuationguidance): Provide funding to state and local public health jurisdictions for preparedness for and response to bioterrorism, other outbreaks of infectious diseases, and other public health threats and emergencies.

Centers for Public Health Preparedness (www.asph.org/acphp): A national system for competency-based training tools for the public health workforce.

Epidemic Information Exchange (www.cdc.gov/mmwr/epix/epix.html): Provides a secure, Web-based communications network for information exchange among CDC, state and local health departments, and other public health professionals.

FDA, Center for Biologics Evaluation and Research (www.fda.gov/cber/flu/ flu.htm): Discussion of influenza vaccines and related information.

FDA, Center for Drug Evaluation and Research (www.fda.gov/cder/drug/ antivirals/influenza): Discussion of influenza antiviral drugs and related information.

HRSA Bioterrorism and Emergency Preparedness Grants and Cooperative Agreements (www.hrsa.gov/bioterrorism): Provide information about HRSA programs for bioterrorism and emergency preparedness activities available for state and local jurisdictions.

The Public Health Preparedness and Response Capacity Inventory (www. dhs.ca.gov/epo/PDF/NPSsmpxv1.pdf): Provides a resource for state and local health departments undertaking comprehensive assessments of their preparedness to respond to bioterrorism, outbreaks of infectious disease, or other public health threats and emergencies.

Strategic National Stockpile (www.bt.cdc.gov/stockpile): Provides information on the availability and rapid deployment of life-saving pharmaceuticals, antidotes, other medical supplies, and equipment necessary to counter the effects of nerve agents, biological pathogens, and chemical agents.

U.S. Agency for International Development (USAID, www.usaid.gov): A leader in the control and prevention of infectious diseases.

REFERENCES

AHRQ. April 2005. Altered standards of care in mass casualty events. Prepared by Health Systems Research Inc. under Contract No. 290-04-0010. AHRQ Publication No. 05-0043. Rockville, MD: Agency for Healthcare Research and Quality.

Blendon RJ, DesRoches CM, Cetron MS, Benson JM, Mekihardt T, Pollard W. 2006. Attitudes toward the use of quarantine in a public health emergency in four countries. *Health Affairs Web Exclusive* 25, W15–W25.

CDC (Centers for Disease Control and Prevention). Avian influenza: CDC response. Available at http://www.cdc.gov/flu/avian/outbreaks/cdcresponse.htm.

Crosby AW. 1989. *America's Forgotten Pandemic: The Influenza of 1918*. Cambridge, UK: Cambridge University Press.

DHS (U.S. Department of Homeland Security). National preparedness guidelines. September 2007. Available at https://www.llis.dhs.gov.

GAO (Government Accountability Office). 2007. Influenza pandemic: Further efforts are needed to ensure clearer federal leadership roles and an effective national strategy. GAO-07-781. Washington, D.C.: August 14, 2007. Available at http://www.gao.gov/new.items/d07881.pdf.

GOARN (Global Outbreak Alert and Response Network, World Health Organization). 2000. Available at http://www.who.int/csr/outbreaknetwork/en/.

Hampton T. 2007. Pandemic flu planning falls short: Many vulnerabilities in healthcare system. *JAMA* 297:1177–1178.

HHS (U.S. Department of Health and Human Services). November 2005. HHS Pandemic Influenza Plan. Available at http://www.hhs.gov/pandemicflu/plan/.

HHS (Department of Health and Human Services). U.S. government pandemic and avian flu information. Managed by the Department of Health and Human Services. Available at http://www.pandemicflu.gov/.

HSA (Homeland Security Act). 2002. Available at http://www.oe.energy.gov/Documentsand-Media/Homeland_Security_Act_of_2002.pdf.

HSC (Homeland Security Council). November 2005. National strategy for pandemic influenza. Washington, D.C. Available at http://www.whitehouse.gov/homeland/pandemic-influenza.html.

HSC (Homeland Security Council). May 2006. National strategy for pandemic influenza implementation plan. Washington, D.C. Available at http://www.whitehouse.gov/homeland/nspi_implementation.pdf.

HSC (Homeland Security Council). July 2007. National strategy for pandemic influenza: Implementation plan one-year summary. Washington, D.C. Available at http://www.whitehouse.gov/homeland/pandemic-influenza-oneyear.html

IMF (International Monetary Fund). 2006. The global economic and financial impact of an avian flu pandemic and the role of the IMF. Available at http://www.imf.org/external/pubs/ft/afp/2006/eng/022806.pdf.

International Health Regulations (IHR). 2005. World Health Organization. Fifty-eighth World Health Assembly. WHA 58.3. Revision of the International Health Regulations. Available at http://www.who.int/CSR/ihr/en.

IPAPI (International Partnership on Avian and Pandemic Influenza). 2005. Available at http://www.hhs.gov/pandemicflu/plan/pdf/AppH.pdf.

North American Plan for Avian and Pandemic Influenza. August 2007. Developed as part of the Security and Prosperity Partnership of North America. Available at http://www.spp.gov/pdf/nap_flu07.pdf.

White House. 2003. Homeland Security Presidential Directive 5: Management of Domestic Incidents. Washington, D.C. Available at http://www.oe.netl.doe.gov/docs/prepare/hspd5.pdf.

White House. 2007. Homeland Security Presidential Directive 21: Public Health and Medical Preparedness. Washington, D.C. Available at http://www.whitehouse.gov/news/releases/2007/10/20071018-10.html.

Whitley RJ, Barlett J, Hayden FG, Pavia AT, Tapper M, Monto AS. 2006. Seasonal and pandemic influenza: Recommendations for preparedness in the United States. *J Infect Dis* 194(Suppl 2):S155–S161.

WHO (World Health Organization). Avian Influenza. Available at http://www.who.int/csr/disease/avian_influenza/en/.

WHO (World Health Organization). Global Pandemic Influenza Action Plan to Increase Vaccine Supply. Available at www.who.int/csr/disease/influenza/pandemic/en.

WHO (World Health Organization). Strategic Action Plan for Pandemic Influenza 2006–2007. Available at www.who.int/csr/disease/influenza/pandemic/en.

7 Defining the Response at the Local Level

Jeffrey R. Ryan, PhD and Jan F. Glarum, EMT-P

> *Life is a race between education and catastrophe.*
>
> **George Orwell**

CONTENTS

7.1   INTRODUCTION

There are four basic phases to comprehensive emergency management: mitigation, preparedness, response, and recovery. Since the World Health Organization (WHO) stepped up attention to the potential of a pandemic due to highly pathogenic H5N1 bird flu and President George Bush released the National Strategy for Pandemic Influenza in 2005, there has been a great deal of activity. At the global level, international public health officials have been focusing their attention on surveillance efforts and the development of infrastructure that should mitigate the threat of pandemic influenza, regardless of where the threat originates. Surely, all eyes are on H5N1 and many believe we are now able to witness the genesis of the next pandemic. At the national level, government officials and public health planners are busy assembling and testing their plans. Plans are a key component of preparedness. Many of the pandemic planners that we encounter express the difficulty in pulling together a functional plan. Some are not even certain what the plan should entail and what "tools in the toolbox" are appropriate for the containment of pandemic influenza. They are often unable to state an overall goal or objective clearly and concisely.

Our response to most of this discussion is, how can you effectively plan and prepare for a pandemic when you haven't defined your response? Furthermore, local plans have to follow the lead of their regions or counties; regional or county plans should be in line with what their respective states have assembled; and state pandemic planners should be following the guidelines of the federal government. Since the President first published his strategy for pandemic influenza, a tremendous amount of money was appropriated for pandemic preparedness and the resultant effort has been impressive. After two solid years we can honestly say that we are better prepared for a pandemic than we were five years ago; however, we must admit that we have a ways to go. After all, how can you be totally prepared for an event that has unlimited potential when you have limited resources?

Pandemic influenza is not just a medical problem. It is a community problem that could undermine an economy (Meltzer, Cox, Fukuda, 1999). Pandemic planning and response requires all public and private sectors to work together. Accordingly, the aim of this chapter is to get the reader to focus on all aspects of community response to pandemic influenza. In essence, we will attempt to outline a goal and define the response. We will do so by stressing the importance of specific emergency services support functions and what role these key players have in dealing with case patients, exposed people, and containing a contagion. We will discuss programs and public health procedures that are necessary to manage an outbreak effectively.

7.2 PRE-INCIDENT PLANNING

For the sake of this chapter, let's say that a pandemic is an incident. Indeed, it's far more than an incident. It goes well beyond emergency, disaster, and well into the realm of catastrophic event. A pandemic is considered to be Mother Nature's WMD (Grigg, Rosen, Koop, 2006). However, if everyone is going to be affected by the same catastrophic event, then each community and agency engaged in planning is expecting to face the incident with what few resources they can currently muster. If history repeats itself, the next pandemic could be as severe as the 1918 Spanish flu, making the enormity of preparedness tasks insurmountable. Given that assurance, many planners would relent by throwing their hands in the air and be willing to admit defeat from the start. However, like the lion faced with the dilemma of having to "eat the elephant," he must do so one bite at a time.

Pre-incident planning is an essential part of emergency preparedness. The fundamental logic that underlies development of emergency plans is that these and related decisions must be addressed before an incident occurs. The development of response plans and a community emergency operations plan (EOP) is required by numerous state and federal laws, including the Stafford Act, the National Response Plan, and Presidential Decision Directive 39. State and local government EOPs must identify available personnel, equipment, facilities, and resources in the jurisdiction, and list the actions to be taken by individuals and government services in the event disaster.

As part of the pre-incident planning process, community and agency officials need to conduct hazard and vulnerability assessments. By combining the information from a hazard assessment with the product from a vulnerability assessment, an overall risk assessment can be determined. This assessment then becomes the basis to establish priorities, which should then improve response capabilities. Once the risk analysis is complete, a community must evaluate its capabilities to meet projected needs.

Two types of resources must be inventoried: equipment and personnel. All equipment used to prevent or respond to an emergency should be noted. A survey should be made of existing communications equipment, medical equipment, supplies, respirators, and personal protective equipment. Training issues should be listed as well. If the survey is done based on inventory logs, a physical inspection must be done to verify the equipment and establish ground truth. When performing this review, it is important to note the lack of required items, which then indicates a shortfall. Once a complete review of capabilities is accomplished, the community will have a better idea of what they have and what they lack. They can then make recommendations to public officials regarding the acquisition of necessary items required to meet their demonstrated shortfall in meeting the challenges posed by a pandemic.

7.2.1 HAZARD ASSESSMENT

The WHO has been monitoring events unfolding in parts of Asia for several years and has sounded a general warning that a pandemic may be imminent. The key to monitoring these events is surveillance. At this point, surveillance systems for influenza virus characterization are quite sophisticated, but they do not extend into every corner of the world. Furthermore, definitive diagnostic tests are costly, technically difficult to perform, and must be conducted in specially equipped facilities. Complete surveillance is impaired by the fact that most cases have occurred in rural areas. Case detection is complicated by the frequent high prevalence in affected countries of other severe respiratory diseases having similar symptoms (WHO, 2005a).

Many activities defined in global and national pandemic response plans are initiated by changes in the behavior of the virus. Detection of these changes and interpretation of their significance depends on timely and reliable epidemiological, clinical, and virological data. Every single human case yields evidence essential for risk assessment. The investigation of clusters of cases, closely related in time and place, provides the first alert to improved transmissibility of the virus. Serological surveys in close contacts of patients, communities where clusters of cases have occurred, and high-risk populations such as poultry or health care workers also provide early alerts to changes in the behavior of the virus. Information on the clinical course of cases is an equally vital signal, as milder disease with lower fatality is anticipated to coincide with improved infection transmissibility (WHO, 2005a).

Since late 2003, the world has moved closer to a pandemic than at any time since 1968, when the last of the previous century's three pandemics occurred. All prerequisites for the start of a pandemic have now been met except the establishment of efficient human-to-human transmission. During 2005, ominous changes in the epidemiology of the disease in animals were observed. Human cases are continuing to occur, and the virus has expanded its geographical range to include countries previously unaffected, thus increasing the size of the population at risk. Each new human case gives the virus an opportunity to evolve toward a fully transmissible pandemic strain (WHO, 2005a).

Currently, it is not feasible for individual communities to establish their own capacity to conduct surveillance at the level previously described. Instead, community public health officials have to rely on the infrastructure already in place and stay in touch with recent developments and findings. Frankly speaking, definitive, strain-specific influenza virus testing is not cost effective enough for hazard assessment to be accomplished locally or in a point-of-care setting. However, current research efforts in the United States are aimed at developing such a capability. Imagine how the advent of a Food and Drug Administration (FDA)-approved, accurate, and inexpensive point-of-care test could change the picture of hazard assessment in a short period of time.

7.2.2 VULNERABILITY

Evidence shows that the H5N1 virus is now endemic in parts of Africa, Asia, and Eastern Europe. So long as we have a close association between sick birds and their human captors, the risk of further human cases will persist, as will opportunities for a pandemic virus to emerge. Outbreaks have recurred despite aggressive control measures, including the culling of hundreds of millions of poultry. Wild migratory birds — historically the host reservoir of all influenza A viruses — continue to die from highly pathogenic H5N1. Domestic ducks can excrete large quantities of highly pathogenic virus without showing signs of illness. Their quiet role in maintaining transmission further complicates control in poultry and makes human avoidance of risky behaviors more difficult (WHO, 2005b).

Given the constantly changing nature of influenza viruses, the timing and severity of the next pandemic cannot be predicted. Reassortment could result in a fully transmissible pandemic virus, announced by a sudden surge of cases with rapid spread from one continent to another in a few days. Adaptive mutation, expressed initially as small clusters of human cases with evidence of limited transmission, will probably give the world some time to take defensive action. It is unknown whether such a "grace period" accompanying adaptive mutation will be granted.

At that point, what community in a developed or developing nation will be vulnerable from the threat of pandemic influenza? The answer is that all communities will be vulnerable. No community will be immune. However, we can reasonably assume that the degree of "connectedness" that a community has with the outside world coupled with its internal mobility will affect the introduction of the threat as well as the spread of the contagion. Nearly every community in the world was affected by the 1918 Spanish flu (Barry, 2004). Those that limited their connectedness prior to introduction of the pathogen into their communities ultimately failed; yet, those that limited contact between community members after introduction fared far better than those that did nothing (Glass, 2006).

7.2.3 CAPABILITIES AND SHORTFALLS

If the WHO fails at efforts to contain isolated outbreaks wherever they occur in the world, global travel would eventually aid in bringing the threat to all four corners of the world. National containment measures would also be difficult to achieve. Hence, the pandemic threat is likely to spread quickly, affecting multiple communities simultaneously, or one after the other in quick succession. Response assets at all levels of government and the private sector would be burdened immediately. Communities will be required to expend all their pandemic response capabilities toward their own needs, and have little to share with others similarly stressed.

As the number of affected communities grows, response assets of the state and federal governments will be stretched to the point of breaking, offering little beyond the initial points of entry where index cases are found. Thousands of communities are likely to be left dealing with the pandemic's wrath with little or no assistance from neighboring communities or higher levels of government. Preparedness planning for pandemic influenza must consider this scenario, move beyond the paper-plan syndrome, and develop a real capacity to take action.

A pandemic is a slow-motion disaster. As such, it will last much longer than most public health emergencies. In addition, past pandemics have occurred in waves, with bouts of morbidity and mortality separated by months. In 20th century pandemics, a second wave of influenza activity occurred three to twelve months after the first wave (Patterson, 1987). In 1957, the second wave began three months after the peak of the first wave and, in 1968, the second wave began twelve months after the peak of the first wave (MMIG: CDC, 2007). The first wave of the 1918 Spanish flu occurred in the spring of that year (Crosby, 2003). That flu was very severe by usual standards, but the second wave beginning six months later was dramatically worse than the first. During the 1918 pandemic, the deadly second wave was responsible for more than 90 percent of the deaths for the entire pandemic. The third wave occurred more than a year later, during the following 1919–1920 winter/spring, and was the mildest of all. So, will the next pandemic manifest with the same wave phenomena or will the first wave be the only wave and the one that takes out your resources? We have no way of knowing. In fact, we really don't know for sure why we experience influenza pandemics in three distinct waves, and if the ones experienced prior to 1889 manifested in the same way. We can only speculate that the first wave enables the emerging virus to adapt more to the human host. Following that round of infection and adaptation, the virus comes back more transmissible between humans and nearly as deadly. That could explain why the second wave is more deadly than the first.

Once a potential pandemic strain of influenza virus is identified, time is needed to perfect a vaccine construct. This is especially true given current technology used to produce influenza vaccines. In fact, public health officials estimate a minimum of six to eight months necessary to produce on a large scale a safe and efficacious vaccine based on a new influenza strain (Fauci, 2006). After inoculation, it takes about two weeks for adults and up to six weeks for children to achieve optimal protection under a one-dose regimen. An additional four weeks is needed if a booster shot is required with a new vaccine construct. [Production of a vaccine after isolation of the circulating strain, and given the capacity of all the current international vaccine manufacturers, means supplies during the following six months would be limited to fewer than a billion doses.] Hopefully, the vaccine will be available for the onset of the second wave. However, the most prudent assumption to make here is that the ideal vaccine will not be available for the second wave of the next pandemic.

7.2.4 THE PANDEMIC SEVERITY INDEX

One of the questions we all would like the answer to is, how bad will the next pandemic be? Even if we had possession of the strain that will cause the next pandemic, no one really could predict this accurately. However, looking back at history we can see that the three pandemics of the 20th century were all different in terms of their severity. We can base our estimates of the severity of the next pandemic on attack rates and case fatality rates. More importantly, we should also be able to predict some of our disease containment measures on the severity of the pandemic. It stands to reason that if the severity of a pandemic is scalable, so might be the measures needed to mitigate it. Accordingly, the Centers for Disease Control and Prevention released its Mitigation Measures Interim Guidance (MMIG; CDC, 2007). This comprehensive document was probably the best thing to come out of the Department of Health and Human Services (HHS) on pandemic planning in the last five years.

Within the MMIG, the CDC detailed a Pandemic Severity Index, which uses case fatality ratio as the critical driver for categorizing the severity of a pandemic (see Figure 7.1). The index is designed to enable estimation of the severity of a pandemic on a population level to allow better forecasting of the impact of a pandemic and to enable recommendations to be made on the use of mitigation interventions that are matched to the severity of future influenza pandemics (see Table 7.1).

According to the MMIG, future pandemics will be assigned to one of five discrete categories of increasing severity (Category 1 to Category 5). The Pandemic

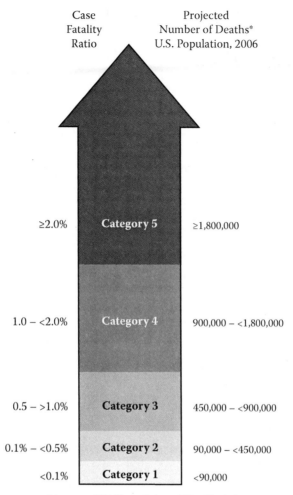

Case
Fatality
Ratio

Projected
Number of Deaths*
U.S. Population, 2006

≥2.0%   **Category 5**   ≥1,800,000

1.0 – <2.0%   Category 4   900,000 – <1,800,000

0.5 – >1.0%   **Category 3**   450,000 – <900,000

0.1% – <0.5%   **Category 2**   90,000 – <450,000

<0.1%   **Category 1**   <90,000

*Assumes 30% Illness Rate and Unmitigated
Pandemic without Interventions

FIGURE 7.1 Pandemic Severity Index. (Courtesy of the Department of Health and Human Services, Centers for Disease Control and Prevention. February 2007. Mitigation Measures Interim Guidance (MMIG). Interim Pre-Pandemic Planning Guidance: Community Strategy for Pandemic Influenza Mitigation Measures in the United States — Early Targeted Layered Use of Non-Pharmaceutical Interventions. http://www.pandemicflu.gov/plan/community/mitigation.html.)

Severity Index provides communities a tool for scenario-based contingency planning to guide local pre-pandemic preparedness efforts. Accordingly, communities facing the imminent arrival of pandemic disease will be able to use the pandemic severity assessment to define which pandemic mitigation interventions are indicated for implementation. The ability to moderate mitigation measures according to the potential severity of the event affords community officials with the opportunity to

TABLE 7.1
The Five Components of the PSI Developed by the CDC

	Pandemic Severity Index				
Characteristics	**Category 1**	**Category 2**	**Category 3**	**Category 4**	**Category 5**
Case fatality ratio (%)	<0.1	0.1 – <0.5	0.5 – <1.0	1.0 – <2.0	≥2.0
Excess death rate (per 100K)	<30	30 – 150	150 – <300	300 – <600	≥600
Illness rate (% population)	20 – 40	20 – 40	20 – 40	20 – 40	20 – 40
Potential number of deaths (based on 2006 U.S. population)	<90,000	90,000 – <450,000	450,000 – <900,000	900,000 – <1.8 million	≥1.8 million
20th century U.S. experience	Seasonal influenza (illness rate 5 – 20%)	1957, 1968 pandemics	None	None	1918 pandemic

Note: The five resultant categories allow pandemic planners to gauge their response on the severity of the event. Category 1, which is the mildest on the scale, represents something reminiscent of a seasonal epidemic outbreak. The 1957 and 1968 pandemics fall into Category 2. The 1918 Spanish flu represents a Category 5 event, which is the most severe. This index has been compared to the categorization of hurricanes, based on wind speed.

minimize social and economic impacts of an intervention scheme. Those measures will be reviewed in detail later in the chapter.

7.2.5 THE OVERALL GOAL

Before we define the overall goal of pandemic planning, let's establish three secondary goals in mitigating a communitywide epidemic. First, we should seek to delay the exponential growth in incident cases and shift the epidemic curve to the right in order to "buy time" for production and distribution of a well-matched pandemic strain vaccine. Second, we would like to decrease the epidemic peak. Third, we should attempt to reduce the total number of incident cases, thus reducing community morbidity and mortality. Ultimately, reducing the number of persons infected is a primary goal of pandemic planning. Disease containment measures, mostly of a nonpharmaceutical nature, should help to reduce influenza transmission by reducing contact.

Many pandemic experts suggest that we have two things on our side: time and distance (Grigg, Rosen, Koop, 2006). If we can establish distance between people in our communities, we can diminish contact between infected and uninfected persons, helping us minimize direct contact spread. Community leaders and public health officials should therefore set their sights on limiting the attack rate of influenza in their community. In addition, if they can lengthen the amount of time over which the pandemic

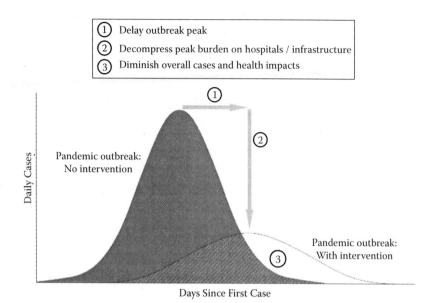

1. Delay outbreak peak
2. Decompress peak burden on hospitals / infrastructure
3. Diminish overall cases and health impacts

FIGURE 7.2 The goal of community pandemic planners is to flatten the pandemic curve. Our mitigation measures should assist us in (1) delaying the outbreak peak, (2) diminishing the peak burden on health care systems, and (3) reducing the number of cases. Delaying a rapid upswing of cases and lowering the epidemic peak to the maximum extent possible would allow a better match between the number of ill persons requiring hospitalization and the nation's capacity to provide medical care for such people. (CDC, 2007.)

wave is experienced in their community, key players and the medical systems in the communities will have more time to deal with the ill, the dead, and the issues that come from them. The MMIG (CDC, 2007) expresses this graphically (see Figure 7.2).

Experience has shown that communities faced with epidemics or other adverse events respond best and with the least anxiety when the normal social functioning of the community is minimally disrupted. Strong political and public health leadership to provide reassurance and to ensure that needed medical care services are provided are critical elements. If either is seen to be less than optimal, a manageable epidemic could move toward catastrophe (Inglesby et al., 2006).

From this initial assessment, one could surmise that the overall goal of a comprehensive pandemic annex we are preparing for our all-hazards plan should be along these lines: employ prudent and timely disease containment measures to limit the rapid spread of illness due to pandemic influenza, preserve the economy, and return the community to normalcy with short- and long-term recovery activities.

7.3 ESTABLISHING TRIGGER POINTS

As mentioned earlier, pandemics are slow-motion disasters. In one of the best papers written on the pandemic threat, Grigg, Rosen, and Koop (2006) put it to us in this way: a pandemic is a story that grows more complex with every new infection. They go on to say that the next pandemic will begin quietly with a single person anywhere in the world. We can only hope that global and national surveillance systems for influenza will serve us well. Regardless of where you are, the pandemic threat will encroach on your community. As to how quickly it will spread from one continent or country to another is a matter of great speculation. Some have suggested that with recognition of the initial cluster, the right resources, and setting, pandemic influenza may be contained at the source (Longini et al., 2005). Regardless of this optimistic assessment, one must prudently prepare for the worst possible outcome.

Being that we view the next pandemic as a slowly encroaching threat on the United States and its citizenry, we should establish actions that are incrementally gauged to where that threat is in relation to our community at any given point in time. For this, we need to establish a set of trigger points that we can invoke as the pandemic takes hold. Each trigger point needs to have a set of well-defined checklists with clear-cut responsibilities. This will help us coordinate key activities throughout all business units and ensure well-managed execution of our emergency plans (DHS, 2007).

Each organization should work diligently with their state, tribal, territorial, and local public health and medical networks, to include veterinary networks, to monitor and evaluate any increase of suspected influenza cases or effects on the local animal population, just as they would for evaluating other emerging infectious diseases within their jurisdiction. Through a coordinated effort, a community will be able to establish its own "trigger-points" to help guide implementation of the plan. (DHS (Department of Homeland Security), April 2007. Pandemic Influenza Best Practices and Model Protocols.)

At the time of this writing, we are in Phase 3 of the WHO's Pandemic Alert Scale. The most likely declared trigger point for a pandemic will become apparent as sustained human-to-human disease transmission emerges. This will prompt the WHO to declare Phase 4. From this point forward, adaptation of the virus and geographic location of the outbreak will constitute specific trigger points in many plans. In addition, other factors may be useful in constituting agency- or entity-specific trigger points. One example that comes to mind here is how some health care systems may wish to factor percentage of surge capacity and workforce reduction into their formularies for appropriate response actions. Refer to Table 7.2 for some examples of commonly used trigger points.

As specified in the MMIG (CDC, 2007), there are several other important considerations. First of all, the decision to use specific tools during a pandemic should be based on the observed severity of the event and its impact on specific subpopulations. In addition, one must estimate the expected benefit of the interventions, the feasibility of their success in a modern setting, the direct and indirect costs associated with such measures and the consequences for critical infrastructure, health care systems, and society should they be implemented (Meltzer, Cox, Fukuda, 1999).

Draconian measures and controversial interventions (e.g., prolonged school closures, imposing travel restrictions, and cancelling public events) won't be needed

TABLE 7.2
Possible Trigger Points and Appropriate Actions for a Health Care Facility or System

Event	Appropriate Actions
Declaration of Phase 4 by the WHO	Implement pandemic communication plan
	Monitor syndromic surveillance system
	Coordination of efforts with governmental and nongovernmental agencies
	Implement employee rapid fit testing
	Initiate employee PPE training
	Implement critical incident stress management support
	Implement financial management plan
First case identified in United States	Activate incident command structure
	Implement pandemic communications plan
	Activate emergency alert system
	Establish influenza hotline
	Implement patient tracking system
	Issue PPE to first receivers
First case identified within 300 miles	Implement infection control plan
	Implement security plan
	Implement employee screening process
First flu patient in county hospital	Begin vacating patient surge areas
	Implement patient management guidelines
	Activate CERT teams
	Implement plan to reduce/cancel elective surgeries
Negative airflow rooms full	Implement patient triage plan
	Implement central staffing plan
	Utilize volunteers
25% Surge capacity	Implement alternative staffing plan
10% Workforce reduction	Implement Phase 1 family/staff support plan
	Implement fatality management plan
50% Surge capacity	Reduce/cancel outpatient routine medical care
20% Workforce reduction	Implement Phase 2 family/staff support plan
	Establish palliative care
75% Surge capacity	Community establishment of alternative care site
30% Workforce reduction	
100% capacity	Activate altered standards of care protocols
40% Workforce reduction	

Note: Preparedness activities and plans should be incrementally phased so that all resources and possibly disruptive actions do not ensue at the onset of the WHO's Phase 4. (Excerpted in part from the North Dakota Department of Health Hospital Template, developed by MeritCare Health System through a grant from the North Dakota Healthcare Association.)

in less severe pandemics (Ferguson et al., 2006). However, these measures, implemented at the appropriate moment, may save lives during severe pandemics. The timing of initiation and termination of various intervention measures will influence their overall effectiveness. Because of this, great thought and careful planning should go into the crafting of clearly defined trigger points and appropriate actions.

Implementing these measures prior to the pandemic may result in economic and social hardship without public health benefit and, over time, may result in "intervention fatigue" and erosion of public confidence and adherence. Conversely, implementing these interventions after extensive spread of pandemic influenza illness in a community may limit the public health benefits of employing these measures. Identifying the optimal time for initiation of these interventions will be challenging because implementation needs to be early enough to preclude the initial steep upslope in case numbers and long enough to cover the peak of the anticipated epidemic curve while avoiding intervention fatigue (CDC, 2007).

7.4 PANDEMIC PREPAREDNESS AND PUBLIC HEALTH

Community leaders, policy makers, and the general public will be looking to public health officials as controlling health authorities. In that regard, public health agency officials need to assert significant leadership to mobilize, enable, and sustain private and public health care resources during a pandemic. One of the underlying principles of the Public Health Incident Command System (PHICS) is that public health commands or directs the medical resources of a community during a public health emergency (Qureshi, Gebbie, Gebbie, 2005.), a role seldom if ever practiced in modern times. Pre-event familiarity with pandemic response policies and protocols; federal, state, and local roles during a pandemic; issues of surge capacity; and pandemic risk communications will better prepare state health officials and their jurisdictions to respond to an influenza pandemic.

Rather than waiting for more-accurate pandemic predictions, the public health community can emphasize pandemic anticipations to spur preparedness activities. Pre-event consideration of agency roles, policy issues, workforce shortages, surge capacity, and risk communications will improve social cohesion and temper the impact of a pandemic (ASTHO, 2002). In a national meeting of federal and state public health officials in February 2007, a great point was made by Dr. Anthony Fauci, Director of the National Institutes of Health: strengthening annual seasonal influenza prevention is the single best way to prepare for a pandemic. He went on to say that it is "the most important thing we can do to prepare for this enormous coming health event." (See Figure 7.3.)

Prepare for the worst. If not, you can expect the worst!

We believe that the only way to ensure proper employee performance for the "big one" is to have them practice their most challenging roles and activities regularly. Doing so in this instance reinforces the value of our seasonal influenza campaigns to allow us to practice for the "big one."

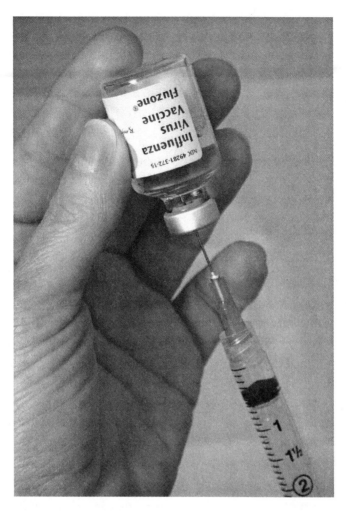

FIGURE 7.3 CDC Clinic Chief Nurse Lee Ann Jean-Louis extracting influenza virus vaccine, Fluzone®, from a vial. (Photo taken by James Gathany; image courtesy of the Public Health Image Library, Department of Health and Human Services, Centers for Disease Control and Prevention (PHIL Image No. 5404).)

Many experts believe that there will be one to six months between the identification of a novel influenza virus and the time that widespread outbreaks begin to occur in the United States. Outbreaks are expected to occur simultaneously throughout much of the country, preventing relocation of human and material resources. Because populations will be fully susceptible to a novel influenza type A virus, rates of illness could peak fairly rapidly within a given community. The effect of influenza on individual communities will be relatively prolonged — six to eight weeks, though possibly up to three months. So, what can be done with this much time, assuming one has it?

The focus of the next section is to discuss the practical measures public health officials can implement prior to and during the pandemic event. Initially, we will explore classic containment measures and examine their practicality, their scientific validity, and relevancy to quelling a pandemic due to influenza.

The United States Responds to a Human H5N1 Cluster

In May 2006, a cluster of human cases in Indonesia raised alarms that H5N1 may have been transmitted between humans. Through prior preparedness planning and through coordination centered in the State Department with the U.S. Naval Medical Research Unit (NAMRU-2), the CDC, and the U.S. Agency for International Development, U.S. scientists, as part of a WHO team, were able to provide emergency support to the Indonesian government. The international team investigated the outbreak, quickly analyzed samples through NAMRU-2 in Jakarta, and performed additional analyses and H5N1 confirmation through the CDC in Atlanta. This coordinated international response allowed the WHO to provide updates quickly and reduce alarm as the cases were confirmed to be isolated incidents of inefficient human-to-human transmission and that the virus was not widely circulating among humans.

The outbreak of avian influenza was not the start of a human pandemic, but the coordinated international response was an opportunity to practice what we intend to do if a pandemic arises. Could it be that actions such as these may well prevent a pandemic, or at least mitigate one?

7.4.1   Containing the Contagion

Controlling the spread of a communicable disease in a community requires a multifaceted approach that includes traditional epidemiology, education of medical providers, cooperation of the public, and provision of treatment and prophylaxis, if available. Specific conditions may dictate the need for more-extensive control measures designed to limit contact among people who are (or may become) contagious and others who are susceptible to infection. Isolation and quarantine are two such measures. The legal authority to impose isolation and quarantine exists in most local health jurisdictions, but the successful implementation of either measure on a broad scale within a community requires careful planning (NACCHO, 2006). However, before you go running off to establish a plan for the emplacement of quarantine barriers, consider that this represents one of the most extreme measures that public health can implement, and that it may not do more than expend precious resources, perturb the situation, and erode public confidence and economic vitality.

7.4.2   Surveillance and the Identification of the Index Case

Disease surveillance capacities of many state and local public health systems depend, in part, on the surveillance capabilities of hospitals and local primary care providers. Whether a disease outbreak occurs naturally or due to the intentional release of a harmful biological agent, much of the initial response will occur at the local level, particularly at hospitals and their emergency departments. Therefore, hospital personnel will be some of the first health care workers with the opportunity to identify an infectious disease outbreak or a bioterrorist event. The same circumstances that place these medical professionals in an optimal position to recognize the onset of an outbreak also places them at greatest risk from the disease event itself.

There is a critical need for an accurate and inexpensive rapid point-of-care assay specific for whatever highly pathogenic strain is making its way between animals and humans. Currently, everyone knows that this is highly pathogenic H5N1. What we have now in the way of a rapid test is not sensitive or specific enough to give us point-of-care capabilities. They are essentially useless for identifying the introduction of an H5N1-infected traveler. What we have to rely on is the Laboratory Response Network and the WHO reference laboratories. To make surveillance work we must educate primary care physicians to know the criteria and case definition for a possible human avian flu case and to rapidly report and send specimens for appropriate lab testing. Rapid recognition of the first importation is vital. A useful acronym from Hong Kong is TOCC, which stands for travel history, occupational risk, case contact, part of a cluster. In other words, did the symptomatic individual recently travel to an H5N1 endemic area? Did he or she have some sort of occupational exposure to H5N1 infected birds? Did he or she have contact with a known H5N1-infected case patient? Is he or she part of a known cluster of cases?

Assuming that we can pinpoint index patients nationally, regionally, or locally, we could identify contacts. Certainly, we would all admit that this important fact, when established, becomes a trigger point for a cascade of activities within each jurisdiction.

Once potential contacts have been identified, there are escalating methods of dealing with limiting the spread of infection from those individuals. Passive monitoring is a process where contacts are asked to perform self-assessment at least twice daily and to inform authorities immediately if respiratory symptoms or fever occurs. This may be useful in situations where the risk of exposure and subsequent development of disease is low, and the risk to others if recognition of disease is delayed is also low, perhaps with a pandemic classified as 2 or lower on the Pandemic Severity Index (PSI). The benefits are that it requires minimal resources and places few constraints on individual freedoms. It does rely on self-reporting, and affected people may not perform an adequate self-assessment. To help assure fulfillment of these responsibilities, the community may want to provide necessary supplies (e.g., thermometer, symptom log, and written instructions) and to staff a hotline to notify authorities about symptoms or needs.

If warranted, the next step in escalation of this process, with a predicted severity of 2 to 3 on the PSI, might include active monitoring by a health care worker designee, such as local EMS providers, without activity restrictions. The contact is evaluated on a regular (at least daily) basis by phone and/or in person for signs and symptoms suggestive of disease. This monitoring may be called for in situations in which the risk of exposure to and subsequent development of disease is moderate to high, resources permit close observation of individuals, and the risk of delayed recognition of symptoms is low to moderate. The benefit is once again few constraints on individual liberties, but it does require trained staffing and a system to track information and to verify monitoring and appropriate actions based on findings.

7.4.3 Pharmaceutical Intervention

Prophylaxis is defined as the medical care or measures provided to individuals to prevent or protect them from disease. This medical care or protective measure may be provided to entire populations or large sectors considered to be at risk. This medical care/prevention is referred to as mass prophylaxis. Traditionally, these measures include dispensing medications or implementing vaccination. Effective public health response to a pandemic hinges on the ability to deliver an appropriate medical countermeasure, recognize the outbreak, mobilize supplies of needed materials to affected populations in a timely manner, and provide ongoing medical care for affected individuals. The dispensing of antibiotics and/or vaccines is a cornerstone of any mass prophylaxis campaign against outbreaks of preventable disease.

However, it is highly unlikely that the most effective tool for mitigating a pandemic (i.e., a well-matched pandemic strain vaccine) will be available when a pandemic begins. This means that we must be prepared to face the first wave of the next pandemic without vaccine and potentially without sufficient quantities of influenza antiviral medications. In addition, it is not known if influenza antiviral medications will be effective against a future pandemic strain. During a pandemic, decisions about how to protect the public before an effective vaccine is available need to be based on scientific data, ethical considerations, consideration of the public's perspective of the protective measures and their impact on society, and common sense. Evidence to determine the best strategies for protecting people during a pandemic is very limited (CDC, 2007).

Public health officials planning mass prophylaxis campaigns should refer to two essential documents. The first is a guidebook published by a group of public health professionals under the direction of Dr. Nathaniel Hupert from Cornell University's Weill Medical College. The guidebook is entitled *Community-Based Mass Prophylaxis: A Planning Guide for Public Health Preparedness*. In it, the authors describe the five components of a mass prophylaxis response to an epidemic. The publication, sponsored by the Department of Health and Human Services, complements the CDC's Strategic National Stockpile (SNS) guidebook and serves to assist public health and emergency management officials in better preparing their communities for mass prophylaxis campaigns. Although the document is strongly rooted in bioterrorism response, its concepts are broadly applicable to pandemic influenza response. One important attribute of this comprehensive guidebook is that the procedures incorporate the incident command system structure, which will be essential for all communities to embrace.

The second essential document is the *Clinic Planning Model Generator* (CPMG), developed by Dr. Jeffrey Herrmann of the Institute for Systems Research at the University of Maryland. The CPMG is essentially a free software program designed to enable public health officials to quickly create an accurate model that will provide immediate assistance with planning for a treatment campaign. The CPMG can be used either in the advance planning stages of a campaign or for support during an active effort. In general, this program is designed to assist in planning a clinic with improved efficiency and performance while enlightening the planners on what to expect in the event of an outbreak. The interactive software model allows clinic planners to enter known population information and set time constraints specific to their application. Immediate results show suggested staff levels and detailed clinic information regarding waiting times, queue lengths, and cycle time. Adjustments can easily be made to staffing levels and other inputs until the user is satisfied with the efficiency of the proposed clinic layout. In July 2006, the CDC required that agencies receiving federal funding use this software to design dispensing and vaccination clinics.

There are two basic approaches to mass prophylaxis — push and pull. The push approach consists of bringing medicine directly to individuals or homes in an affected community. The pull approach requires that individuals leave their homes or places of work in order to travel to specially designated centers where they can receive medications or vaccinations.

Each approach has strengths and weaknesses. The push approach may enable faster and more widespread coverage of an affected community, but it has little flexibility to handle medical evaluation for contraindications or dosage adjustment and may be infeasible for vaccination campaigns. The pull approach may increase efficient use of scarce health care providers and resources, enable medical evaluation of potential victims, and provide opportunities for centralized data collection. However, these advantages must be weighed against the delays and logistical challenges of setting up sufficient dispensing centers to handle high patient volumes. Finally, what message do we send to our citizens when we bring them together en masse while at the same time we recommend social distancing?

Elements of both push and pull strategies are likely to be used in pandemic influenza response. For example, in addressing the needs of homebound or institutionalized individuals in a community, a push approach may be preferred to avoid complex transportation requirements in the midst of a public health crisis. Alternatively, even if a push approach is used to provide the majority of community residents with antibiotic prophylaxis, a small number of dispensing centers may be established to handle specific subpopulations (e.g., first responders and their families, tourists, health care providers, etc.).

7.4.4 Vaccine Strain and Supply

There is currently an FDA-approved vaccine for an early isolate of the H5N1 strain (FDA, 2007a). By the end of 2007, the HHS procured 26 million doses of prepandemic H5N1 vaccines from Sanofi Pasteur (Parker, 2007). The stock of H5N1 vaccine is now part of the Strategic National Stockpile; HHS has a plan that addresses how the stockpile will be used and when the prioritization scheme will be implemented. Essentially, the vaccine stock will be put to use when the WHO declares Phase 4 of the Pandemic Alert Scale. At that time, Tier I and Tier II prioritizations will be employed. Initial pandemic vaccine stocks will be used to vaccinate designated priority groups (e.g., health care providers, EMS personnel, first responders, very old, very young, etc.). After vaccination of these priority groups, vaccination of all those who desire it will be phased in, depending on available supplies (HHS, 2006).

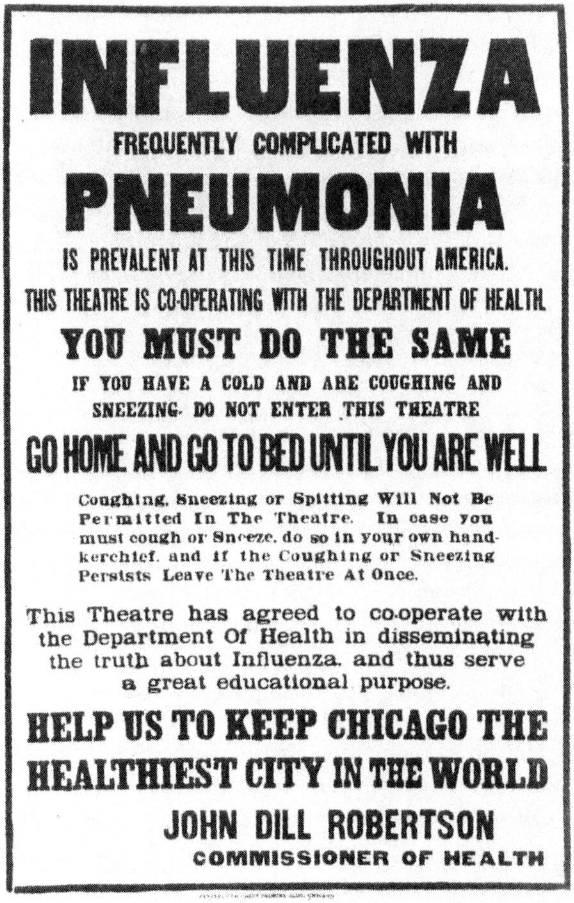

FIGURE 7.4 During the Spanish flu of 1918, local health departments warned those who were ill to stay away from theaters and other public places. (Image courtesy of the Office of the Public Health Service Historian, Department of Health and Human Services.)

Food for Thought

Ideally, we'd all like to have the perfect vaccine for the next pandemic on hand and be able to administer it several months before the first case arrives in the country. But, is that likely to be the case? No, it is very unlikely that we will be able to protect our citizenry with the perfect vaccine; most likely we will already be experiencing the second wave of the pandemic before we have a protective and safe vaccine. Alternatively, we could move to vaccinate all our citizens with a seasonal flu vaccine (Figure 7.4) when faced with a pandemic threat. There is not likely to be any cross-protection or direct benefit to individuals except to protect them from seasonal strains that will be circulating at the same time as a pandemic strain.

So, why do it? Well, seasonal influenza will present one more confounding element for public health officials and health care providers to deal with. Reducing it to near-extinction at the time of a pandemic will eliminate a lot of the confusion when someone with true flu-like illness presents at a medical treatment facility. This might also quell public fears and act as a good dress rehearsal for the next mass prophylaxis campaign. This is merely presented as food for thought, not doctrine.

The number of persons who may be protected by vaccination depends on the manufacturing capacity, the amount of antigen per dose needed for a protective immune response, and the number of doses required. Although annual influenza vaccine is immunogenic in older children and adults with a single 15-microgram (µg) dose, a higher antigen concentration (90 µg) and/or two doses may be needed for pandemic vaccine where persons have no previous exposure to the influenza subtype and lack any immunity. Recent clinical trials conducted with the FDA-approved H5N1 vaccine showed that healthy adults require two doses of 90 µg for evidence of protective immunity (FDA, 2007b).

In accordance with the president's National Strategy for Pandemic Influenza, every American will be vaccinated in the event of an influenza pandemic. That means the nation will vaccinate approximately 300 million people in a short period of time. Given that it may require two injections for each person, there would be a need for 600 million syringes and the same number of needles. To some, these do not seem like significant figures. However, each community must do its part to ensure adequate on-hand stocks of needles and syringes. These purchases should not be attempted while we are in the midst of a public health crisis.

7.4.5 Antiviral Drugs

As discussed in chapter 4, antiviral drugs (adamantanes and neuraminidase inhibitors) are useful in the treatment and prevention of influenza. In fact, Tamiflu® (oseltamivir) and Relenza® (zanamivir) have shown their effectiveness if given early in the course of the infection. Antiviral medications such as oseltamivir and zanamivir have been shown to reduce the severity and duration of seasonal influenza, typically reducing the duration of illness by one or two days (Cooper et al., 2003). Tamiflu is used to treat adults, adolescents, and pediatric (one-year-old and older) influenza patients whose flu symptoms started within the previous one or two days. Tamiflu is also used to reduce the chance of contracting the flu in people aged one-year-old and older who have a higher chance of getting the flu because of time spent with an infected person. The use of Tamiflu to reduce the chance of getting flu has been studied up to 42 days in adults and up to 10 days in children. Tamiflu may also reduce the chance of contracting the flu if there is an outbreak in the community (Longini et al., 2004).

The FDA approved Relenza for people seven-years-old and older for the treatment of uncomplicated influenza illness. This product is also approved to treat types A and B influenza, the two types most responsible for flu epidemics. Clinical studies showed that for the drug to be effective, patients needed to start treatment within two days of the onset of symptoms (Cooper et al., 2003). The drug seemed to be less effective in patients whose symptoms were not severe or did not include a fever. Relenza is approved for preventive use, to decrease the risk of developing influenza illness, for people five-years-old and older.

The HHS Pandemic Preparedness Implementation Plan (2006) called for the purchase of enough antivirals — oseltamivir and zanamivir — to treat 25 percent of the population. Efforts center on the federal purchase of 44 million courses of antiviral drugs for treatment, with another 6 million courses for containment. However, the federal plan contained a strategy to leverage state tax dollars to purchase the remaining 31 million courses of antiviral drugs with a 25-percent federal subsidy. Few state officials have embraced this part of the plan. There is considerable doubt that antiviral drugs will be effective and easily dispensed in any mass prophylaxis schemes (Inglesby et al., 2006). A highly debated concept known as "quenching" assumes that public health officials could establish two concentric rings around an index case of influenza once the pandemic threat arrives in their community. This follows "ring prophylaxis" strategies for smallpox containment, where we would vaccinate all primary and secondary contacts from the index case. Furthermore, we recognize that influenza strains can become resistant to antivirals, especially with selective pressure applied by mass dispensing schemes. Some have the opinion that, given the short incubation period of influenza and the nondescript nature of the clinical syndrome, it is highly doubtful we will recognize the index case of influenza in a timely manner. That would seem to undermine quenching. The employment of quenching and targeted prophylaxis schemes is one of the most contentious issues in pandemic planning. Our recommendation: use them if you've got them. Come to the fight with everything you've got at your disposal. What will really be the harm in surrounding the index case with layers of prevention? On the other hand, you could always sit and wait to see how it develops. The choice is yours — as a community!

7.5 NONPHARMACEUTICAL MEASURES

The most effective intervention for influenza is vaccination with a safe and effective vaccine. However, it is highly unlikely that a well-matched vaccine will be available when a pandemic begins unless a vaccine with broad cross-protection is developed (Fedson, 2005). So, if you can't rely on the vaccine and you can't afford enough antivirals to protect your population for the entire pandemic period, what can you do? What you can do pretty much takes us back to what some communities did manage during the height of the second wave of the 1918 Spanish flu.

Recall that one of our primary goals is to delay introduction of the pandemic strain into our communities and to slow transmission once cases begin to appear. Classical public health disease containment measures such as individual case investigations, contact tracing, and mandatory isolation or quarantine may be feasible and perhaps even effective for pandemic influenza. This may be practical for public health agencies to grapple with, but only when there are very few cases and when such measures are likely to have a substantial impact on slowing transmission (Bell, 2006). Determining when case-specific investigation and response measures are no longer useful and when attention should shift to population-level interventions is a difficult decision and one that must be well coordinated and agreed upon by all stakeholders.

Population-level interventions referred to as nonpharmaceutical intervention (NPI) measures may be the best and most practical tools in the toolbox, especially during the first wave. A number of recent studies and publications provide evidence for the effectiveness of NPI. Bootsma and Ferguson (2007) reviewed the mortality data and public health records from the fall of 1918 for 16 U.S. cities. The study showed that if NPI measures were introduced early on and left in place for the duration of the pandemic wave, they were effective at reducing transmission rates by up to 30 to 50%.

Nonpharmaceutical measures discussed in this chapter include:

- Hand hygiene and cough etiquettes
- Isolation of persons with confirmed or probable pandemic influenza
- Voluntary home quarantine of members of households with confirmed or probable influenza case
- School closures and snow days
- Use of social distancing measures to reduce contact between adults in the community and workplace including, for example, cancellation of large public gatherings and alteration of workplace environments and schedules to decrease social density and preserve a healthy workplace to the greatest extent possible without disrupting essential services

7.5.1 HYGIENE AND COUGH ETIQUETTE

Direct transmission involves direct body-to-body surface contact. Indirect transmission occurs via contact with contaminated intermediate objects such as contaminated hands or inanimate objects such as nonporous surfaces. The most common way to catch the flu is by touching something that has been contaminated by an infected person. Consider a scenario that affects nearly every person weekly: use of a shopping cart at the grocery store. Before you arrived at the store, a person recently infected and now shedding virus handles the very same cart that you are now pushing down the aisles. That infected store patron covered his mouth with his hand when he coughed, then used that very hand to push the cart around the store. Now your hands are touching the same cart. Without thinking while shopping, you scratch your nose, thereby introducing virus to one of the most vulnerable points of entry for infection. Good hand-washing does more to prevent the spread of flu than anything else. Therefore, emphasize hand-washing and properly covering one's cough often and through multiple forms of media. This emphasis will go a long way, especially with children still in their formative years.

Practical and common-sense measures (e.g., frequent hand-washing, covering the mouth and nose while sneezing or coughing, and staying home from work or school if ill with influenza-like illness) may be important to help prevent the spread of pandemic influenza. All such community-based strategies should be used in combination with individual infection control measures, such as hand-washing and cough etiquette. Implementing these interventions in a timely and coordinated fashion will require advance planning. Communities must be prepared for the cascading second- and third-order consequences of the interventions, such as increased workplace absenteeism related to child-minding responsibilities if schools dismiss students and childcare programs close.

7.5.2 ISOLATION

Isolation means separation of a person infected with a communicable disease in a place and under conditions to prevent direct or indirect transmission of an infectious agent to others, during the period of communicability. It may mean extremely limited contact with an ill person who is diagnosed with, or suspected of having, a communicable disease. Formal isolation is a medical procedure that occurs in a hospital setting in a negative airflow room. Formal isolation procedures require health care workers and visitors to use gowns, masks, respirators, goggles, and gloves as a means of protecting the visitors, but also to protect the patient from exposure to new diseases their weakened immune system may not be able to overcome.

7.5.3 QUARANTINE

Quarantine means restrictions of activities or travel of an otherwise healthy person who likely has been exposed to a communicable disease, during or immediately prior to a period of communicability. The restrictions are intended to prevent disease transmission during the period of communicability or incubation period of the disease. This means they have been exposed to an individual with a communicable disease and may be developing the disease as well. Remember that the incubation period for influenza is typically two to four days and that infected individuals normally shed the virus before they are symptomatic.

Restrictions may be voluntary or legally mandated; confinement may be at home or in an appropriate facility. Whenever possible, contacts should be quarantined at home. Home quarantine requires the fewest additional resources, although arrangements must still be made for monitoring patients, reporting symptoms, transporting patients for medical evaluation if necessary, and providing essential supplies and services.

Quarantine can be accomplished by a variety of means including having the person stay at home and avoid contact with others (including family members) to having the person or group of people stay in a designated facility, to restricting travel out of an impacted area. The contact remains separated from others for a specified period (generally 10 days after potential exposure), during which he or she is assessed on a regular basis (in person at least once daily) for signs and symptoms of disease. People with fever, respiratory, or other early influenza symptoms require immediate evaluation by a trained health care provider. Restrictions may be voluntary or legally mandated; confinement may be at home or in an appropriate facility.

No specific precautions are required for those sharing the household with a person in quarantine as long as the person remains asymptomatic. However, because onset of symptoms may be insidious, it may be prudent to minimize interactions with household members during the period of quarantine. This more-aggressive approach may be appropriate in situations in which the risk of exposure and subsequent development of disease is high and the risk of delayed recognition of symptoms is moderate.

A working quarantine may be an option with improved compliance potential over other mandatory measures. Individuals are permitted to work, but must observe activity restrictions while off work. Self or active monitoring for fever or influenza-like illness-type symptoms prior to going to work is required. PPE must be worn while at work. This type of quarantine may be useful for critical workers or others for whom compliance by other measures is not possible. This method helps to reduce the risk of spread, while at the same time provides minimal disruption of community life.

Analysis shows that concern about lost wages was the single factor in Toronto that caused the most hesitation when people were asked by health officials to quarantine themselves. At such moments, employers must be prepared to send clear signals to workers early in an emergency so that sick-leave policies are coordinated with the messages from health authorities.

7.5.4 COMMUNITY QUARANTINE

In extreme circumstances, public health officials may consider the use of widespread or communitywide quarantine, which is the most stringent and restrictive containment measure. Strictly speaking, widespread community quarantine is a misnomer, since quarantine refers to separation of exposed people only and (unlike snow days) usually allows provision of services and support to affected people. Like snow days, widespread community quarantine involves asking everyone to stay home. It differs from snow days in two respects — it may involve a legally enforceable action, and it restricts travel into or out of an area circumscribed by a real or virtual sanitary barrier or *cordon sanitaire* except to authorized people, such as public health or health care workers.

You know, "quarantine" is a word that has a lot of bad meanings for many people. We talk about modern quarantine as a way of creating some common-sense steps to decrease the chance that disease will spread from one person to another. If a pandemic evolves in one part of the world, there are some immediate things that we will do, in support with our international partners, including isolating the people who are sick so they don't spread to others, and perhaps quarantining their immediate contacts. And by that, we just mean asking them to stay home or to separate themselves from other people in the community.

The old-fashioned concept of quarantine, involving military forces or law enforcement agents, forcing people to do something that they wouldn't ordinarily do, is really an outdated concept. We think of it more today as social distancing, where we would close schools or sometimes close large meetings, asking people to avoid as much face-to-face contact with others in the community. But I don't think any of us are thinking about those kind[s] of draconian measures to really completely quarantine a community or even quarantine a country.

(Director Julie L. Gerberding, Centers for Disease Control and Prevention, January 1, 2006 interview with Bernard Schieffer, "Face the Nation" (CBS News) transcript.)

The community must be clear about local, state, and federal legislation (i.e., restriction of movement of individuals for the purposes of controlling communicable diseases) and about which authority can declare a public health emergency in the jurisdiction. In some cases, connecting the implementation of isolation and/or quarantine to a declaration of an emergency may be beneficial. Once imposed, there is a clear means of notification for individuals, businesses, other response partners, and the media. What measures will a community accept? What means may be used to monitor and enforce restrictions or penalize noncompliance?

The short incubation period for influenza makes it difficult to identify and quarantine contacts of pandemic influenza-infected persons before they become ill and have spread infection to others. By contrast, the longer incubation periods for smallpox (about 14 days) and SARS (up to 10 days) make this a more-effective control strategy for those infections. Consequently, quarantine is unlikely to be an effective measure in controlling pandemic influenza (Inglesby et al., 2006). In general, quarantine has been ineffective, at the most postponing epidemics of influenza by a few weeks to two months, and even the most-severe restrictions on travel and trade have gained only a few weeks. In the United States, no large-scale quarantine has been employed in the last eight decades, and few if any strategies currently exist to guide such a response.

7.5.5   Social Distancing

Dr. Julie Gerberding of the CDC alluded to social distancing as a substitute to quarantine. Social distancing measures are designed to increase the distance between people in an outbreak zone and to reduce the opportunities for disease transmission to occur. Like quarantine, these measures are socially disruptive and may cause economic discomfort. Of greater interest is the lack of clear scientific studies that measure the actual impact of such measures. In the absence of data, a difference of opinion will undoubtedly arise and be difficult to solve without collaboration and careful thought. Those responsible for managing schools or businesses may simply elect to shut down their facilities in the face of an absent workforce, student body, or clientele. Likewise, churches may cancel services, and other community organizations may cancel programs, regardless of advice from the government.

Two ways of increasing social distance activity restrictions are to cancel events and close buildings or to restrict access to certain sites or buildings (refer to Figure 7.5). These measures are sometimes called focused measures to increase social distance. Closures of office buildings, stores, schools, and public transportation systems may be feasible community containment measures during a pandemic. All of these have significant impact on the community and workforce; however, careful consideration should be focused on their potential effectiveness, how they can most effectively be implemented, and how to maintain critical supplies and infrastructure while limiting community interaction. Widespread acceptance of social distancing concepts depends largely on the public health official's ability to explain the concept in a way that the average citizen can put into practice. The populace is more likely to abide by this advice as morbidity and mortality rates increase.

Snow days can effectively reduce transmission without explicit activity restrictions (i.e., quarantine). Implementation of snow days involves the entire community

FIGURE 7.5 Days after Philadelphia's Liberty Loan parade in September 1918, which was attended by 200,000 people, hundreds of cases of influenza were reported. There are numerous anecdotal reports that suggest large public gatherings promoted morbidity and mortality during the Spanish flu. A number of studies indicate that social distancing, like limiting large public gatherings, will be essential in the limiting transmission. (Image courtesy of the United States Naval Historical Center.)

in a positive way, is acceptable to most people, and is relatively easy to implement. A snow day would be declared to reduce public gatherings and limit contact among people. Snow days may be declared for up to 10 days to give public health officials time to assess the local situation. In advance of such a declaration, local authorities need to consider how they would deliver the message and what recommendations they would pass along to the public for them to have adequate provisions. Very few families stock a 10-day supply of food in their homes.

7.5.6 SCHOOL CLOSURES

Questions surrounding school closures are illustrative of the challenges confronting public health officials in considering the imposition of social distancing strategies to slow or limit the spread of influenza. Determining when to close and open schools and enlisting parental cooperation is essential (Kahn, 2007). Children are known to be efficient transmitters of seasonal influenza and other respiratory illnesses (Heymann et al., 2004). School closures may be effective in decreasing the spread of influenza and reducing the overall magnitude of disease in a community. In addition, the risk of infection and illness among children is likely to be decreased, which would be particularly important if the pandemic strain causes significant morbidity and mortality rates among children. Anecdotal reports suggest that community influenza outbreaks may be limited by closing schools (Inglesby et al., 2006). During the first wave of the Asian flu pandemic of 1957–1958, the highest attack rates were seen in school-aged children; this has been attributed to their close contact in crowded settings (Davis et al., 1970). During a pandemic period, parents would be encouraged to consider child care arrangements that do not result in large gatherings of children outside the school setting (Kahn, 2007). If the children are not in school, they have to be somewhere. Over a short period, most parents will be able to adapt in some way to this inconvenience. However, over longer periods, this becomes untenable for most families, especially with single parents. Closing schools would force many parents to stay home from work. There may be alternatives or variations in this approach that may be more useful (e.g., voluntary versus optional school attendance, requiring documentation of pandemic-strain vaccination, screening students on arrival at school, or use of Web-based or other approaches to support home-based schooling). It is also possible there are unintended consequences of school closures such as adolescents congregating elsewhere, which suggests that school closures may need to coincide with other social distancing interventions at locations where students may meet.

Limiting public gatherings can be an effective preventive measure for diseases that are transmitted through airborne transmission, such as influenza. In making a decision to close gathering places, the impact on the economy, education, and access to essential commodities needs to be balanced with the ability to protect the public effectively through such means. There is a big difference between recommending limited public gatherings and enforcing a more-specific and uniform requirement.

In September 1918, the city of Philadelphia held a Liberty Loan parade, which was attended by 200,000 people (Crosby, 2003). Days after that parade hundreds of cases of influenza were reported (see Figure 7.5). During the 1957-1958 pandemic, a WHO expert panel found that spread within some countries followed public gatherings, such as conferences and festivals (WHO, 2005b). This panel also observed that in many countries the pandemic broke out first in camps, army units, and schools, suggesting that the avoidance of crowds may be important in reducing the peak incidence of an epidemic.

Hatcher and colleagues (2007) systematically examined the timing of NPI measures in 17 U.S. cities during the 1918 Spanish flu. Early implementation of closures of schools, churches, and theaters was associated with lower peak death rates, but no single intervention showed an association with improved aggregate outcomes for the 1918 phase of the pandemic.

Referring [to the] bureau wire [on] this date indications are influenza will become epidemic here soon unless active measures [are] taken [to] prevent. If city will adopt my recommendation relative closing theaters, picture shows, and other crowded places, there will be no necessity for emergency hospital. This demonstrated in previous outbreak. At present time, all places [of] amusement [are] excessively crowded and reports show marked daily increase in cases and deaths. (Telegram from a New Orleans PHS Officer to Surgeon General Rupert Blue, January 1919.)

7.5.7 Applying the Pandemic Severity Index

From a pre-pandemic planning perspective, the steps between recognition of a pandemic threat and the decision to activate a response are critical to successful implementation. Recalling what was said in the Introduction to this chapter, plans at the local level have to fall in line with the regional plan, regional plans have to be synchronized with the state plan, and so on. The CDC's MMIG represents the federal government's true attempt to bring all levels of government together into a cohesive pandemic response. Accordingly, there is now a cascading effect that starts with the federal government. State, regional, and local plans must include this strategy if we're all going to work together. Since the PSI was outlined nicely for us in the MMIG, this section will follow the CDC's guidance in helping us understand and appreciate the application of the PSI.

Scenario-specific contingency plans for pandemic response must be developed so that we can identify key personnel, critical resources, and processes. To emphasize the importance of this concept, the MMIG (CDC, 2007) introduces us to the terminology of Alert, Standby, and Activate, terms used to escalate response actions. Alert includes notification of critical systems and personnel of their impending activation. Standby is a term that signals initiation of decision-making processes for imminent activation and mobilization of resources and personnel. Activate refers to implementation of the specified pandemic mitigation measures (CDC, 2007). Pre-incident pandemic planning should be geared toward lessening transition times between alert, standby, and activate modes. Characteristics of the pandemic strain and speed of transmission will drive the amount of time decision makers are given for each mode, as does the amount of time it takes to implement the intervention fully once a decision is made to activate. Refer to Table 7.3 for application of the terminology.

For Category 1, 2, and 3 pandemics, alert is declared during U.S. Government Stage 3, with stepwise progression by states and regions to Standby based on U.S. government declaration of Stage 4 and the identification of the first human pandemic influenza case(s) in the United States. Progression to Activate by a given state or region occurs when that state or region identifies a cluster of laboratory-confirmed human pandemic influenza cases, with evidence of community transmission in their jurisdiction (CDC, 2007).

For Category 2 and Category 3 pandemics, planning for voluntary isolation of ill persons is recommended; however, other mitigation measures (e.g., voluntary quarantine of household members and social distancing measures for children and adults) should be implemented only if local decision makers determine their use is warranted due to characteristics of the pandemic within their community. Pre-pandemic planning for the use of mitigation strategies within these two Pandemic Severity Index categories should be done with a focus on duration of four weeks or less, distinct from the longer time frame recommended for the more-severe Category 4 and Category 5 pandemics. For Category 1 pandemics, voluntary isolation of ill persons is generally the only communitywide recommendation, although local communities may choose to tailor their response to Categories 1 through 3 pandemics by applying NPI measures on the basis of local epidemiologic parameters, risk assessment, availability of countermeasures, and consideration of local health care surge capacity. Thus, from a pre-pandemic planning perspective for Category 1, 2, and 3 pandemics, capabilities for assessing local public health capacity and health care

TABLE 7.3

Recommendations Arrayed by the PSI and U.S. Government Stage for Stepwise Escalation of Action

Pandemic Severity Index	WHO Phase 6/U.S. Government Stage 3[a]	WHO Phase 6/U.S. Government Stage 4[b]/First Human Case in the United States	WHO Phase 6/U.S. Government Stage 5[c]/First Laboratory-Confirmed Cluster in State or Region
1	Alert	Standby	Activate
2 and 3	Alert	Standby	Activate
4 and 5	Standby[c]	Standby/Activated	Activate

Note: These triggers for implementation of nonpharmaceutical intervention measures will be most useful early in a pandemic.

[a] Outbreaks in multiple locations overseas.

[b] First case in North America.

[c] Spread throughout the United States.

Source: CDC (U.S. Centers for Disease Control and Prevention). February 2007. Mitigation Measures Interim Guidance (MMIG). Interim Pre-Pandemic Planning Guidance: Community Strategy for Pandemic Influenza Mitigation in the United States — Early Targeted Layered Use of Non-Pharmaceutical Interventions. http://www.pandemicflu.gov/plan/community/mitigation.html

surge, delivering countermeasures, and implementing these measures in full and in combination should be assessed (CDC, 2007).

For the most severe pandemics (Categories 4 and 5), Alert is implemented during WHO Phase 5/U.S. Government Stage 2 (confirmed human outbreak overseas), and Standby is initiated during WHO Phase 6/U.S. Government Stage 3 (widespread human outbreaks in multiple locations overseas). Standby is maintained through Stage 4 (first human case in North America), with the exception of the state or region in which a cluster of laboratory-confirmed human pandemic influenza cases with evidence of community transmission is identified. The recommendation for that state or region is to Activate the appropriate NPI measures when identification of a cluster with community transmission is made. Other states or regions activate appropriate interventions when they identify laboratory-confirmed human pandemic influenza case clusters with evidence of community transmission in their jurisdictions (CDC, 2007).

For Categories 4 and 5 pandemics, a planning recommendation is made for use of all listed NPI measures. In addition, planning for dismissal of students from schools and school-based activities and closures of child care programs, in combination with means to reduce out-of-school social contacts and community mixing for these children, should encompass up to 12 weeks of intervention in the most severe scenarios. This approach to pre-pandemic planning will provide a baseline of readiness for community response. Recommendations for use of these measures for pandemics of lesser severity may include a subset of these same interventions and potentially for shorter durations, as in the case of social distancing measures for children. Refer to Table 7.4 for CDC recommendations on the application of nonpharmaceutical interventions based upon the Pandemic Severity Index.

TABLE 7.4
This Table Allows Pandemic Planners to Perform a Cross-Walk of NPI Measures with the PSI

Interventions[a] by Setting	1	2 and 3	4 and 5
Home			
Voluntary isolation of ill at home (adults and children); combine with use of antiviral treatment as available and indicated	Recommend	Recommend	Recommend
Voluntary quarantine of household members in homes with ill persons (adults and children); consider combining with antiviral prophylaxis if effective, feasible, and quantities sufficient	Generally not recommended	Consider	Recommend
School: Child Social Distancing			
Dismissal of students from schools and school-based activities and closures of child care programs	Generally not recommended	Consider: ≤4 weeks	Recommend: ≤12 weeks
Reduce out-of-school social contacts and community mixing	Generally not recommended	Consider: ≤4 weeks	Recommend: ≤12 weeks
Workplace/Community: Adult Social Distancing			
Decrease number of social contacts (e.g., encourage teleconferences, alternatives to face-to-face meetings)	Generally not recommended	Consider	Recommend
Increase distance between persons (e.g., reduce density in public transit, workplaces)	Generally not recommended	Consider	Recommend
Modify, postpone, or cancel selected public gatherings to promote social distance (e.g., postpone indoor stadium events, theatre performances)	Generally not recommended	Consider	Recommend
Modify workplace schedules and practices (e.g., telework, staggered shifts)	Generally not recommended	Consider	Recommend

[a] All these interventions should be used in conjuction with other infection control measures, including hand hygiene, cough etiquette and personal protection.

Note: The most restrictive NPI measures are only recommended for the most-severe pandemic categories (4 and 5).

Source: CDC (U.S. Centers for Disease Control and Prevention). February 2007. Mitigation Measures Interim Guidance (MMIG). Interim Pre-Pandemic Planning Guidance: Community Strategy for Pandemic Influenza Mitigation in the United States — Early Targeted Layered Use of Non-Pharmaceutical Interventions. http://www.pandemicflu.gov/plan/community/mitigation.html

7.6   POSTURING FOR MEDICAL SURGE

The three influenza pandemics of the 20th century shared a similar theme. In each outbreak approximately 30% of the population developed severe illness and approximately half of those ill individuals sought medical care. The greatest secondary hazard will be the problems caused by shortages of medical supplies (e.g., vaccines and antiviral drugs), equipment (e.g., mechanical ventilators), hospital beds, and health care workers. Also of particular concern is the likelihood that health care systems, particularly hospitals, will be overwhelmed. Having a detailed plan for allocating or adjusting scarce medical resources can potentially reduce such difficulties. Ideally, this plan should be in place well before the next pandemic occurs.

During a pandemic, there will be a need to expand the capacity of the existing health care system rapidly in order to provide triage and medical care. This expansion is termed medical surge. Medical surge includes the need for more personnel (clinical and nonclinical), support functions (laboratories and transport), physical space (beds and alternate care facilities), and logistical support. This section of the chapter will discuss strategies to expand the capabilities of existing facilities.

Historically speaking, hospitals were built for the poor; other patients got their care at home. They were well staffed and administratively simple, making it possible to deal with larger numbers of patients during outbreaks. Over time, hospitals came to acquire costly, immobile technology that had to be located in hospitals, thereby centralizing more and more patients out of the home care arena and into the hospital. Patient-days rose as patients were kept in beds for observation and rest. Hospitals became multi-disciplinary medical care department stores (Tussing, 1996). Today, observation and bed rest have lost favor with modern medicine, and technology is increasingly decentralized. Declining inpatient utilization and pressures to increase administrative efficiency and profitability have resulted in the closure and consolidation of many hospitals. In fact, there are approximately 900 fewer hospitals in the United States today than there were 25 years ago (AHA, 2002).

Demand for hospital services is soaring, especially as the baby boom generation begins to age, and the remaining hospitals are struggling to keep up. Nowhere is this trend more evident than in the hospital's portal — the Emergency Department (ED). Here, patients receive critical care for a multitude of acute conditions and injuries. Emergency departments also serve as a safety net for indigents and people with no medical insurance. Rising rates of ambulance diversion indicate that capacity has become constrained in many parts of the country. Patients are already ear-to-ear and toe-to-toe in EDs as they wait for access to hospital care because the hospitals lack the staff and space to care for additional patients. Consider the implications of this overcrowding situation when attempting to minimize contact between the infected and noninfected.

Despite a smaller patient base, rural hospitals still have to maintain a broad range of services to meet the health care needs of their communities. With fewer patients over which to spread these high-fixed costs, costs per case tend to be higher. Often the only health care resource in a community, a greater percentage of rural hospitals offer home health and skilled nursing services (AHA, 2002).

TABLE 7.5
Number of Episodes of Illness, Health Care Utilization, and Death Associated with Moderate and Severe Pandemic Influenza Scenarios

Characteristics	Moderate (1958/1968-like)	Severe (1918-like)
Illness	90,000,000(30%)	90,000,000(30%)
Outpatient medical care	45,000,000(50%)	45,000,000(50%)
Hospitalization	865,000	9,900,000
ICU care	128,750	1,485,000
Mechanical ventilation	64,875	742,500
Deaths	209,000	1,903,000

Note: Estimates are based on extrapolation from past pandemics in the United States. Note that these estimates do not include the potential impact of interventions not available during the 20th century pandemics.

Pandemic influenza will place a tremendous burden on the health care system. Estimates for the next pandemic, based on the two lesser pandemics of the 20th century, indicate that the United States could experience between 839,000 to 9,625,000 hospitalizations, 18 to 42 million outpatient visits, and 20 to 47 million additional illnesses. However, when one bases estimates on extrapolation from the more-severe 1918 pandemic, there are more-substantial numbers of hospitalizations and deaths (see Table 7.5). The demand for inpatient and intensive care unit (ICU) beds and assisted ventilation services could increase by more than 25 percent under the less-severe scenario. In the United States, there are 105,000 mechanical ventilators, between 75,000 and 80,000 of which are in use at any given time. During a normal influenza season, the number in use climbs to 100,000. In an influenza pandemic, there may be a demand for an additional several hundred thousand ventilators (Osterholm, 2005). In the midst of a growing health care crisis, how would an already-broken system manage to care for the flux of influenza patients on top of the workload they already shoulder?

The Center for Biosecurity at the University of Pittsburgh Medical Center has estimated that the minimum costs of realistic readiness for a severe (1918-like) pandemic are at least $1 million for the average size hospital (164 beds). The component costs to achieve minimal preparedness include:

- Developing specific pandemic plan: $200,000
- Educating/training staff: $160,000
- Stockpiling minimal personal protective equipment: $400,000
- Stockpiling basic supplies: $240,000
- Total: $1 million per hospital

Using these estimates, the total for the nation's 5,000 general acute care hospitals for initial pandemic preparedness is about $5 billion. The Center for Biosecurity estimates recurring annual costs to maintain preparedness to be approximately $200,000 per year per hospital.

These figures exclude stockpiling antivirals, since there is a separate national plan to acquire these drugs. In addition, this estimate does not include funds for the purchase of expensive equipment such as mechanical ventilators, since it is not clear that extra ventilators would be useful if there were no trained personnel to operate them. (Testimony of Nancy Donegan on behalf of the American Hospital Association before the U.S. Senate Special Committee on Aging, "Preparing for Pandemic Flu," May 25, 2006.)

7.6.1 SURGE CAPACITY

Surge capacity refers to the health care system's ability to expand rapidly beyond normal services to meet the increased demand for qualified personnel, medical care, and public health in the event of large-scale public health emergencies or natural disasters. Surge capacity is not defined by the number of beds available in a health care system. It encompasses potentially available space that may be converted for use to triage, manage, vaccinate, and hold patients. Surge capacity also includes personnel of all types who contribute to the operation, as well as necessary medications, supplies, and equipment. During the planning process, medico-legal professionals should address barriers to the provision of such services beyond normal capacity, licensure, certification, or authority during times of extreme need.

7.6.2 INCREASING SURGE CAPACITY

HHS recommends that hospitals develop their own response plans, which include components on hospital surveillance, hospital communication, staff education and training, triage and admission procedures, staffing and bed capacity, consumable and durable supplies, and planning for provision of care in nonhospital settings. In order to plan for and meet the surge need, communities should work with health care facilities to anticipate emergency staffing needs, increased demand for isolation wards, alternate care sites, maintenance of day-to-day health care systems, ICUs, assisted ventilation services, and consumable and durable medical supplies (Toner et al., 2006). For the care of influenza patients during a pandemic, HHS has established a goal for communities to create 500 additional beds per million in population. This physical capacity translates to 1,624 additional personnel (e.g., physicians, nurses, respiratory therapists, lab technicians, administrative assistants, food workers, engineers/maintenance, and security). These additional skilled staff must be found in the middle of thousands of unfilled positions now. Without community involvement, this will be impossible to achieve.

7.6.3 TRIAGE

During a pandemic, communitywide triage should be conducted to identify persons who meet the case definition of infection with the pandemic strain and separate those from others to reduce the risk of disease transmission, and identify the type of care they require (e.g., home care, outpatient facility, or hospitalization). This will reduce unnecessary congestions at hospitals and help people avoid illness, but it requires community cooperation. Phone triage is one way to keep the sick away from those not ill. Hospitals, clinics, physicians' offices, pharmacies, and 9-1-1 operators need simple lines of questioning to identify patients who need emergency care, possible influenza cases, and those who can be referred to an alternate site for their service.

7.6.4   HEALTH CARE PERSONNEL SHORTAGES

Exactly where a community might find the additional personnel requires innovative and collaborative solutions. Increased cross-training of personnel provides support for essential patient care areas at times of severe staffing shortages (e.g., in emergency departments, ICUs, and medical surgical units). Discussions with the state health department on plans for rapidly credentialing health care professionals during a pandemic are crucial. Together, state health departments and members of the health care community can determine a definition of an emergency staffing crisis and when it can be declared, as well as identification of emergency laws that allow employment of health care personnel with out-of-state licenses.

Health care facilities and businesses that support them need to create a list of essential-support personnel that are required to maintain hospital operations. Nonessential personnel are also identified as potential candidates for cross-training to be reassigned to support critical hospital services, shared to maintain other critical operations in the community, or placed on administrative leave to limit the number of people in the hospital (HHS, 2006).

Insurance and liability issues related to the use of nonfacility staff will have to be addressed. Handling the health care needs will require recruiting of personnel from other health care settings, (e.g., medical offices, dental offices, and day surgery centers). Health care facilities should consult public health partners about existing state or local plans for recruitment and deployment of local personnel (HHS, 2006). Hospital emergency preparedness coordinators should work with prehospital providers and home health care agencies to arrange at-home follow-up care for patients who have been discharged early and for those whose admission was deferred because of limited bed space or acuity. The utilization of emergency medical technicians (EMTs) and paramedics, resources not in existence in 1918, could prove invaluable to help meet surge needs. These medical professionals are used to working in homes and, with proper PPE and scope-of-practice enhancements, could help limit movement of ill community members, while still providing appropriate medical assessment and care.

7.6.5   ALTERNATIVE CARE SITES

Hospitals are licensed for a certain number of beds. Hospital officials must work with their licensing agencies to develop a process that allows for the expansion of bed capacity during crises. These efforts should take into account the need to provide staff and medical equipment and supplies to care for the occupant of each additional hospital bed. In some cases, staffing levels may fall below minimum standards,

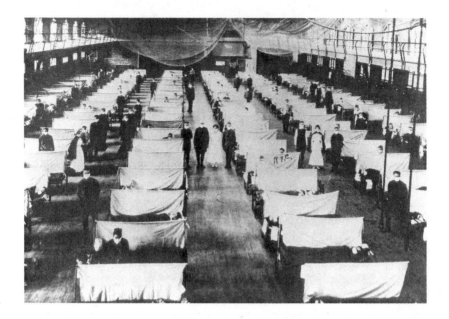

FIGURE 7.6 Iowa Fever Hospital during the 1918 Spanish Flu. Here, a gymnasium was used as an alternate care facility. Health care providers wore masks and the patients were tented to limit the spread of the contagion. This open, airy facility is another way of looking at infection control and isolation in a grand fashion. (Image courtesy of the Office of the Public Health Service Historian, Department of Health and Human Services.)

and health care regulators must decide when and how altered standards of care or sufficiency of care will be allowed during a pandemic event. This may involve grouping patients based on stage of recovery and infectivity (HHS, 2006). If an influenza pandemic causes severe illness in large numbers of people, hospital capacity will most likely be overwhelmed. In that case, communities could provide care in alternative sites (e.g., temporary shelters, convention centers, indoor stadiums). The selection of alternative care sites for pandemic influenza should specifically address infection control and patient care needs. Routine care of influenza patients may allow for the establishment of a fever hospital, such as was the case in 1918 (see Figure 7.6). Open, airy spaces, as seen in the figure, may actually be an equally effective infection control environment than negative airflow rooms, which will not be available.

7.6.6 HEALTH AND WELFARE OF THE WORKFORCE

The ability to deliver quality health care is dependent on adequate staffing and optimum health and welfare of staff. During a pandemic, the health care workforce will be stressed physically and psychologically. Health care facilities must be prepared to protect healthy workers from exposures in their occupational setting through the use of recommended infection control measures. The facilities must also provide psychosocial services to health care workers and their families to help sustain the workforce. Part of maintaining a healthy workforce may be the provision for antiviral drugs to hospital staff and quickly manage symptomatic and ill health care personnel. Facilities may want to consider assigning staff who have recently recovered from influenza to care for influenza patients. Rehabilitation of personnel is a function of incident command. A pandemic will create a tremendous workload; in order to sustain a response for weeks or months, personnel must be rotated out of high-stress positions and get rest. Reassignment of personnel who are at high risk for complications of influenza to low-risk duties or placing them on furlough may be necessary.

The community planning process should identify mental health and faith-based resources for counseling of health care personnel during a pandemic. Counseling should include measures to maximize professional performance and personal resilience by addressing grief, exhaustion, anger, and fear management; physical and mental health care for employees and their families; and resolution of ethical dilemmas brought on by altered standards of care.

7.6.7 ALTERED STANDARDS OF CARE

Under normal conditions, current standards of care might be interpreted as calling for the allocation of all appropriate health and medical resources to improve the health status and/or to save the life of each individual patient. However, in a pandemic the demand for care provided in accordance with current standards would exceed system resources. The duration of the pandemic event is likely to occur in waves over a period of many weeks or months. In an event involving so many severely ill patients, the preservation of our health care systems may require a paradigm shift toward some altered standards of care (HHS, 2005). Naturally, this concept is extremely controversial and difficult for many clinicians to grasp. The term "altered standard of care" has not been legally defined, but generally is assumed to mean a shift to providing care and allocating scarce equipment, supplies, and personnel in a way that saves the largest number of lives in contrast to the traditional focus on saving each and every individual. Given the highly contentious nature of this subject, it is essential that community health care professionals create a forum of discussion to determine the feasibility of this measure at the local level. If accepted, it then becomes important to establish clear authority to activate the use of altered standards of health and medical care to ensure consistency across a region (HHS, 2005).

7.7 RISK COMMUNICATIONS

During a pandemic, a single or very limited number of credible spokesperson(s) should be used to improve public understanding of and maintaining support for disease containment measures. In keeping with the concept that seasonal flu preparedness leads to pandemic flu preparedness, emphasis now on public health education and communications should be improved to help limit the spread of influenza. Communications preparedness for an influenza pandemic incorporates the following key risk communications concepts: prepare with information, encourage action steps to prepare now, provide frequent updates, use a trusted messenger, coordinate to ensure a consistent message, and address rumors and inaccuracies.

Effective risk communications preparedness involves assessing the communications strengths and challenges, including capacity and needs. Collaborative planning ensures strong and well-integrated working relationships between communications professionals in the public and private sectors. Critical elements of a comprehensive domestic communications plan include:

- Coordinating training and other preparedness activities that include options for backing up key communications personnel in the event of personal illness or emergency
- Coordinating with partner agencies to prepare for appropriate public, health care provider, policy, and media responses to outbreaks of pandemic influenza
- Considering how and when to use federal assistance when available (e.g., background information and frequent updates will be available on www. pandemicflu.gov and through other official mechanisms)
- Identifying and engaging credible local resources as partners (e.g., local chapters of nonprofit health organizations may assist with urgent communications to community groups)
- Affirming processes with news media representatives to optimize working relationships during pandemic phases
- Ensuring that communications professionals have opportunities to participate with other public health and emergency staff in tabletop exercises and drills to identify and resolve potential problems early

During the interpandemic and pandemic alert periods, standard state and local procedures for disseminating information should be developed and tested prior to a pandemic influenza outbreak. Locally tailored interpandemic messages and materials should also be developed, tested, and disseminated (HHS, 2005).

7.8 CONCLUSION

Pandemics create more than medical problems — they affect every sector of a community and it takes a community effort to assemble a functional plan. An effective and comprehensive response to a fast-moving, contagious, and potentially fatal disease with limited possibilities for prevention, treatment, or other medical intervention will require the unprecedented coordination and collaboration of a wide range of governmental and nongovernmental parties. Government officials must provide leadership, but they cannot provide all of the services required to contain a disease and support an affected community.

Response to a public health crisis will and must rely heavily on public health, medical, and scientific experts. It will also require support from law enforcement personnel, mental health providers, transportation authorities, emergency management directors, and other key service providers who may know little about disease transmission or control measures. Finally, as devastating as the pandemic may be, early and aggressive support for the economic foundations in a community must be part of the community action plans.

No intervention by itself, short of mass vaccination, will dramatically reduce influenza transmission. Mathematical modeling of pandemic influenza scenarios in the United States indicate that pandemic mitigation strategies utilizing multiple nonpharmaceutical intervention may decrease transmission substantially and that even-greater reductions may be achieved when such measures are combined with the targeted use of antiviral medications for treatment and prophylaxis. Recent preliminary analyses of cities affected by the 1918 pandemic show a highly significant association between the early use of multiple NPI measures and reductions in peak and overall death rates. The rational targeting and layering of interventions may mitigate the effects of a severe pandemic. It will be critical for us to apply many of these measures in layers to reduce transmission to the greatest extent possible.

Any community that fails to prepare and expects the federal government to come to the rescue will be tragically wrong. (Michael Leavitt, Secretary, Department of Health and Human Services.)

If estimates and model predictions hold true for the next pandemic, there will be a critical need for the expansion and alteration of health care. Medical surge includes the need for more personnel, support functions, physical space, and logistical support. It can be accomplished through creative pre-planning, extension of existing medical treatment facilities and personnel, movement to alternate facilities, and use of federal assets if sufficient pre-planning is accomplished.

Communities need operational and functional plans to move them strategically and tactically through the next pandemic. These plans must involve all key components of society, not just traditional response entities. Government officials, public health officials, health care managers, and business leaders must partner with the more-traditional response community of emergency management, police, fire, EMS, and public works.

After an extended public health emergency, significant organizational fatigue and psychological burnout will come to weigh heavily on every person in the community. When disasters terminate, there is a tendency for everyone to stand down, recuperate, and return to normalcy as soon as possible. It is important for both the public and private sectors to maintain sufficient focus to capture quickly the lessons learned while memories are still fresh and the unique personal networks that developed during the emergency are still active. The arrival of a pandemic organism will set the stage for leaders across the globe to assess their commitment to the welfare of their constituents. Furthermore, public servants in every community will be judged by one important statistic: the mortality rate of their constituents. This statistic, coupled with the attack rate and case fatality rate that their populace experienced, will be a testament to the investment each community made in recognizing the seriousness of the threat and the steps they took to mitigate it. The next influenza pandemic seems inevitable. Unfortunately, it is likely to provide ample pain and suffering even for the best-prepared communities. The time it takes for a community to rebound will be directly dependent upon the investment made today to prepare. This is a decisive point in time, and communities must act with resolve.

REFERENCES

AHA (American Hospital Association). 2002. Cracks in the Foundation: Averting a Crisis in America's Hospitals. Chicago, IL. www.aha.org.

ASTHO (Association of State and Territorial Health Officials). 2002. Preparedness Planning for State Health Officials. Nature's Terrorist Attack: Pandemic Influenza. Washington, D.C.

Barry J. 2004. *The Great Influenza: The Epic Story of the Deadliest Plague in History.* New York: Viking.

Bell D. 2006. Non-pharmaceutical interventions for pandemic influenza, national and community measures. *Emerg Infect Dis* 12:88–94.

Bootsma, M., and N. Ferguson. 2007. The effect of public health measures on the 1918 influenza pandemic in U.S. cities. *Proc Natl Acad Sci.:* USA 104: 7588–7593.

CDC (U.S. Centers for Disease Control and Prevention). February 2007. Mitigation Measures Interim Guidance (MMIG). Interim Pre-Pandemic Planning Guidance: Community Strategy for Pandemic Influenza Mitigation in the United States — Early Targeted Layered Use of Non-Pharmaceutical Interventions. http://www.pandemicflu.gov/plan/community/mitigation.html.

Clinic Planning Model Generator. May 22, 2007. User's Guide. Version 2.03. Institute for Systems Research. University of Maryland. Developed by Dr. Jeffrey Herrmann.

Cooper N, Sutton A, Abrams K, Wailoo A, Turner D, Nicholson K. 2003. Effectiveness of neuraminidase inhibitors in treatment and prevention of influenza A and B: systematic review and meta-analyses of randomised controlled trials. *BMJ* 326:1235.

Crosby A. 2003. *America's Forgotten Pandemic: The Influenza of 1918,* Second Edition. Cambridge: Cambridge University Press.

Davis L, Caldwell G, Lynch R, Bailey R, Chin T. 1970. Hong Kong influenza: the epidemiologic features of a high school family study analyzed and compared with a similar study during the 1957 Asian influenza epidemic. *Am J Epidemiol* 92:240–247.

DHS (U.S. Department of Homeland Security). 2006. Implementation Plan for the National Strategy for Pandemic Influenza. May 2006. http://www.whitehouse.gov/homeland/nspi_implementation.pdf.

DHS (U.S. Department of Homeland Security). 2007. Pandemic Influenza Best Practices and Model Protocols. http://www.usfa.dhs.gov/downloads/pdf/PI_Best_Practices_Model.pdf.

Fauci A. 2006. Pandemic influenza threat and preparedness. *Emerg Infect Dis* 12: 73-77.

FDA (U.S. Food and Drug Administration). 2007a. Center for Biologics Evaluation and Research. Product Approval Information — Licensing Action. April 17, 2007. Message No. BL 125244/0.

FDA (U.S. Food and Drug Administration). 2007b. FDA Approves First U.S. Vaccine for Humans Against the Avian Influenza Virus H5N1. FDA News No. P07-68. April 17, 2007.

Fedson D. 2005. Preparing for pandemic vaccination: an international policy agenda for vaccine development. *J Public Health Pol* 6:4–29.

Ferguson N, Cummings D, Fraser C, Cajka J, Cooley P, Burke D. 2006. Strategies for mitigating an influenza pandemic. *Nature* 442(7101):448–452.

Germann T, Kadau K, Longini I, Macken C. 2006. Mitigation strategies for pandemic influenza in the United States. *Proc Natl Acad Sci USA* 103(15):5935–5940.

Glass R. 2006. Targeted social distancing design for pandemic influenza. *Emerg Infect Dis* 12:1671–1681.

Grigg E, Rosen J, Koop CE. 2006. The biological disaster challenge: Why we are least prepared for the most devastating threat and what we need to do about it. *J Emergency Manage* January/February:23–35.

Hatchett, R., C. Mecher and M. Lipsitch. 2007. Public health interventions and epidemic intensity during the 1918 influenza pandemic. PNAS. 104: 7582–7587.

Heymann A, Chodick G, Reichman B, Kokia E, Laufer J. 2004. Influence of school closure on the incidence of viral respiratory diseases among children and on health care utilization. *Pediat Infect Dis J* 23:675–677.

HHS (U.S. Department of Health and Human Services). 2004. Agency for Healthcare Research and Quality. Community-Based Mass Prophylaxis: A Planning Guide for Public Health Preparedness. http://www.ahrq.gov/research/cbmprophyl/cbmpro.htm.

HHS (U.S. Department of Health and Human Services). 2005. Agency for Healthcare Research. Altered Standards of Care in Mass Casualty Events. http://www.ahrq.gov/research/altstand/altstand.pdf.

HHS (U.S. Department of Health and Human Services). 2006. Pandemic Influenza Implementation Plan. http://www.pandemicflu.gov

HSC (U.S. Homeland Security Council). National Strategy for Pandemic Influenza Implementation Plan. 2006. Available from: http://www.whitehouse.gov/homeland/nspi_implementation.pdf.

Inglesby T, Nuzzo J, O'Toole T, Henderson DA. 2006. Disease mitigation measures in the control of pandemic influenza. *Emerg Infect Dis* 41:1–10.

Kahn L. 2007. Pandemic influenza school closure policies [letter]. *Emerg Infect Dis* 13:344.

Longini I, Halloran M, Nizam A, Yang Y. 2004. Containing pandemic influenza with antiviral agents. *Am J Epidemiol* 2004 159(7):623–633.

Longini I, Nizam A, Xu S, Ungchusak K, Hanshaoworakul W, Cummings D, et al. 2005. Containing pandemic influenza at the source. *Science* 309:1083–1087.

Meltzer M, Cox N, Fukuda K. 1999. The economic impact of pandemic influenza in the United States: priorities for intervention. *Emerg Infect Dis* 5(5):659–671.

NACCHO. 2006. National Association of County and City Health Officials. *Isolation and Quarantine: Issues to consider.* Washington. D.C.

Osterholm MT. 2005. Preparing for the next pandemic. *Foreign Affairs* 1 July 2005.

Parker G. 2007. Testimony before Committee on Homeland Security and Governmental Affairs, United States Senate. Tuesday, October 23, 2007. Accessed on 9 January 2008. http://www.hhs.gov/asl/testify/2007/11/t20071023e.html.

Patterson K. 1987. *Pandemic Influenza, 1700–1900; A Study in Historical Epidemiology.* New Jersey: Rowman & Littlefield.

Qureshi K, Gebbie K, Gebbie E. 2005. *Public Health Incident Command System: A Guide for the Management of Emergencies or Other Unusual Incidents within Public Health Agencies, Volume I.* October 25, 2005.

Toner E, Waldhorn R, Maldin B, Borio L, Nuzzo J, Lam C, et al. 2006. Hospital preparedness for pandemic influenza. *Biosecur Bioterror* 4:207–217.

Tussing A. 1996. The decline of hospitals and the rise of managed care organizations: medical care in the twenty-first century. *AHSR FHSR Annual Meeting Abstract Book* 13:135.

WHO (World Health Organization). 2005a. Responding to the Avian Influenza Pandemic Threat: Recommended Strategic Actions. Geneva, Switzerland. http://www.who.int/csr/resources/publications/influenza/WHO_CDS_CSR_GIP_05_8-EN.pdf.

WHO (World Health Organization). 2005b. WHO global influenza preparedness plan. The role of WHO and recommendations for national measures before and during pandemics. Geneva, Switzerland. http://www.who.int/csr/resources/publications/influenza/ who_cds_csr_gip_2005_5.pdf.

8 Service Continuation Planning for Businesses

Onalee Grady-Erickson, BS, CEM

American businesses are beginning to recognize that a pandemic flu outbreak would present a clear and present danger to their employees, their operations, and their bottom lines.

Tommy G. Thompson
Former Secretary of the U.S. Department of Health and Human Services

CONTENTS

8.1   INTRODUCTION

World leaders and government officials from the United States believe in having an overall effective plan in order for the continuation of national and governmental functions and activities to survive after any sort of catastrophic event. Naturally, the same holds true for the private sector. Businesses concerned about continuity planning for a pandemic can refer to *Federal Preparedness Circular 65, Federal Executive Branch Continuity of Operations* (FPC–65) and *Interim Guidance on Continuity of Operations Planning for State and Local Governments.* These guidelines will assist businesses in maintaining and recuperating in the event of a flu pandemic. Businesses should understand that although a flu pandemic could be tragic, there will be no direct physical affect to the infrastructure. There will be an impact on human capital, possibly removing personnel from the workplace for days, weeks, or even months (HSC [Homeland Security Council], 2005).

The federal government stated that 40 percent of staff within government entities and private sectors may be gone for about two weeks during the height of the pandemic. Employees may be out of work because they are sick, caring for sick family members or for children who are out of school, or they may be subject to public health or hospital containment measures. Private sector entities need to have a plan in order for continuity of business operations. This plan should "(1) identify and ensure continued performance of essential functions, and (2) provide for continued supply of products and services at as close to normal levels as possible" (HSC, 2005). The Centers for Disease Control and Prevention (CDC) and the U.S. Department of Health and Human Services (HHS) developed a business checklist (http://www. pandemicflu.gov), which recognizes specific actions that businesses can and should take in order to secure their business, employees, and customers.

8.2   CONTINUITY PLANNING FOR BUSINESS

The ability for a business to survive a pandemic will depend upon the preparedness measures undertaken from this day forward. The preparation of a strong all-hazard response plan includes dedication to exploring the planning, responding, mitigating, and recovery issues that will affect business. In the September 2007 *Journal of Infection Control,* a paper was published entitled "Pandemic influenza preparedness: A survey of businesses" (Smith et al., 2007). The authors surveyed Omaha businesses on pandemic preparedness and all-hazard preparedness. The survey found that a majority of businesses (63 percent) had started pandemic influenza preparedness planning, although 22 percent had not begun planning, and 15 percent were not certain. Additionally, 63 percent had a business continuity plan, although 4.2 percent were aware of the continuity plan having been exercised, and 46 percent felt that the plan would be effective. This chapter will not detail how to develop an all-hazard response plan. For information on the development of this type of plan, the Federal Emergency Management Agency (FEMA) has a detailed document for businesses on their Web site (http://www.fema.gov) entitled "Emergency Management Guide for Business and Industry: A Step-by-Step Approach to Emergency Planning, Response and Recovery for Companies of All Sizes."

What this chapter will delve into is the concept of service continuation. Pandemic planning presents unique differences from current continuity of operations templates. Instead of loss of physical structures, the nation will be faced with reduction of workforce and significant human health concerns in the workplace environment. Due to these particular circumstances, the State of Minnesota (2007) built upon the federal government's pandemic considerations and developed the concept of "service continuation." This chapter will describe this approach and provide guidance on the development of trigger points, planning assumptions, and human capital concerns, and how to prioritize day-to-day objectives and services.

Regardless of whether you are from a large corporation or a small, privately owned business, the concepts and principles presented in this chapter are relevant and scalable to any setting. However, if you are with an organization with diverse holdings and thousands of employees, the service continuation plan that you will develop will be significantly different than the plan developed by an organization with three employees. The major difference between the large corporate entity and a small business is that big business can delegate the planning responsibility to numerous individuals throughout the organization. In addition, they will have significantly more human capital resources than smaller organizations.

Owners of small businesses won't have the ability to delegate the planning responsibility completely throughout the organization, nor will they have the human capital to draw from. However, by developing the plan themselves and building the relationships that will be needed within their communities for additional human capital support, they will have more of an in-depth knowledge of the interdependencies of their service continuation plan with others.

In March 2007, the Trust for America's Health (TFAH, 2007) published a report entitled "Pandemic Flu and Potential for U.S. Economic Recession." The report based its outcomes on a severe pandemic outbreak per the Pandemic Severity Index (CDC, 2007). The report stated that about 90 million Americans will fall ill, and of those who suffer from the flu more than 2 million will die. When considering this estimate, please keep in mind that there are up to three pandemic infection waves and the pandemic may last up to a year. Not everyone will fall ill and/or die at once. The report stated that a severe pandemic could result in the second-worst recession in the United States since World War II, resulting in an estimated loss in revenue of $683 billion.

Most businesses do not have pandemic preparedness plans in place. Business plans need to cover issues including absenteeism policies for pandemic-related situations (such as closed schools, ill family); social distancing policies; remote work opportunities; reinforced workforce availability and trained flexibility for supply sources, production, and distribution; and a communications plan for pandemic response and to notify employees regarding applicable public health advisories.

Although CDC/HHS has released a Business Pandemic Influenza Planning Checklist to provide guidance to businesses in preparing for pandemic influenza, additional education is needed at the state and local level. State and local government is preparing to respond to the threat to the public's health while keeping the community's economy in mind.

There are no federal legal requirements for paid sick leave. Although companies are subject to the Family and Medical Leave Act (FMLA), which requires them to offer unpaid sick leave, most employees without a paid sick leave benefit do not have the financial security that would allow them to stay home from work when they are ill. This issue could be especially problematic in the event of pandemic flu. Over 15 million first-responder personnel, including health care and law enforcement workers, may be required to protect the public from and manage a pandemic outbreak in the United States. Other workers may be occupationally exposed prior to awareness of a pandemic outbreak, depending on their relationship to the infected individual.

Finally, workers who provide priority services will be needed to continue working throughout a pandemic. Priority services are dependent upon the need for certain services to continue nonstop for a pandemic and are not solely based upon categorization of employment. Priority services will be found in health care, laboratories, transportation, critical infrastructure, institutions such as prisons and group homes, child and elder care professionals, law enforcement, emergency management, and mortuary workers. The workers performing priority services with direct contact with individuals will face enormous risks and make great sacrifices on the public's behalf. Protecting them from occupational risks goes beyond a moral obligation; the U.S. public depends upon these workers. There is no program in place that would ensure that governmental resources address increased workplace expenses for pandemic preparedness and for providing exposure controls, mental health support, and assistance with family and outside commitments. There are no federal job or workers' compensation protections for ill workers, increasing the likelihood that individuals might continue to work while contagious. In addition, many health care workers tend to continue to come to work, especially in the very early phases of any illness. Although Occupational Safety and Health Administration (OSHA) OSHA has issued "Guidance for Protecting Workers against Avian Flu," which focuses primarily on H5N1 avian influenza, it lacks a standard specifically relevant to infection control during an influenza pandemic. Mandatory provisions for emergency response personnel are needed because of the urgency to protect workers and remove barriers to their participation in response efforts.

The National Strategy for Pandemic Influenza Implementation Plan does not provide adequate worker protection. The plan does not recommend respiratory protection at the level required in the OSHA Respiratory Protection Standard, including NIOSH-certified respirators provided with training and fit-testing. The plan instead recommends surgical masks, which are not actually intended to protect the wearer from a virus. This plan also does not recommend comprehensive infection control plans, as have been required for other agents. Further, the plan relies only on voluntary compliance.

When the pandemic occurs, the viability of our nation not only lies in the hands of the government, but in the hands of the communities in which we live and the business and nongovernmental agencies within those communities. A favorite saying that has been floating around these days in regard to preparedness is "YOYO," which means "you're on your own." Originally, it meant that we'll all be in the same situation — a catastrophic event affecting everyone — therefore, don't look to neighboring communities or the federal government to rescue you from the situation. More disturbing, it left one with the premonition that nobody is planning for anything and we're all doomed. The more appropriate acronym and way of looking at this is represented by "WITT," which means "we're in this together." Have no doubt; governmental agencies are planning for a pandemic. The key component to their plans is the formation of partnerships between businesses, nongovernmental groups, and community agencies. This response model — community based — is the key to survivability in a pandemic or any other type of disaster.

The Department of Homeland Security's National Response Framework (NRF) is one means that the government is using to get the nation better prepared for a pandemic. The NRF (in draft form as of December 2007) discusses the interplay between government, nongovernmental organizations and businesses (DHS, 2007). The Framework states "Government agencies are responsible for protecting the lives and properties of their citizens and promoting their well-being. However, the government does not, and cannot, work alone. In all facets of emergencies and disasters, the government works with private sector groups as partners in emergency management" (DHS, 2007).

Businesses have three main goals during times of disaster — any disaster. The first goal is the safety and security of employees, because without the people that run your business, you may only have four walls and not much of a livelihood. The second goal of the business should be to assist the community in any way possible during a disaster. Without community members spending money for goods and services, businesses are once again left with four walls and no livelihood. Last of the three goals for businesses is to preserve the economic viability of the business. Investors and owners: if there wasn't a return on an investment, how long could money continue to flow? Owners would declare bankruptcy and investors would pull out and yes, once again businesses have four walls, only now there is a CLOSED sign out front. Finding the balance between the aforementioned goals and keeping businesses afloat is precarious and ever changing in a disaster. Without thriving businesses, communities can't survive and without communities, businesses won't be able to survive either:

Much has been written on preparing businesses for a pandemic. Generally speaking, most of these documents center on continuity of operations plans (COOP). Per National Security Presidential Directive 51 — Homeland Security Presidential Directive 20, COOP is defined as "an effort within individual executive departments and agencies to ensure that primary mission-essential functions continue to be performed during a wide range of emergencies, including localized acts of nature, accidents, and technological or attack-related emergencies." In a memo to federal executive branch departments and agencies, dated March 1, 2006, Charles L. Hopkins III, Director, Office of National Security Coordination, FEMA, stated:

> It is the responsibility of FEMA and the Office of National Security Coordination to provide planning assumptions and guidelines to Federal departments and agencies for pandemic planning. While preparing these guidelines and developing and understanding of the potential impact of a pandemic, FEMA has concluded that planning for a pandemic requires a state of preparedness that is beyond traditional Federal Government COOP planning.

The memo also includes information on additional considerations to the eleven key COOP planning elements (Federal Preparedness Circular 65 *Federal Executive Branch Continuity of Operations* (COOP), which will need to be addressed in a pandemic influenza outbreak. The memo provides a table (see Table 8.1) and takes the 11 key COOP planning elements and guidance from the *National Strategy for Pandemic Influenza Implementation Plan* and brings to light additional continuity measures to help address pandemic influenza planning assumptions.

8.3 THE PLANNING CYCLE

Service continuation/continuity of operations includes all activities conducted by businesses to ensure that their priority service functions can be performed. This includes plans and procedures that detail priority service functions, specify succession to office and emergency delegation of authority, provide for the safekeeping of vital records and databases, identify alternate operating strategies, provide for interoperable communications, and validate such capabilities through drills, training, and exercises. COOP planning facilitates the performance of priority service functions during an emergency situation that disrupts normal operations and/or the timely resumption of normal operations once the emergency has ended. Figure 8.1 illustrates the planning cycle that should be used when developing any type of all-hazard service continuation/COOP plans. The process begins with Step 1 "Initiate the COOP Planning Process" and moves through the subsequent steps of the cycle. The process is a cycle and doesn't end with the completion of Step 5. COOP effectiveness relies upon habitually testing, revising, and updating plans.

8.3.1 PLANNING ASSUMPTIONS

When developing a pandemic service continuation plan, it is necessary to develop a list of assumptions regarding the type of incident that you are planning for. The assumptions that are developed establish the framework to begin the development of the plan The following are a list of general pandemic planning assumptions taken from the *Service Continuation Planning Guide for Businesses* compiled by the Minnesota Department of Public Safety, Division of Homeland Security and Emergency Management (HSEM, 2007):

- Each pandemic wave could last six to eight weeks. Several waves could occur over the course of a year.
- Up to 30 percent of the workforce could be out sick during a pandemic. Absenteeism could reach 40 percent during the peak of a pandemic. People may decide to stay home to care for ill family members or for children when schools are closed. Fear of exposure may lead to higher rates of absenteeism before an actual outbreak begins.
- Management flexibility will be necessary. Possible strategies might include establishing staggered shifts, expanding physical space between work stations, or allowing employees to work from home.
- Leave policies may need to be flexible.

TABLE 8.1
Key Elements from the Federal Preparedness Circular (FPC) 65 *Federal Executive Branch Continuity of Operations (COOP)*, Guidance from the *National Strategy for Pandemic Influenza Implementation Plan*, and Additional Continuity Measures to Help Address Pandemic Influenza Planning Assumptions

FPC-65 COOP Elements	National Strategy Implementation Guidance	Pandemic Influenza Continuity of Operations (COOP) Considerations
Plans and procedures	To reduce the impacts of a pandemic threat on an organization, a portion of the COOP plan's objectives should be to minimize the health, social, and economic impact on the U.S.	Plans must be capable of sustaining operations until normal business activity can be reconstituted, which may be longer than 30 days. D/As will continue operations indefinitely until the situation returns to normal. Review and update plans to ensure essential services can be provided if employee absenteeism reaches 40%. Different activation phases will be based on pandemic alert levels, proximity of outbreak to organization's offices/facilities, and reoccurring outbreaks. Appoint a senior manager and identify essential stakeholders as part of an Influenza Team that addresses issues related to pandemic influenza planning. Health focus will be needed to minimize the effects of a pandemic on staff and operations.
Essential functions	During a pandemic, or any other emergency, these essential functions must be continued to facilitate emergency management and overall national recovery. Particular attention must be given to Primary Mission Essential Functions of an organization.	Continue to perform essential functions beyond the existing 30-day requirement. Consider additional business services critical to meeting an organization's missions. Review the effect of a pandemic on essential contract and support services and organizational operations, and develop mitigation strategies.

(Continued)

TABLE 8.1 (CONTINUED)
Key Elements from the Federal Preparedness Circular (FPC) 65 *Federal Executive Branch Continuity of Operations (COOP)*, Guidance from the *National Strategy for Pandemic Influenza Implementation Plan*, and Additional Continuity Measures to Help Address Pandemic Influenza Planning Assumptions

FPC-65 COOP Elements	National Strategy Implementation Guidance	Pandemic Influenza Continuity of Operations (COOP) Considerations
Delegations of authority	Because absenteeism may reach a peak of 40% at the height of a pandemic wave, delegations of authority are critical.	Plan for delegations of authority that are at least three deep per responsibility to take into account the expected rate of absenteeism. Plan for geographical dispersion of delegations of authority, taking into account the regional nature of an outbreak.
Orders of succession	Because a pandemic influenza may affect regions of the U.S. differently in terms of timing, severity, and duration, organizations with geographically dispersed assets and personnel should consider dispersing their order of succession.	Plan for orders of successions that are at least three deep per position to take into account the expected rate of absenteeism. Plan for geographical dispersion of orders of succession, taking into account the regional nature and possibility of different orders of succession depending on the spread of the pandemic.
Alternate operating facilities	Because a pandemic presents essentially simultaneous risk everywhere, the use of alternate operating facilities must be considered in a non-traditional way. COOP planning for pandemic influenza will involve alternatives to staff relocation/co-location such as "social distancing" in the workplace through telecommuting or other means.	Determine which essential functions and services can be conducted from a remote location (e.g., home) and those that need to be performed at a designated department or agency facility. Consider the need for reliable logistical support, services, and infrastructure systems at facilities that remain open, to include alternate operating facilities: Prioritization/determination of accessible facilities/buildings (as alternative to relocating to remote facility) Necessary support staff Social distancing policies Public health guidance for operation of facilities and safety of employees

		Sanitation
		Essential services
		Food/water
		Consider impact of local quarantines on open/accessible facilities and operating plans.
Interoperable communications	Systems that facilitate communication in the absence of person-to-person contact can be used to minimize workplace risk for essential employees and can potentially be used to restrict workplace entry of people with influenza symptoms.	Planning should carefully consider the use of laptops, high-speed telecommunications links, PDAs, and other systems that enable employees to perform essential functions while teleworking. This includes the identification, availability, redundancy, and testing of critical communications systems that support connectivity to internal organizations, external partners, critical customers, and other key stakeholders. Test and exercise telework impact on internal networks.
Vital records and databases	Pandemic influenza COOP planning must identify and ensure the integrity of vital systems that require periodic maintenance or other direct physical intervention by employees.	Identify records needed to sustain operations for longer than 30 days since vital records at alternate facilities may not be accessible. Determine whether files can be accessed electronically from a remote location (e.g., an employee's home). Identify and plan for maintenance of vital systems that rely on periodic physical intervention/servicing.
Human capital	Each organization must develop, update, exercise, and be able to implement comprehensive plans to protect its workforce. Although an influenza pandemic will not directly affect the physical infrastructure of an organization, a pandemic will ultimately threaten all operations by its impact on an organization's human resources. The health threat to personnel is the primary threat to COOP during a pandemic.	Coordinate directly with the D/A's human resources office and the Office of Personnel Management as appropriate to determine the impact of pandemic influenza on workforce capabilities, including: Compensation policy for nonessential and essential employees; Sick leave policy; Fitness for duty policy; Family medical leave policy; Grievance policy; Telework policy; Family assistance programs. Coordinate modifications to human capital policies and plans with labor relations. Review terms and conditions of contract work to ensure contractor responsibility for essential functions (where relevant) and to suspend nonessential work.

(Continued)

TABLE 8.1 (CONTINUED)
Key Elements from the Federal Preparedness Circular (FPC) 65 *Federal Executive Branch Continuity of Operations (COOP)*, Guidance from the *National Strategy for Pandemic Influenza Implementation Plan*, and Additional Continuity Measures to Help Address Pandemic Influenza Planning Assumptions

FPC-65 COOP Elements	National Strategy Implementation Guidance	Pandemic Influenza Continuity of Operations (COOP) Considerations
Human capital (cont.)		In accordance with current guidance, evaluate need for hygiene supplies, medicines, and other medical necessities to promote the health and wellness of personnel.
		Develop and/or modify an employee accountability system.
		Promote guidance developed by public health and safety authorities, including:
		Occupational risk reduction strategies
		Infection control
		Personal hygiene
		Social distancing techniques
		Travel restrictions.
		Provide employees and families with relevant information and advisories about the pandemic, via:
		Hotlines
		Web sites
		Voice Messaging System
		Alerts
		Consider the need for cross-training to ensure essential staff is available to perform functions and services.

Test, training, and exercises	Pandemic influenza COOP plans should test, train, and exercise sustainable social distancing techniques that reduce person-to-person interactions within the workplace.	Testing, training, and exercising should include social distancing techniques, including telework capabilities and impacts of a reduced staff on facilities and essential functions and services.
Devolution of control and direction	Because local outbreaks will occur at different times, have variable durations, and may vary in their severity, devolution planning may need to consider rotating operations between regional field offices as the pandemic wave moves throughout the U.S.	Take into account how an organization will conduct essential functions and services if pandemic influenza renders leadership and essential staff incapable or unavailable to execute those functions. Full or partial devolution of essential functions and services may be necessary to ensure continuation. Develop detailed guidance for devolution, including: Essential functions and services; Rotating operations geographically as applicable; Supporting tasks; Points of contacts; Resources and phone numbers
Reconstitution	Because a pandemic will not harm the physical infrastructure or facilities of an organization, and because long-term contamination of facilities is not a concern, the primary challenge for organizations after a pandemic will be the return to normal and bringing their systems back to full capacity.	Develop plans for replacement of employees unable to return to work and prioritize hiring efforts. In conjunction with public health authorities, develop plans and procedures to ensure the facilities/buildings are safe for employees to return to normal operations.

Note: This table is useful for COOP-trained people, who are already using the FPC as a basis for their plans. This table provides a bullet pointed list of additional considerations that will need to be addressed in a pandemic.

Source: Taken from a March 1, 2006, memo written by Charles L. Hopkins III, Director, Office of National Security Coordination, FEMA. The memo provided guidance to federal executive branch departments and agencies on incorporating pandemic influenza considerations into COOP planning.

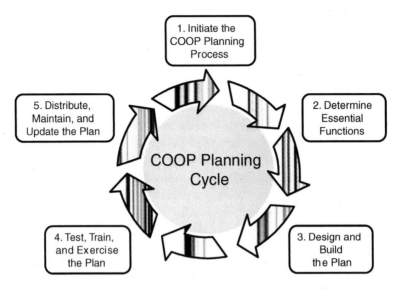

FIGURE 8.1 Graphic depiction of the Continuity of Operations Plans planning cycle, which involves 5 main components. (Taken from FEMA (Federal Emergency Management Agency). 2008. Guidance on Continuity of Operations Planning for State, Local, Tribal, Territorial, and Private Sector Organizations.)

- Employees may need personal protective equipment (PPE) to maintain priority service functions. Such an action requires implementation of PPE policies and procedures as well as ensuring the required training and fit testing is done.
- Availability of supplies will be limited because of stockpiling, limited production, and transportation limits.
- Administrative rule waivers and alternate service delivery systems may be necessary to maintain priority service functions. Businesses should develop policies for reduced service and product delivery.
- Assistance from outside organizations and county, state, and federal governments will be limited.

8.4 PRIORITIZATION OF SERVICES

A pandemic will impact the ability of businesses to provide products and services, while demand for some products and services will increase. Governmental and nongovernmental organizations must clearly communicate the level of service that businesses will be providing to the public to ensure that the public knows the operating environment of the businesses. Additionally if there are co-dependencies with other organizations that have been identified, each knows the prioritization of service is to each other.

The World Health Organization (WHO) has the Pandemic Alert Phases, the United States has the U.S. Stages, and additionally, each state may have developed its own response phases. It is up to businesses to do the leg work and find out what

TABLE 8.2

A Cross-Walk of the WHO's Pandemic Phases and the U.S. Pandemic Response Stages for COOP planners

WHO Phases	U.S. Stages
WHO Phase 1 Low Risk of Human Cases	**U.S. Stage 0** New Domestic Animal Outbreak in At-Risk Country
WHO Phase 2 Higher Risk of Human Cases	
WHO Phase 3 No or Very Limited Human-to-Human Transmission	**U.S. Stage 1** Suspected Human Outbreak Overseas
WHO Phase 4 Evidence of Increased Human-to-Human Transmission	**U.S. Stage 2** Confirmed Human Outbreak Overseas
WHO Phase 5 Evidence of Significant Human-to-Human Transmission	
WHO Phase 6 Efficient and Sustained Human-to-Human Transmission	**U.S. Stage 3** Widespread Human Outbreaks in Multiple Locations Overseas
	U.S. Stage 4 First Human Case in North America
	U.S. Stage 5 Spread Throughout the U.S.
	U.S. Stage 6 Recovery and Preparation for Subsequent Waves

trigger points have been developed in their states. Businesses must clearly identify the level of service they intend to provide throughout the response phases of their particular state. See Table 8.2 for a correlation between the WHO Pandemic Phases and the U.S. Response Stages.

When determining the priority service levels for businesses, the following factors are good examples of considerations:

- Economic and safety impacts of not providing service
- Health, welfare, and safety of employees and customers
- Ability to provide services during a pandemic
- Availability of alternate methods of delivering products and services

Each department within an organization needs to determine the priority service level for all services that department provides. Departments are not themselves classified as a single priority service level. Each separate departmental function needs to be vetted against the definitions of priority service levels being utilized by the business as a whole.

Priority Service Level One are core community-based services, or ones in which an immediate threat to employee and/or customer safety/welfare, or the economic well-being of the company and its shareholders, would result if not continually performed. These activities must remain uninterrupted or be performed every few hours to prevent an immediate negative impact. Here are some examples of Priority Service Level One functions:

- Computer room operations
- Security
- Facility maintenance
- Fraud detection and monitoring
- Information security
- 24-hour call center operations
- Credit card support
- Delivery service
- Employee and visitor screening
- Human resource helpline

Priority Service Level Two services are those that, if stopped or delayed, would cause a major negative impact to the company and its shareholders. Some services may be required by contractual obligations with vendors, employees, and/or customers, both external and internal. These are activities that can be disrupted temporarily or might be periodic in nature, but must be reestablished within 24 to 48 hours. Here are some examples of these key functions:

- Benefit payment to individuals
- Payroll processing
- Vendor payments
- Internal communications
- Workers' compensation
- Phone and internet communication services
- Distribution/shipping and receiving
- Public relations

Priority Service Level Three services are those that are required by contractual obligations with vendors, employees, and/or customers, both external and internal, that can be suspended or delayed, causing a minor negative impact to the company and its shareholders. These activities may be disrupted temporarily (a few days or weeks) but must be re-established some time before the pandemic wave is over (<6 weeks). Here are some examples of these activities:

- Collective bargaining with labor unions
- Filling job vacancies

- Project management
- Advertising
- Maintaining Web sites for information
- Investigation of complaints
- General maintenance programs
- Legal issues

Priority Service Level Four services are made up of all other services that could be suspended during an emergency and resumed as possible. Here are some of the activities that can be deferred for the entire duration of a pandemic influenza:

- Training marketing
- Construction/real estate
- Grounds keeping
- Education program
- Education program
- Research and development
- Pre-employment testing/drug testing

Refer to Figure 8.2 for a matrix that is designed to assist in the designation of priority service and prioritization into the four categories previously discussed.

8.5 DEVELOPMENT OF A PANDEMIC INFLUENZA COMMITTEE

Businesses should establish a Pandemic Influenza Committee and assign one individual to oversee the development of the service continuation plan. The Pandemic Influenza Committee should be comprised of key department heads (human resources, information technology, finance, etc.). Depending on the size of the business, these responsibilities are scalable in order to match the needs of the individual organization. The following is an outline of key responsibilities of the Pandemic Influenza Committee.

8.5.1 Establish an Overall Mission Statement

The Pandemic Influenza Committee will be tasked with developing an overall mission statement for the business. This mission statement will serve as the basis for the development of the priority service levels to be vetted against. If a service doesn't fit into the mission statement, it is not a valid prioritization of a service.

8.5.2 Develop Relationship/Contacts at the Local Governmental Level

Businesses should develop a relationship with their local government before any type of disaster occurs, including a pandemic influenza outbreak. By developing a relationship now and exploring mutual prioritization of services, both government and businesses will have a better understanding of the operating environment of each organization in times of disaster. As the saying goes, "It is better to exchange

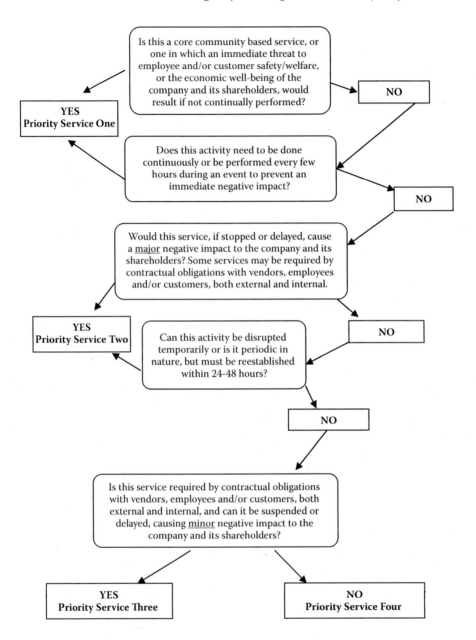

FIGURE 8.2 Pandemic Priority Service Continuation Determination Matrix, to help COOP planners decide what services must receive priority within their organizations should a pandemic event occur.

business cards now instead of during a response." Government will be able to provide businesses with trigger points for their response, the level of service they are going to be providing, potential nonpharmaceutical interventions (and when they will occur), as well as the possibility of integration into their notification system.

8.5.3 IDENTIFY PRIORITY SERVICE FUNCTIONS

The Pandemic Influenza Committee will request departments to work within their structure to prioritize their day-to-day services. Information on how to prioritize and examples of priority service functions have been provided in the previous section.

8.5.4 DEVELOP A PRIORITY SERVICE FUNCTION SKILL MATRIX

The Pandemic Influenza Committee will oversee the creation of skill matrix for priority service functions one and two. This task matrix will be cross-matched with individual employee qualifications and certifications. This matrix will facilitate the reallocation of workers within a department or to other departments as needs arise to maintain priority service one and two functions.

8.5.5 ENSURE PANDEMIC INFLUENZA PLANS ARE UPDATED AND EXERCISED

The Pandemic Influenza Committee will ensure that the creation of an overarching service continuation plan is developed for the business. The plans must define, in detail, the operations, actions, trigger points, services, and structure of the department in the event of an influenza pandemic event. The committee must also ensure that the developed plans are implemented; employees are informed as to their duties and exercised.

8.5.6 STRESS FAMILY AND PERSONAL PREPAREDNESS

It is likely there will be a high level of anxiety regarding a pandemic influenza outbreak among employees, which will contribute to increased absences and/or increased distress. Assisting employees ahead of time by promoting family preparedness is one way to alleviate some of the employees' stress. If employees feel that their families are taken care of, they are more apt to come to work. Refer to http://www.ready.gov for a downloadable document to assist families in personal preparedness efforts.

8.6 DEVELOPMENT OF A COMMUNICATIONS PLAN

The Pandemic Influenza Committee will also need to develop an all-hazard communications plan if one has not yet been developed. When developing the plan, include additional avenues to disseminate status information to employees, vendors, suppliers, and customers via hotlines and/or dedicated Web sites. The communications plan should include the following notifications.

8.6.1 INTERNAL NOTIFICATIONS

- Identification of key contacts (three deep) and chain of communications (including suppliers and customers).

- Accurate and prompt communication to departments and employees within the company regarding business status.
- Communicate the possibility of a pandemic — and your organization's preparedness to manage it — very early to staff.
- Discuss possible health and safety issues, prioritization of services, and human resource considerations.
- Upon activation of your business service continuation plan, provide clear, timely, and pro-active communications to employees, including how your organization is handling the situation.
- Utilize and disseminate local public health information regarding pandemic fundamentals (e.g., signs and symptoms of influenza, modes of transmission), hand hygiene, and coughing/sneezing etiquette.
- Identify and distribute community sources for timely and accurate pandemic information.

8.6.2 EXTERNAL NOTIFICATIONS

- Media relations and public statements associated with the current level of business service during an all-hazard event, including a pandemic.
- In the *National Strategy for Pandemic Influenza Implementation Plan*, Appendix A lists several aspects of communication planning for employers, schools, and universities:
  - Assess readiness to meet communications needs in preparation for an influenza pandemic, including review, testing, and updating of plans
  - Develop a dissemination plan for communication, including lead spokespeople and links to other communications networks
  - Ensure language, culture, and reading level appropriateness in communications by including community leaders representing different language and/or ethnic groups on the committee
  - Develop and test platforms (e.g., hotlines, telephone trees, dedicated Web sites, and local radio or television statements) for communicating pandemic status and actions
  - Develop and maintain up-to-date communications of key public health and education stakeholders and use the network to provide regular updates as the pandemic unfolds
  - Ensure the provision of redundant communication systems/channels that allow for the expedited transmission and receipt of information
  - Advise people where to find updated and reliable information from federal, state, and local public health sources
  - Disseminate information from public health sources covering routine infection control, pandemic influenza fundamentals, as well as personal and family protection and response strategies
  - Anticipate the potential fear and anxiety of the public as a result of rumors and misinformation and plan communication accordingly

8.7 HUMAN RESOURCE POLICIES TO BE IMPLEMENTED DURING A PANDEMIC

Many policies will need to be created or updated to account for human capital loss. Policy decisions will need to be made regarding:

- Vacation and sick leave policies
  - Employees themselves are ill
  - Employees need to look after family members who are ill
  - Employees need to stay home due to closure of schools and/or day care centers
- Additional policies
  - Employee compensation policy
  - Flexible worksite policy
  - Travel policy

8.7.1 ACTIVATION OF SERVICE CONTINUATION PLAN

The Pandemic Influenza Committee will need to establish a strategy for activating the businesses service continuation plan. The Pandemic Influenza Committee will also need to monitor absenteeism, geographic proximity of outbreaks, and the federal and state governments' current operational status to determine when to activate their individual plan.

8.7.2 REALLOCATION OF PERSONNEL

The Pandemic Influenza Committee will need to establish a single point of contact (possibly Human Resources) to develop procedures to reallocate available resources. Accomplish the reallocation of individuals via the task matrix and individual certification and training in order to accomplish priority service one and two functions.

If reallocation can't be done within the company due to licensure or certifications, coming up with a unique plan will be necessary. Contacting the local chamber of commerce or other local business groups can be done in an effort to pool resources during a pandemic. Such action could prove to be mutually beneficial to many aspects within the community.

8.7.3 DONATIONS OF HUMAN CAPITAL, GOODS, AND SERVICES

During an influenza pandemic or any other all-hazard event, it is not uncommon for businesses to want to offer up not only goods and services, but people to assist whenever possible. Per the National Response Framework:

> Incidents must be managed at the lowest possible jurisdictional level and supported by additional response capabilities when needed. It is not necessary that each level become overwhelmed, or fail, prior to surging resources from another level. Just the contrary, a tiered response will also be a forward-leaning response. Most incidents begin and end locally and are wholly managed at the community level.

During any type of all-hazard event, including an influenza pandemic, it is important for businesses that decide to offer up goods, services, or human capital to do so at the local level to the emergency operations center. If that jurisdiction is not accepting or doesn't need the donation, it will refer the donation to either the regional multiagency response group or the state emergency operation center.

8.8   CONCLUSION

The ultimate goal of any business, big or small, during a pandemic is to survive. Some business are moving from bricks to clicks (store shopping to Internet-based shopping); some business are looking into utilization of nonpharmaceutical interventions now (hand sanitizing wipes for the grocery carts, dots with a six-foot separation on the floor of the store for social distancing measures); and some are stockpiling antivirals (employee use) and N95 masks (employee and customer use).

Is one measure more right than the other? Does one measure say "I care about my employees"? Does another say "shop here because we care about making the customer feel safe"? Or is each measure a good measure and dependent upon the current situation and the time that it is used?

Service continuation or continuity of operations plan — the name isn't important. What is important is the time that a business puts in to develop the service continuation plan and the relationships that are developed during the process. Government, nongovernmental organizations, and private sector businesses are all part of a community. Cooperation among these organizations will sustain a community during a pandemic and the community will sustain the business and the individual.

REFERENCES

CDC (Centers for Disease Control and Prevention). February 2007. Mitigation Measures Interim Guidance (MMIG). Interim Pre-Pandemic Planning Guidance: Community Strategy for Pandemic Influenza Mitigation in the United States — Early, Targeted, Layered Use of Non-Pharmaceutical Interventions. http://www.pandemicflu.gov/plan/community/mitigation/html.
DHS (U.S. Department of Homeland Security). September 2007. National Response Framework. Family Emergency Plan. http://www.ready.gov/america/_downloads/family-emergencyplan.pdf.
FEMA (Federal Emergency Management Agency). 2007. Guidance on Continuity of Operations Planning for State, Local, Tribal, Territorial and Private Sector Organizations.
HSC (Homeland Security Council). 2005. National Strategy for Pandemic Influenza. http://www.whitehouse.gov/homeland/pandemic-influenza.html.
HSC (Homeland Security Council). 2006. National Strategy for Pandemic Influenza Implementation Plan. http://www.whitehouse.gov/homeland/nspi_implementation.pdf.
HSEM (Minnesota Department of Public Safety, Division of Homeland Security and Emergency Management). January 2007. Service Continuation Planning Guide for Businesses, version 1.0.
National Security Presidential Directive 51 and Homeland Security Presidential Directive 20. May 2007.
Smith PW, et al. September 2007. Pandemic influenza preparedness: A survey of businesses. *American Journal of Infection Control.* September 2007.
TFAH (Trust for America's Health). 2007. Pandemic Flu and Potential for U.S. Economic Recession.

9 Fatality Management during a Pandemic

Lori J. Hardin, MFS and John P. Ahrens, MPA

*Show me the manner in which a nation or a community cares for its dead,
and I will measure with mathematical exactness the tender sympathies of
its people, their respect for the laws of the land, and their loyalty to high ideals.*

William Gladstone
Prime Minister of England

CONTENTS

9.1   INTRODUCTION

Each year in the United States approximately 2.4 million people die from a variety of causes (Miniño et al., 2004). Estimates for the number of dead that will result from a severe pandemic vary widely. However, one such estimate from the Department of Health and Human Services (HHS) predicts that hundreds of thousands of deaths could result from a pandemic influenza outbreak (HSC, NSPI, 2005). This is in addition to the number of people that will die from all other causes. During an influenza pandemic, state and local authorities must be prepared to manage additional deaths over and above the number of fatalities from all causes currently expected during the interpandemic period. One of the best pieces of advice you can get to manage the increased number of deaths is to manage everyone's expectations for fatality management. In other words, what reasonably can be accomplished efficiently and respectfully to put to rest the tremendous number of dead that we will be faced with?

Within any locality, the total number of fatalities from the outbreak (including influenza and all other causes) occurring during a six- to eight-week pandemic wave is estimated to be equal to that which typically occurs over six months in the interpandemic period (Virginia Department of Health, 2006). Few communities are prepared to handle this increased number of deaths. The public and private agencies that manage fatality issues in communities today are already operating at maximum capacity.

Daryl Sensing, a training officer for a Disaster Mortuary Operational Response Team (DMORT), stated, "When you think of fatality management, you have to start thinking in terms of days, weeks, months, and years as your response time; not hours" (Sensing, 2004). As a testament to this statement, six years after the World Trade Center bombing on September 11, 2001, the New York City Office of the Chief Medical Examiner was still collecting, examining, and identifying human remains from the site and the landfill. In addition, two years after Hurricane Katrina, bodies were still being found and attempts to identify the remains were ongoing.

The greatest obstacle in pandemic influenza fatality management planning is a lack of knowledge on death management in the United States. People do not want to talk about it; they see it as a failure. In the words of the historian Philippe Ariès, when discussing the emergence of hospitals and subsequently funeral homes, "Death ... ceased to be accepted as a natural, necessary phenomenon. Death is a failure, a 'business lost.' This is the attitude of the doctor, who claims the control of death as his mission in life. But the doctor is a merely a spokesman for society. When death arrives, it is regarded as an accident, a sign of helplessness or clumsiness that must be put out of mind" (Ariès, 1991).

9.2 MYTHS SURROUNDING FATALITY MANAGEMENT

Myth 1: Persons who die from natural disease outbreaks will pose the threat of additional disease-causing epidemics (WHO, 2006).

Reality: According to the World Health Organization, "there is a minimal risk for infection from dead bodies." In a document published in 2002, the WHO established that "dead or decayed human bodies do not generally create a serious health hazard, unless they are polluting sources of drinking water with fecal matter, or are infected with plague or typhus, in which case they may be infested with the fleas or lice that spread these diseases" (WHO, 2006).

Myth 2: The fastest way to dispose of bodies and avoid the spread of disease is through mass graves or cremations. This can create a sense of relief among survivors (WHO, 2006).

Reality: The risk of disease from general handling of human remains is low and should not be used as a reason for mass graves. Mass graves do not allow individual family members to grieve and perform religious or final acts for their loved ones as individual, private ceremonies. Cremations may violate certain ethnic or religious practices, resulting in increased anguish and anger for the survivors (Morgan, Tidbal-Binz, van Alphen, 2006).

Myth 3: It is best to limit information to the public on the magnitude of the tragedy (WHO, 2006).

Reality: Restricting information to the public during a disaster creates distrust and a lack of confidence by the population in our government (Virginia Department of Health, 2006). Pandemic influenza public information releases should be informative about the death predictions and the death management plans. The public should be assured that they will have choices on the final disposition of their family members, but realistic time frames (mostly delays) will have to be discussed to give realistic expectations.

Myth 4: Pandemic influenza is likely to be a mass fatality event. Therefore, the Medical Examiner/Coroner (ME/C) is responsible for all the dead bodies.

Reality: Each state and U.S. territory has different laws on jurisdictional authority over dead bodies (who may pronounce death, who may or will be required to certify death, who directs the final disposition of the body, etc.). The ME/C may not have jurisdictional authority over naturally occurring disease deaths. Physicians licensed in a state are normally required to sign death certificates for the patients they treat who die of natural disease. Regardless of who has jurisdiction, assuming the dead body is positively identified through investigation, the most efficient natural disease fatality plan is to keep the remains available locally to the physicians, families, and the funeral service personnel who will manage the remains (Virginia Department of Health, 2006).

Myth 5: It is impossible to identify a large number of bodies after a tragedy.

Reality: With the advancements in forensic procedures such as fingerprinting and DNA technology, identification of human remains has become much more precise (WHO, 2006). Visual identification and comparison can and have been utilized in "normal" death cases; however, there are circumstances where scientifically based identification methods must be applied, such as fingerprints, dental, medical implants, etc. Law Enforcement Forensic, Medical Examiner/Coroner with their dental staffs can apply forensic studies on individual identification cases when needed.

Myth 6: Eliminating the requirements to complete and certify death certificates for disaster victims will speed up the response as well as the healing process for the victims' families.

Reality: A death certificate is a permanent legal document that records the fact of death. It is admissible in court as evidence when a question of death arises (CDC, 1994). In addition, registered death certificates are required to collect insurance, settle estates, award guardianship of minors and ownership of property, re-marriage as well as many other legal issues that will benefit survivors. Failure to document and certify an individual's death properly will cause severe hardships on the surviving family members.

Myth 7: The ME/C runs and operates the state funeral director's associations as well as the crematories and cemeteries.

Reality: Components of the funeral service industry, which includes funeral homes, funeral directors, embalmers, cemetery owners, crematories, casket companies, and embalming equipment and supply companies, are mostly privately owned and operated. Some governmental jurisdictions have cemeteries (e.g., the City Cemetery, commonly called Potters Field, operated by the Department of Corrections, in the Bronx, New York), but the jurisdiction must still follow existing state laws to operate the facility. This collective is generally very community oriented and interested in disaster planning, response, and coordination. Community planners should include their funeral service providers in their plans and ensure that the local public health offices provide the work-specific education and medications the funeral service workers need for a disease outbreak.

Myth 8: The ME/C or public health department specifies requirements for disposing of all human remains following a disaster.

Reality: State laws governing funeral director operations generally have an authority matrix associated with them. Generally, the "legal next-of-kin" enters into a contract with a funeral home and the contract shall govern the disposal of the body. There may be occasions when an ME/C will not allow cremation or burial at sea because the death was very unusual and the cause and manner of death could not be determined, or the next-of-kin has not been found, or the body is unidentified. In the examples given, when burial is mandated, there is a reasonable possibility that the body may be exhumed and relocated to the family's desired funeral home or re-examined later for cause and manner of death.

Some states have followed the example of the Model State Public Health Act (2003), a tool for assessing public health laws, and have passed laws to protect the fatality management workers by limiting the medico-legal death investigation's autopsy procedures, funeral providers, and/or final disposition options. In these circumstances, the bodies are considered to be highly contaminated or infectious due to the circumstances of death. In these cases, public health officers may have the authority to mandate the disposition of the bodies if there is a threat of the body harboring a contagious disease or contaminated materials.

An influenza pandemic will not result in highly contaminated remains (AFMIC, 2006). Those who have direct contact with remains will be at some risk to other infectious agents and should use standard mortuary precautions based upon the task they perform (e.g., collection and securing in body bag versus medico-legal autopsy).

Myth 9: During a known pandemic influenza (PI) event, all deaths can be assumed to be from the PI disease process and no medico-legal death investigations are necessary.

Reality: During a PI event, communities will experience cases where their citizens die from accidents, suicides, homicides, and sudden unexplained deaths not related to the PI event. Basic investigations into each death by community resources are necessary to differentiate between deaths from PI versus other activity (violence, suicide, etc.). Claiming the death of a family member will entitle some to become recipients of insurance benefits. Disaster brings out the best and worst in people. Unfortunately, some unscrupulous individuals may see the pandemic as an opportunity to hide someone's untimely death. Therefore, we must be vigilant for acts of homicide that may occur during a PI event.

Myth 10: All deaths occur in hospitals.

Reality: Vital records data show 55 percent of the deaths in Virginia are outside of medical treatment facilities (Virginia Department of Health, 2003). Local police, fire, and/or EMS (emergency medical services) are normally involved in each of these deaths to verify that death has actually occurred and to ensure the death is from a natural cause and not a result of suspicious or violent activity or, in other words, an ME/C's case. In a pandemic, only the sickest people will be admitted into hospitals until the space runs out. There is still a possibility that large numbers of deaths will be occurring outside of medical facilities.

Myth 11: HIPAA regulations prevent the Red Cross, medical staff, and institutions from releasing information to the public, police, funeral directors, and other governmental agencies even during disasters.

Reality: Under the exceptions portion of the HIPAA regulations, the following paragraphs are copied verbatim (Public Health Law 104-191, 1996):

a. Coroners and medical examiners. A covered entity may disclose protected health information to a coroner or medical examiner for the purpose of identifying a deceased person, determining a cause of death, or other duties as authorized by law. A covered entity that also performs the duties of a coroner or medical examiner may use protected health information for the purposes described in this paragraph (US 45 CFR §164.512 (g)(1)).

b. Funeral directors. A covered entity may disclose protected health information to funeral directors, consistent with applicable law, as necessary to carry out their duties with respect to the decedent. If necessary for funeral directors to carry out their duties, the covered entity may disclose the protected health information prior to, and in reasonable anticipation of, the individual's death (US 45 CFR §164.512 (g)(2)).

c. Following Hurricane Katrina, the CDC and the U.S. Public Health Service conceded that law enforcement officials may also receive patients' demographic data for the purposes of solving missing persons reports in a disaster (US 45 CFR §164.512 (f)(2)).

9.3 FACTS BEARING ON FATALITY MANAGEMENT

9.3.1 First Fact

Under normal conditions, the vast majority of the fatalities in the United States are not ME/C cases because these deaths occur under normal circumstances.

ME/Cs are charged by their individual state laws to investigate deaths that are due to violence, specifically accident, homicide, or suicide, or those due to natural disease processes when the death occurred suddenly and without warning or when the decedent was not being treated by a physician. In 2004, ME/C offices assumed jurisdiction over approximately 20 percent of the deaths in the United States (Hickman, Hughes, Strom, 2007). Approximately 80 percent of the deaths in the United States were managed by treating physicians.

Non-ME deaths are managed by medical facility staff, the local law enforcement (if death occurred out of medical treatment facilities), ME/Cs who may conduct preliminary investigations only to decline jurisdiction in accordance with their governing laws, EMS, treating physicians, hospitals, funeral directors, cemetery or cremation owners, and the individual families.

Natural disease outbreaks occurring under normal circumstances (e.g., not terrorist related) do not normally fall under the legal jurisdiction of ME/Cs. In these circumstances, the determination of cause and manner of death as well as the certification of death is expected (and sometimes legally required) to be completed by the decedent's treating physicians in accordance with state and local laws. For planning purposes, the fact that licensed physicians can manage the death determination and certification in their facilities or by coordinating with local law enforcement or other investigators at the scene, significantly increases the manpower staffing resources

- Representatives from the following:

Department of Finance	Local health care facilities
Department of Social Services	Local medical associations
Department of Public Works	Local religious and ethnic groups
Department of Environmental Quality	Local law enforcement
Department of Transportation	Local fire and EMS

During a pandemic, it is important that planners do not presume that all deaths are the result of the virus. Law enforcement usually conducts the initial investigation of death, and then contacts the ME/C. A complete investigation into the circumstances of death is always necessary, even during a pandemic event. Refer to Table 9.2 for some planning guidance for Mortuary Affairs Systems.

Also, planners must establish an Incident Command System (ICS) for the event. Refer to Figures 9.1 and 9.2 for a suggested ICS structure that is NIMS compliant and incorporates a Mortuary Affairs Branch under Operations. In a mass fatality incident, more direct communications with Incident Command, or more likely Unified Command will be necessary. This communication will be more effectively facilitated by placing Mortuary Affairs under the Operations Section.

9.6 DEATH MANAGEMENT PRACTICES AND POSSIBLE SURGE SOLUTIONS

In order to identify planning needs for the management of mass fatalities during a pandemic, it is important to examine each step in the management of human remains under normal circumstances and then to identify what the limiting factors will be when the number of dead increases over a short period of time.

9.6.1 DEATH REPORTING AND MISSING PERSONS

When individuals die in the community, 9-1-1 is normally the first number dialed. However, 9-1-1 centers will not be able to adequately handle the large number of calls that are inevitable in a PI event. During a PI event, families, friends, and neighbors will be calling government officials and hospitals for various reasons: to find their loved ones, request police to check on the welfare of family or neighbors, etc. Communities should establish separate numbers to complete these tasks with linkage to hospitals, shelters, ME/C and Vital Records offices to check on the status of individuals. Public information messages to call this center should be made frequently and in many venues so hospitals and 9-1-1 centers are not overwhelmed. This center should manage a database that is shared with ME/Cs, law enforcement missing persons units, and police/EMS dispatchers who can dispatch resources as needed. After the illness part of the event, this data will be required to identify deceased, insurance fraud, and other legal matters.

It is anticipated that most fatal influenza cases will seek medical services prior to death. However, whether or not people choose to seek medical services will partly depend on the lethality and the speed at which the pandemic strain kills. Under normal conditions, the majority of deaths (55.2 percent) occur in the place of residence, including nursing homes and other long-term care facilities (NORTHCOM, 2006a).

TABLE 9.2
Mortuary Affairs System Planning Guide

Steps	Requirements	Limiting Factors	Possible Solutions/Expediting Steps
Death reporting/ missing persons	If death occurs in the home/business/community, then a call in system needs to be established Citizens call local 9-1-1 to request a check on the welfare call for others 9-1-1 or other system needs to be identified as the lead to perform this task	Availability of people able to do this task, normally 9-1-1 operators Availability of communications equipment to receive and manage large volumes of calls/inquiries Availability of trained "investigators" to check into the circumstances of each report and to verify death is natural or other	Provide public education about the call centers, what information to have available when they call, and what to expect from authorities when a death or missing persons report is made Consider planning an on-call system 24 hours a day, 7 days a week specifically for this task to free up operators for 9-1-1 calls on the living Provide a system to have medical treatment facilities, ME/C, vital statistics, and law enforcement report and sort data for the call center staffs
Search for remains	If death occurs in the home/business, then law enforcement and possibly ME/C (if required) will need to be contacted Person legally authorized to perform this task	Law enforcement officers and ME/C availability	Consider deputizing and training (through the investigations units of law enforcement) of people whose sole responsibility is to search for the dead and report their findings Consider having community attorneys involved in the legal issues training for the groups identified (e.g., breaking into locked homes/businesses, etc.)
Recovering remains	Personnel trained in recovery operations and the documentation required to be collected at the "scene" Personal protection equipment such as coveralls, gloves, and surgical masks Equipment such as stretchers and human remains pouches	Availability of trained people to perform this task Availability of transportation assets Availability of interim storage facility	Consider training volunteers ahead of time Consider refrigerated warehouses or other cold storage as an interim facility until remains can be transferred to the family's funeral service provider for final disposition

Death certified	Person legally authorized to perform this task If a death due to a natural disease and decedent has a physician, physician notified of death If trauma, poisoning, homicide, suicide, etc., ME/C case with police investigation Ability to identify the deceased based upon sound investigative techniques	The lack of availability or willingness of primary treating physicians to certify deaths for their patients The lack of willingness to pay for a certification of death as imposed by some physicians The lack of ME/C staff and limited police resources	When possible, arrange for "batch" processing of death certificates for medical facilities and treating physicians Consider investing in electronic death certificate software and distributing to the entire MAS community that manages the certification process Induce fines for those treating physicians or medical institutions that refuse to sign for their patients or charge a family (funeral home) for such services Conduct training on human remain identification procedures to MAS personnel Establish policy to collect at least a thumb print and a buccal swab (or other DNA sample) from each decedent that will be maintained in a case file in the event identity becomes an issue in the future
Decedent transportation to the morgue	In hospital: trained staff and stretcher Outside hospital: informed person(s), stretcher and vehicle suitable for this purpose	Availability of human and physical resources Existing workload of local funeral directors and transport staff Possible requirement for transportation services to be registered with a state agency	In hospital: consider training additional staff working within the facility Consider keeping old stretchers in storage instead of discarding
Transportation	To cold storage, Mortuary Affairs holding location and/or burial site From hospitals to morgue, funeral home, or other location Suitable covered, refrigerated vehicle and driver	Availability of human and physical resources Existing workload of local funeral directors and transport staff Possible requirement to have a transport certificate to transport dead bodies over the roadway (this is state-specific)	Identify alternative vehicles that could be used for this purpose Identify ways to remove or completely cover (with a cover that won't come off) company markings of vehicles used for MA operations Consider use of volunteer drivers Consider setting up a pickup and delivery service for all the hospitals with set times, operating 24 hours a day, 7 days a week Consider finding resources to assist funeral homes in transporting remains so they can concentrate on remains preparations for the families

(Continued)

TABLE 9.2 (CONTINUED)
Mortuary Affairs System Planning Guide

Steps	Requirements	Limiting Factors	Possible Solutions/Expediting Steps
Cold storage	Suitable facility that can be maintained ideally at 34 to 37°F	Availability of facilities and demand for like resources from multiple localities Capacity of such facilities Inability to utilize food storage or preparation facilities after the event	Identify and plan for possible temporary cold storage sites and/or equipment close to where the body originated for the convenience of identification, family, and funeral home[a]
Autopsy if required or requested	Person qualified to perform autopsy and suitable facility with equipment	Availability of human and physical resources May be required in some circumstances	Ensure that physicians and families are aware that an autopsy is not required for confirmation of influenza as cause of death when the outbreak is identified Review state laws as to who may authorize autopsies as usually restrictions do apply
Funeral service	Appropriate location(s), casket (if not cremated) Funeral director availability Clergy availability Cultural leaders availability	Availability of caskets Availability of crematories Availability of locations for service and visitation	Contact suppliers to determine lead time for casket manufacturing and discuss possibilities for rotating 6-month inventory Consult with the local funeral director associations to determine surge capacity and possibly the need for additional sites (use of religious facilities, cultural centers, etc.)
Body preparation	Person(s) trained and licensed to perform this task	Supply of human and material resources, embalming fluids, powders, etc. Supply of human remains pouches If death occurs in the home: the availability of these requirements	Consider developing a rotating 6-month inventory of body bags and other supplies, given their shelf life Consider training or expanding the role of current staff to include this task Provide public education on the funeral service choices during a pandemic Amend regulations to eliminate restrictions on transporting remains that have not been embalmed

Cremation	Suitable vehicle of transportation from morgue to crematorium Availability of cremation service A cremation certificate issued by the ME/C or other authorized agent in accordance with state law	Capacity of crematorium and speed of process Availability of local medical examiner/coroner to issue cremation certificate	Identify alternate vehicles to be used for mass transport Examine capacity of crematoriums within the jurisdiction Discuss and plan for appropriate storage options if the crematoriums are backlogged Discuss and plan expedited cremation certificate completion processes Provide human resources to assist crematory owners Allow crematory operators to operate 24 hours a day, 7 days a week if there are local restrictions in place
Embalming	Suitable vehicle for transportation from morgue Trained person to perform Embalming Equipment and supplies Suitable location	Availability of human and physical resources Capacity of facility and speed of process	Consult with service provider regarding the availability of supplies and potential need to stockpile or develop a rotating 6-month inventory of essential equipment/supplies Discuss capacity and potential alternate sources of human resources to perform this task, such as retired workers or students in training programs Consider "recruiting" workers who would be willing to provide this service in an emergency
Temporary storage	Access to and space in a temporary vault Use of refrigerated warehouses, or other cold storage facilities	Temporary vault capacity and accessibility	Expand capacity by increasing temporary vault sites
Burial	Grave digger and equipment Space at cemetery	Availability of grave diggers and cemetery space	Identify sources of supplementary workers Identify sources of equipment such as backhoes and coffin lowering machinery Identify alternate sites for cemeteries or ways to expand cemeteries

(Continued)

TABLE 9.2 (CONTINUED)
Mortuary Affairs System Planning Guide

Steps	Requirements	Limiting Factors	Possible Solutions/Expediting Steps
Temporary interment (if authorized by the governor)	Person to authorize temporary interment Location for temporary interment Grave diggers and equipment	Availability of grave diggers and temporary interment space Availability of funeral directors, clergy, and cultural leaders for guidance and community acceptance Specific criteria as to when authorization may occur and procedures to follow prior to the interment Availability of resources after the event to disinter and to place remains into family plots	Identify locations that will be suitable for temporary interment space Consider using the global positioning system for individual remains location
Behavioral health	Prepare public and responders for mass fatality possibilities prior to pandemic Assist responders and other MA workers during pandemic and in post-pandemic periods	The pandemic will virtually affect the entire nation; a shortage of mental health people will complicate the ability to assist people Many people will be doing MA tasks that they are mentally unprepared for and will require assistance	Train first responders and some Citizen Corps people in crisis intervention techniques to assist MA teams during the pandemic Set up clinics to assist the public separate from the MA workers and first responders
Event and community recovery	Persons to authorize re-interment Grave digger and equipment Clergy and cultural leaders	Availability of funeral directors, clergy, and cultural leaders for guidance Existing code requirements to have a court order for the disinterment of human remains	Consider that the public may want to erect a monument at the temporary interment site(s) after the pandemic is over

aFor areas that have a forestry re-seeding capability, check to see if there are cold storage seedling buildings available to store remains. Get trucks for the seedlings because you can clean those and put them back into service for food and other items. Refrigerated trucks used for bodies may never be utilized for food again. A community may have to buy the trucks.

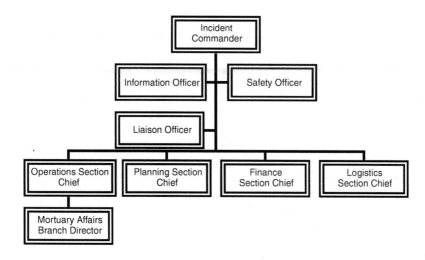

FIGURE 9.1 Incident command structure with fatality management included.

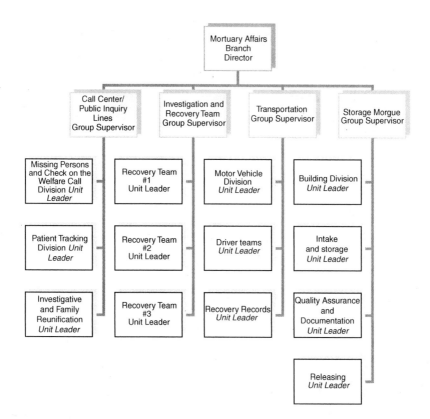

FIGURE 9.2 Suggested mortuary affairs branch structure in a natural disease event within the incident command system.

Hospitals, nursing homes, and other institutions (including nontraditional sites) must plan for more-rapid processing of human remains. These institutions should work with local pandemic planners to gain access to the additional supplies (e.g., human remains pouches) and to expedite the steps necessary for efficient human remains management during a pandemic, including the completion of required documents.

9.6.2 SEARCH AND RECOVERY OF REMAINS

During the event, as more and more calls come in, more human resources will be needed. Normally EMS and law enforcement are dispatched to locations first. If a dead body is found, the law enforcement and/or ME/C conduct the medico-legal death investigation. If the body is identified at the scene, death is reasonably expected, a natural manner of death, and there is a treating physician, the body is released to the family's funeral home and the doctor will sign the death certificate. Otherwise, the ME/C assumes jurisdiction and completes the death certificate.

Few things in our democracy are as important as ensuring that citizens have confidence in their institutions in a crisis. For many individuals the death of a loved one is just such a crisis. Ensuring that the proper steps and procedures are taken at the scene of that death to reassure family members that the death was a natural one, a suicide, or a homicide is a key element in maintaining citizen confidence in local officials. (Jeanne M. Adkins, Colorado State Legislature Representative, quoted in NIJ, 1999.)

In preparation for a pandemic event, communities should consider identifying additional groups of individuals to train and coordinate with the lead search and recovery groups. Retired police, ME/C, and funeral directors could lead teams of other qualified volunteers to assist in this effort and ensure all of the data required for tracking the remains and completing death certificate is compiled.

Detailed case files should be maintained for every human remain during a pandemic, regardless of the cause of death, the location of death, and the signing physician. With an increased number of dead bodies to be managed, the possibility of mistakes and liability for misidentification, loss of personal property, loss of a body, physicians refusing to sign death certificates, and funeral home mix-ups is only increased. Detailed records can eliminate nearly all human mistakes.

9.6.3 PRONOUNCEMENT OF DEATH

State laws dictate who is legally authorized to pronounce death. Community planners should review existing laws and identify current resources to determine if expanded capabilities are required. For example, if state laws mandate that coroners must pronounce deaths out of medical facilities, it may be helpful to expand this capability to EMS and law enforcement or other individuals who have specific recognition of death training, provided the deaths are still reported to the coroner.

The date, time, and place of death (including name and address of institution), and the name and contact information of the individual who pronounced death should be recorded in the case file. This information is required to be documented on the state death certificate (CDC, 1994).

9.6.4 DECEDENT IDENTIFICATION REQUIREMENTS

Identification parameters will have to be established. State and/or county laws will normally identify who is responsible for the identification of the dead and the notification of the death to the next-of-kin. Normally law enforcement, ME/Cs, and/or hospitals perform this function. In some cases, it will be impossible to utilize conventional means to identify the dead because of the lack of identification on the body or reliable witnesses, decomposition, or mitigating circumstances. Local police departments should attempt to find fingerprint files on the unidentified persons in their database. Many ME/C offices do not normally have access to this database (Gursky et al., 2007) and if unsuccessful, they can request identification support from law enforcement agencies. In some cases, known personal items (e.g., a razor, a toothbrush, etc.) of the missing person or presumed deceased can be used to compare prints and/or DNA profiles for identification.

Localities will normally be asked to assist in the antemortem data collections including the sharing of missing persons reports, patient tracking information, and the retrieval of medical and dental records during the identification process conducted by ME/Cs.

Foreign, undocumented nationals and homeless individuals will require much greater effort. The ME/Cs may have to develop a method of separating those that will pose significant identification problems requiring a longer time to identify. These remains may have to be put into temporary storage or be temporarily interred awaiting identification at a later date. The fact that some remains will never be identified must be planned for.

Even in those cases where the identification of remains is reasonably certain, it is recommended that some form of personal identifier should be collected and maintained in a record following death. A simple fingerprint or a buccal swab dried and filed could be completed by trained funeral homes and filed with the Public Health Vital Records offices or elsewhere. Complete physical characteristics as well as DNA collections should be taken for files to be compared with missing person data at a later date if required. The expectation here is that the samples are available if needed. It would be unreasonable and much too costly to process all samples taken for all decedents.

The following identifying information should be collected for the case files: full legal name, sex, date of birth, age, and social security number or other government issued identification number, if available.

9.7 GENERAL DEATH SURVEILLANCE FOR DISEASE OUTBREAK

To determine if avian influenza agent has arrived in the locality, it is recommended that the ME/C take jurisdiction in a limited number of cases to establish the index case in the following situations (Virginia Department of Health, 2006):

- A death that meets criteria for an emerging infection and needs to be confirmed by culture of blood and tissues. This includes the first "native" cases of pandemic flu.
- Illness and death in a poultry worker where illness is suspected as flu to confirm flu has been contracted from poultry.
- Any flu-like illness resulting in the death of a family member/companion of a poultry worker to prove human to human transmission. The worker should also be tested if not done so previously.
- A death of a traveler from elsewhere suspicious for flu or a citizen from the locality who has traveled elsewhere and has been at risk (e.g., China).
- The first diagnosed case in a hospital that needs documentation of virus in tissue.

The ME/C should assume jurisdiction over all of the deaths described in the specific scenarios above based upon the code in their operational area. Additionally, as a pandemic develops and becomes established within the community, the ME/C will normally take jurisdiction over the following deaths:

- Cases in which there is no attending physician (e.g., the decedent had no physician or medical treatment facility that treated the decedent or the decedent's physician is licensed out of state).
- The identity of the decedent is unknown and the normal investigative procedures completed by hospital, social services, police or law enforcement agencies, including fingerprinting, have not positively identified the deceased.
- The death is sudden and unexplained (e.g., does not meet the normal flu case definition).
- Death of an inmate or person in correctional custody.
- Assisting the interest of the public health department, when an individual who was sequestered into a private residence or public facility through the isolation or quarantine procedures and dies outside of a medical treatment facility. (This does not apply if an entire community is impacted by the public health order.)
- Normal ME/C cases as defined by state/local code.

9.7.1 Death Certification

Certification of the cause of death is a legal issue. State laws dictate who may certify a death and each state is different. The medical officer or the medico-legal authority is responsible for certifying the medical part of the death certificate (CDC, 1994). When death is a result of natural disease, primary physicians or other doctors who have access to the medical record of the deceased are normally authorized to sign the death certificate. "The medical certification includes information on the cause and manner of death and related factors, such as place of death and the date and time of the legal pronouncement" (CDC, 1994).

Consideration for handling remains other than death due to pandemic influenza must be taken into account. There will still be other diseases, traffic accidents, suicides, homicides, and natural-cause deaths (CDC, 1994). There will be individuals who have underlying diseases or are frail prior to an influenza exposure. The influenza may have brought on the death of a person who was ill due to another disease or injury. There may be an increase in suicides and euthanasia by family members as well as elder abuse and child abuse cases during the event.

After responders confirm who is certifying the death, the name and contact information of the certifying medical official should be recorded in the case file. Careful records should be kept here because the certificate of death will normally be completed at a later time and the funeral director will have to find the physician or ME/C to complete the medical portion of the legal document.

Funeral directors generally have standing administrative policies that prohibit them from collecting a body from the community or an institution until there is a completed certificate of death. In the event of a pandemic with many bodies, it seems likely that funeral directors could develop a more-flexible practice if directed to do so by a central authority such as the Funeral Directors' Association, the Attorney General's Office, or possibly the Registrar of Vital Statistics. These special arrangements must be planned in advance of the pandemic and should include consideration of the regional differences in resources, geography, and population. The Board of Medicine in the states should support this effort by educating their members of the responsibility to complete the death certificate for their patients and forcing compliance with the state codes.

In hospitals or other medical institutions, a position should be established whose sole responsibility is to complete the certification of death of those patients who die there. Having a completed death certificate available at the time funeral directors pick up remains will put the directors at ease. There will not be time in a pandemic to track down doctors to complete their required tasks of death certification.

9.7.2 Transportation of Bodies

Once it has been determined that the death is natural and a physician or ME/C has determined who will certify the death, transportation of the remains from the place of death to an appropriate facility will be required. Normally, if the death is natural and the ME/C is not assuming jurisdiction over the remains, the family will choose a funeral home and the body will be transported by that funeral home or their agent to the funeral home preparation facility.

During a pandemic, the death rate may overwhelm the funeral director's transportation resources. To further complicate this shortfall, most ME/C offices in this country rely upon the same funeral director resources to transport their cases to their autopsy suites or storage facilities. Community planners should plan for supplementing the funeral directors and human remain transporters for a wide-scale event.

Some states regulate who may transport human remains and require specific licenses to do so. Ambulances should be used to care for the living and remain in that status.

Based upon what is known from influenza virus in general, it is presumed human remains can be transported and stored (refrigerated) in impermeable bags (double-bagging is preferable), after wiping visible soiling on outer bag surfaces with 0.5 percent hypochlorite solution (AFMIC, 2006).

9.7.3 COLD STORAGE

Additional temporary cold-storage facilities may be required during a pandemic for the storage of remains prior to their transfer to funeral homes. Cold-storage facilities require temperature and biohazard control, adequate water, lighting, rest facilities for staff, and office areas, and should be in communication with patient tracking sites and the emergency operations center. A cold-storage facility should maintain temperatures between 34 to 37°F. Decomposition of remains slows when a body is cooled at this temperature range and can normally be stored for up to six months (NORTHCOM, 2006d).

Communities could work together on a regional basis as there will be high demand for cold-storage facilities and few resources. Each jurisdiction should make pre-arrangements for cold-storage facilities based on local availability and require-ments. The resource needs (e.g., human remains pouches) and supply management for cold-storage facilities should also be addressed. The types of temporary cold storage to be considered may include refrigerated trucks, cold-storage lockers, or refrigerated warehouses. Refrigerated trucks can generally hold 25 to 30 bodies without additional shelving.

To increase storage capacity, temporary wooden shelves can be constructed of sufficient strength to hold the bodies. Shelves should be constructed in a way that allows for safe movement and removal of bodies (i.e., storage of bodies above waist height is not recommended) but may be required (ensure enough staffing is available to avoid injuries). These shelves will be contaminated with biological material and will require special handling after the event.

To reduce any liability for business losses, using trucks with markings of a supermarket chain or other companies should be avoided, as the use of such trucks for the storage of corpses may result in negative implications for business. If trucks with markings are used, the markings should be painted or covered over to avoid negative publicity for the business. It should be noted that refrigerated trucks used for corpses are usually not permitted to be utilized for any food transportation afterward.

Using local businesses for the storage of human remains is not recommended without considering the total cost implications (loss of business, rental costs, and if a food company the rebuilding of their facilities). The post-pandemic implications of storing human remains at these sites can be very serious and may result in negative impacts on business with ensuing liabilities.

When considering ice rinks, have a refrigeration engineer help in the planning. The ice cooler will do exactly as it was designed to do. If you place warm bodies on the ice, it will melt and the water will be a biohazard. The coolers will turn on due to the melting and freeze the water and the remains into ice. With the assistance of refrigeration experts, this scenario could be avoided.

There should be no media, families, friends, or other onlookers permitted on the temporary storage site. Families should make arrangements with their funeral homes to conduct viewings of the remains at the funeral home or medical facility of death, prior to removal, at the grave site, or at the crematory. If responders can take a facial photograph, when appropriate for viewing, and keep the photo in the case files, the photo could be utilized to meet families' needs of viewing or viewing for identification purposes. Utilizing black and white photography is sometimes preferred to lessen the impact on the family.

Complete and detailed records on who is stored in each cooler will need to be maintained for the community leadership.

9.7.4 Autopsy

Most deaths in an influenza pandemic would not require autopsies since autopsies are not indicated for the confirmation of influenza as the cause of death. However, for the purpose of public health surveillance (e.g., confirmation of the first cases at the start of the pandemic), respiratory tract specimens or lung tissue for culture or direct antigen testing could be collected postmortem. Pathologists should contact their local or regional public health consolidated laboratory network prior to the examination to get the most-recent testing requirements and packaging standards for influenza testing. Permission will be required from the next-of-kin if a private or public hospital performs this function. The ME/C offices do not require permission from the next-of-kin if the case meets the criteria as a ME/C case under state or local laws.

9.7.4.1 Autopsy Risks

Biosafety is critical for autopsy personnel who might handle human remains contaminated with a pandemic influenza virus. Infections can be transmitted at autopsies by percutaneous inoculation (i.e., injury), splashes to unprotected mucosa, and inhalation of infectious aerosols. Since no one knows what exact strain of influenza will cause a pandemic, the highest level of precautions, like those used by the laboratory workers, should be used during the autopsy.

All autopsy facilities should have written biosafety policies and procedures; autopsy personnel should receive training in these policies and procedures, and the annual occurrence of training should be documented (Nolte et al., 2004).

9.7.4.2 Waste Handling

Liquid waste (e.g., body fluids) can be flushed or washed down ordinary sanitary drains without special procedures. Pretreatment of liquid waste is not required and might damage sewage treatment systems. If substantial volumes are expected, the local wastewater treatment personnel should be consulted in advance. Solid waste should be appropriately contained in biohazard or sharps containers and incinerated in a medical waste incinerator (AFMIC, 2006).

9.7.5 Death Registration

Death registration is a process governed by its own set of laws, regulations, and administrative practices. Moreover, there is a legal distinction between the practices of pronouncing, certifying, and registering a death. Death registration is normally done by the funeral directors. Funeral directors normally receive the death certificate from the certifying official with the cause and manner of death completed. A space for the presumed name of the deceased is completed by the certifying official. The funeral directors will normally sit with a family member and collect demographic data, including the deceased's full legal name, date of birth, etc. (CDC, 1994). After the funeral director receives all of the required information from the family, he/she will file the death certificate with the Vital Records office. In many states, the death certificate must be filed with the Vital Records office in the county of death. In a pandemic, states could work with the Vital Statistics offices and allow for either electronic filing of death certificates or filing of paper death certificates in any state Vital Records office.

9.7.6 FUNERAL HOMES, CEMETERIES, AND CREMATORIA

In an influenza pandemic, each individual funeral home could expect to handle about six months of work within a six- to eight-week period (Virginia Department of Health, 2006). That may not be a problem in some communities, but funeral homes in larger cities may not be able to manage the increased demand. Individual funeral homes should be encouraged to make specific plans during the interpandemic period regarding the need for additional human resources during a pandemic situation. For example, volunteers from local service clubs or churches or even contractors with heavy equipment may be able to take on tasks, such as digging graves, under the direction of current staff. In addition, many localities have received grant funding for citizen response groups such as CERT teams or auxiliary police teams that could provide assistance with training.

Localities should conduct a gap analysis that includes the private mortuary sector and determine if their funded volunteer groups could fill gaps identified in the funeral service industry. Crematoriums will also need to look at the surge capacity within their facilities. Most crematoriums can handle about one body every four hours and could probably run 24 hours to manage the increased demand (NORTH-COM, 2006b); however, licensing and local operating restrictions on crematories may have to be lifted.

9.7.7 EMBALMING

If the legal next-of-kin is not going to have the remains cremated, and authorizes embalming, plans to expedite the embalming process should be developed since, in the case of a pandemic, bodies may have to be stored for an extended period of time. In counties where a timely burial is not possible due to frozen ground or lack of facilities, corpses may need to be stored for the duration of the pandemic wave (NORTHCOM, 2006b).

Local emergency management agencies, funeral directors, and the state and local health departments should work together to determine in advance the local capacity (bodies per day) of existing crematoriums and soil and water table characteristics that might affect interment. For planning purposes, a thorough cremation produces approximately three to six pounds of ash and fragments and takes approximately four hours to complete (NORTHCOM, 2006b).

FIGURE 9.3 Traditional funerals, such as this one in 1910, typically included many friends and relatives of the deceased. During the pandemic, fears that mourners could spread influenza led many communities to ban public funerals. It is doubtful that such a practice would be adopted today. (Image courtesy of the Office of the Public Health Service Historian, Department of Health and Human Services.)

9.7.8 FUNERAL PRECAUTIONS

Visitations could be a concern in terms of influenza transmission among funeral attendees. It is the responsibility of Public Health to place restrictions on the type and size of public gatherings if this seems necessary to reduce the spread of disease. This may apply to funerals and religious services. The Public Health Department should plan in advance for how such restrictions would be enacted and enforced, and for consistency and equitability of the application of any bans. The Consensus paper (Gursky et al., 2007) recommends immediate family members at grave site or the new concept being seen, the virtual funeral service a Web-based program for the memorial services. During the 1918 Spanish flu some people believed that mourners could spread influenza, which led many communities to ban public funerals (see Figure 9.3). It is doubtful that such a practice could be adopted today.

Family members should take some precautions when viewing their loved ones. The following recommendations may reduce the potential risk of virus transmission from a decedent to a living individual (AFMIC, 2006):

- Family members may view the human remains. If an individual died while infectious, family members should wear gloves and gowns, and perform hand hygiene.

- Before touching the human remains, the area should be disinfected (e.g., 70 percent alcohol).
- Special attention should be given to funerals, where mourners of the decedent, potentially having acquired the disease from the decedent or in the community, are now congregating, potentially allowing for transmission of pandemic influenza.
- Alcohol-based sanitizers and tissues should be made available.
- Funeral homes should consider environmental cleaning.
- Other strategies should be considered during the funeral process (e.g., videoconferences).

9.7.9   TEMPORARY INTERNMENT

If the death rate from the pandemic is far beyond the capabilities of the community and surge capacities cannot be met, political leaders and responders may opt to store human remains in the ground temporarily. This procedure is known as temporary interment and is meant to be a temporary option. The bodies are normally placed in double body bags and buried in a known secure plot of land.

The bodies stored in the temporary graves are done so in a manner where each individual tagged body can be located with global positioning systems (GPS) and disinterred for movement into a family plot as time permits. The Department of Defense has very detailed requirements for establishing temporary interment sites (Joint Publication 4-06, 1996), which could be utilized by community planners if the ground is not frozen.

The decision to conduct temporary storage will have to be a political decision. If this is done in a community, the exact GPS location of the deceased will be required to be placed into the case file.

9.7.10   PROPHYLAXIS FOR MORTUARY WORKERS

If first responders and health care providers are receiving prophylaxis (antiviral drugs or vaccination) during a pandemic, mortuary personnel should be included as a priority group since they will be having direct contact with bodies of the deceased. Moreover, mortuary personnel will have contact with surviving family members of individuals known to have had the disease. Not providing prophylaxis to the mortuary workers may be a disincentive for them to stay on the job when needed most. Furthermore, those who do remain on the job without priority for prophylaxis may become ill and add to the number of incapacitated or deceased.

9.7.11   SUPPLY MANAGEMENT

Counties should recommend to funeral directors that they not order excessive amounts of supplies such as embalming fluids, human remains pouches, etc., but that they have enough on hand in a rotating inventory to handle the first wave of the pandemic (that is enough for six months of normal operation). Fluids can be stored for years, but human remains pouches and other supplies may have a limited shelf-life. Cremations generally require fewer supplies since embalming is not required.

Families experiencing multiple deaths are unlikely to be able to afford multiple higher-end products or arrangements. Funeral homes could quickly exhaust lower-cost items (e.g., inexpensive caskets) and should be prepared to provide alternatives (NORTHCOM, 2006b).

9.7.12 Social and Religious Considerations

Most religious and ethnic groups have very specific directives about how bodies are managed after death, and such needs must be considered as a part of pandemic planning. Christian sects, Hindus, Indian Nations, Jews, and Muslims all have specific directives for the treatment of bodies and for funerals. The wishes of the family will provide guidance; however, if no family is available local religious or ethnic communities can be contacted for information. Counties should contact the religious and cultural leaders in the pandemic planning stages and develop plans. The plan should address not being able to meet expectations of some groups and support from the religious or cultural leadership should be solicited to face this fact. Counties should document what is culturally and religiously expectable, what can be compromised, and what practices are strictly forbidden.

As a result of these special requirements, some religious groups maintain facilities such as small morgues, crematoria, and other facilities, which are generally operated by volunteers. Religious groups should be contacted to ensure these facilities and volunteers are prepared to deal with pandemic issues. Religious leaders should also be involved in planning for funeral management, bereavement counseling, and communications, particularly in ethnic communities with large numbers of people who do not speak English.

9.7.13 Community Healing Processes

When the pandemic event is over, community leaders should already have a plan in place to memorialize the dead. Communities should have plans in place to identify a suitable location to erect an appropriate nondenominational memorial for the dead and the families left behind.

As we have seen in past disasters in America, families will want to be part of the planning group in the community and have input into the process and location of the memorial. The political leadership of the community should establish this planning group and have the memorial event declared a very public and very solemn annual occasion.

For a civilization to deserve that name, all of life must be valued, including the absent life of the dead. (Reyes Mate, *Memorial de Auschwitz*, 2003.)

9.8 CONCLUSION

The current death rates for the H5N1 virus as of November 2007 have a case fatality rate of over 61 percent (WHO, 2007). Should an influenza strain evolve into a full pandemic, communities will need to manage very large numbers of deaths in a short time period. To be fully prepared, communities must partner with both public and private groups to ensure each case is properly managed and documented to avoid future problems (i.e., insurance fraud, homicides, misidentification, etc.). Managing expectations through public information for all segments of society must be a top priority of the government's public information releases. The mortuary affairs community is not robust enough to manage large numbers of deaths and chances are very high that religious and cultural expectations will not be met. Yet we must strive to ensure the dead are treated with utmost respect and families are given the assurance that they still have choices in the final disposition decisions.

Reviews of existing laws, capabilities, and resources in the community should be a primary function of emergency planners. Developing pre-event emergency declarations to identify streamlining legal processes should be explored and discussed by the stakeholders in the community. Investigative resources, recovery personnel, missing persons capabilities, transport capabilities, storage, and funeral service providers will require augmentation and standard practices to ensure cross-referencing capabilities and decedent tracking and reporting.

ACRONYMS

ANSI: American National Standards Institute
CERT: Community Emergency Response Team
CFR: Code of Federal Regulations
DEM: Department of Emergency Management
DMORT: Disaster Mortuary Operations Response Team
DOT: Department of Transportation
DPMU: Disaster Portable Mortuary Unit
EMS: emergency medical services
EOC: Emergency Operations Center
EP&R: Emergency Preparedness and Response Division
GPS: global positional system
HAN: health alert network
HEPA: high-efficiency particulate air
HIPAA: Health Insurance Portability and Accountability Act
HVAC: heating, ventilation, and air conditioning system
ICS: Incident Command System
MA: Mortuary Affairs
MACPs: Mortuary Affairs collection points
MAS: Mortuary Affairs System
MMRS: Metropolitan Medical Response System
NFDA: National Funeral Directors Association
NIMS: National Incident Management System
NIOSH: National Institute of Occupational Safety and Health
NOK: next-of-kin
NRP: National Response Plan
OCME: Office of the Chief Medical Examiner
PAPRs: powered air-purifying respirators

PI: pandemic influenza
PIO: Public Information Office
PPE: personal protective equipment
WHO: World Health Organization

REFERENCES

AFMIC. 2006. Bodies of Dead H5N1 Avian Influenza Patients Pose Minimal Risk for Virus Spread. Medical Intelligence Note 030-06, DI-1812-1105-06, March 3, 2006.

Ariès, P. 1991. *The Hour of Our Death.* Oxford University Press.

CDC (U.S. Centers for Disease Control and Prevention). 1994. National Center for Health Statistics, Medical Examiner's and Coroner's Handbook on Death Registration and Fetal Death Reporting.

DHS (U.S. Department of Homeland Security). December 2004. The National Response Plan.

DHS (U.S. Department of Homeland Security). 2007 Mass Fatality Target Capability.

Gursky EA, et al. July 2007. A Working Group Consensus Statement on Mass-Fatality Planning for Pandemics and Disasters. *Journal of Homeland Security.*

Hickman MJ, Hughes KA, Strom KJ. 2007. Medical Examiners and Coroners' Offices, 2004. *Bureau of Justice Statistics Special Report,* NCJ 216756.

HSC (Homeland Security Council). November 2005. National Strategy for Pandemic Influenza (NSPI).

Joint Tactics, Techniques, and Procedures for Mortuary Affairs in Joint Operations, Joint Publication of U.S. Department of Defense 4-06, 28 August 1996.

Miniño AM, Heron M, Murphy SL, and Kochanek, Division of Vital Statistics. Deaths: Final Data for 2004.

Model State Public Health Act: A Tool for Assessing Public Health Laws. 2003. Public Health Statute Modernization National Excellence Collaborative.

Morgan O, Tidbal-Binz M, van Alphen D, Editors. 2006. *Management of Dead Bodies after Disasters: A Field Manual for First Responders.* Washington, D.C.: Pan American Health Organization.

NIJ (National Institute of Justice). 1999. Death Investigation: A Guide for the Scene Investigator, Research report, NCJ 167568, Washington, D.C.

Nolte K, et al. 2004. Medical examiners, coroners, and biologic terrorism, a guidebook for surveillance and case management. Weekly Morbidity and Mortality Report, CDC, 53(RR08), June 11, 2004.

NORTHCOM (U.S. Northern Command). 2006a. Fatality Management Pandemic Influenza Working Group White Paper. Scene Operations, to Include Identification and Medico-legal Investigation Protocols and Command and Control of Mass Fatalities Resulting from a Pandemic Influenza (PI) in the United States.

NORTHCOM (U.S. Northern Command). 2006b. Fatality Management Pandemic Influenza Working Group White Paper. Funeral Services and Final Disposition of Mass Fatalities Resulting from a Pandemic Influenza (PI) in the United States.

NORTHCOM (U.S. Northern Command). 2006c. Fatality Management Pandemic Influenza Working Group White Paper. The Provision of Family Assistance and Behavioral Health Services in the Management of Mass Fatalities Resulting from a Pandemic Influenza (PI) in the United States.

NORTHCOM (U.S. Northern Command). 2006d. Fatality Management Pandemic Influenza Working Group White Paper. Morgue Operations, Identification, and Medico-legal Investigation Protocols and Command and Control of Mass Fatalities Resulting from a Pandemic Influenza (PI) in the United States.

Public Health Law 104-191, Health Insurance Portability and Accountability Act of 1996, 104th Congress, August 21, 1996.

Sensing D. 2004. Disaster Mortuary Operations Response Team Training. Region Three Training, Gettysburg, PA, March 2004.

Virginia Department of Health. 2003. Death Certificate Data. Division of Vital Records.

Virginia Department of Health. 2006. Virginia Natural Disease Outbreak and the Pandemic Influenza Mass Fatality Response Plan. Office of the Chief Medical Examiner, Commonwealth of Virginia.

WHO (World Health Organization). 2005. WHO Global Influenza Preparedness Plan: The Role of WHO and Recommendations for National Measures Before and During Pandemics. Department of Communicable Disease Surveillance and Response Global Influenza Programme,

WHO (World Health Organization). 2006. Myths and Realities in Disaster Situations. Geneva.

WHO (World Health Organization). 2007. Cumulative Number of Confirmed Human Cases of Avian Influenza A/(H5N1) Reported to WHO. http://www.who.int/csr/disease/avian_influenza/country/cases_table 2007_11_12/en/index.html (accessed 12 November 2007).

10 Epilogue
Putting It All Together

Jeffrey R. Ryan, PhD and Jan F. Glarum, EMT-P

Failing to plan is planning to fail.

Proverb

CONTENTS

10.1 INTRODUCTION

Pandemics happen. They cause widespread disease, death, and social disruption; a perfect storm of global proportion if you will. They vary widely in severity and their timing cannot be predicted. However, we know that we are overdue and ill-prepared for the next pandemic. Advance preparations can reduce the number of people who become ill or die, and can minimize the economic and community infrastructure impacts. They can make weathering a pandemic better, but by no means easy.

Pandemic flu preparation is very much a collaborative process and requires extensive discussions on how various functional areas — including human resources, finance, legal, and employee health — will work together to ride out the storm. It also requires collaboration with outside parties such as vendors, suppliers, and surrounding health care facilities to ensure that we all successfully navigate the next pandemic together. Even the best-prepared facilities will be severely tested in a pandemic. Now is not the time to be complacent — once the outbreak begins, it will be too late to plan. As the proverb says, "He who fails to plan, plans to fail."

Pandemic flu planning, like preparing to sail a ship across the ocean, requires serious forethought and effort, and should build upon and strengthen all hazard planning already well underway at local, regional, and state levels. Should such

237

coordination activities not already exist between entities likely to be intertwined and impacted by a pandemic, the journey is doomed before it ever casts off from the dock. The benefit of an existing strong community all hazard planning team concept is that much of this work will assist with pandemic response. Likewise, well coordinated and comprehensive efforts toward pandemic influenza planning should advance all hazard plans.

The Department of Health and Human Services (HHS) estimates a burden of seasonal flu results in approximately 226,000 hospitalizations, 36,000 deaths, and direct health care costs of 1 to 3 billion dollars annually. The real benefit of preparing for pandemic influenza is the opportunity to institutionalize influenza mitigation activities and help us all to reduce the burden of common seasonal influenza.

Pandemic influenza planning and preparedness must be based on sustainable systems and activities, which is another strong argument to build a program off of a foundation designed to influence morbidity and mortality from seasonal influenza. Assuming that history repeats itself, pandemics will occur sporadically several times a century. While highly pathogenic H5N1 is a serious virus, it is by no means certain that it will evolve into a pandemic strain of virus. The next pandemic could evolve anywhere from several months to many years from now. What does appear to be certain is that it will eventually happen.

Responsibility for preparing and responding to pandemic influenza spans all levels and sectors. Governmental entities, health care, business, faith-based organizations, schools and universities, volunteer groups, businesses, and individuals all have very critical roles to play in pandemic as well as other emergency preparedness. While federal and state agencies play critical roles in preparedness and response, emergencies arise and response is operationalized at the local level. Pandemics, like other natural disasters can be catastrophic events and individuals have significant responsibility to ensure positive outcomes for the communities they live in. This is troublesome to contemplate when considering the wide array of individual preparedness competencies displayed in recent disasters. Federal, state, and local governments will be unable to address all needs, resources will be insufficient, and decisions complex. Pandemics are unlike any other significant emergency. The normal progression of communities asking for help when overwhelmed goes next to the county or parish level, followed by state and federal assistance. When all communities are impacted at nearly the same time, state and federal support will be an issue. There are no resource pools deep enough to address the simultaneous requests. The proverb that led off this chapter applies clear down to the individual level and perhaps it will be providence in the end for those that heed its simple message.

10.2 EXPECTATIONS AND RESPONSIBILITIES

Not all people and entities are accustomed to responding to health crises nor do they understand the actions and priorities required to prepare for and respond to a pandemic. A critical element of pandemic planning is to ensure that all groups (including political leadership at all levels of government, nonhealth components of government, and members of the private sector) are informed and trained. Essential planning also includes the coordination of efforts between human and animal health authorities (HSC, 2005).

The private sector and critical infrastructure entities must have clear and achievable guidance on their roles in the pandemic response. Likewise, the health care community must grant considerations to the private sector that are necessary to maintain essential services and operations despite significant and sustained worker absenteeism as predicted by some (HSC, 2005).

An influenza pandemic will strain public health and health care systems; the nature of the demands of a pandemic will vary over its course. Public health, medical, business, and government authorities at all levels must take actions to mitigate the potentially catastrophic consequences of a pandemic. Specific capabilities are developed through preparedness activities prior to the beginning of a pandemic. The following are response actions and capabilities deemed necessary for implementation of an effective response.

Public health and some health care agencies have been considering issues around pandemic influenza for the past two to three years. Given the complex issues that surround pandemic influenza and the potential for major societal and economic disruption, many others need to be engaged. Preparedness and response must be multidiscipline and community based. Institutional, agency, local, and state emergency operations plans should be looked at and adapted to address pandemic influenza through development of incident specific annexes or other routes.

In a moderate to severe pandemic, absenteeism due to illness, caring for ill family members, and fear of infection may reach 40 percent during the peak weeks of a community outbreak. These could be higher with certain public health measures implemented (school closures, voluntary quarantine, "snow days," etc.). Continuity of operations planning for such reduced workforces or disruptions in supply chains is needed to minimize the impact on economic and community infrastructure.

It is estimated that 85 percent of critical infrastructure is maintained through the private sector. Links with the business community are critical both to support their planning for continuity of operations and to identify other roles they can play in response and recovery. Such roles may include helping sustain community infrastructure, establishing policies that better enable staff to follow public health control measures, communicating credible information to their employees, and helping communities recover from the economic and societal impacts of pandemics or other disasters. As such, we must strive to identify an ongoing forum to work with the business community around pandemic flu and broader emergency preparedness. Our economy is built upon supply and demand. If a demand for services is correctly perceived and prepared for, business has an opportunity to actually prosper during a pandemic by being influenza ready.

Early identification of pandemic virus upon arrival in the United States allows a quicker and more effective response. Knowing who is most impacted by the disease helps direct how best to use any appropriate vaccine and antivirals. Tracking the number of cases helps know when it is best to apply or relax different containment measures and to learn better the effectiveness of different measures. This involves capturing information on disease as it occurs and strong lab testing capabilities. We could all benefit from strengthening surveillance systems to detect a pandemic and to track the effectiveness of containment measures. Having a good point-of-care diagnostic test is crucial in building that capability.

The number of health care visits, hospitalizations, and deaths will depend on the virulence of the virus that causes the next pandemic. Bird flu due to H5N1, though not at this point a pandemic virus, currently causes severe disease similar to that seen in the 1918 influenza pandemic. Pandemic viruses in 1957 and 1968 caused at least tenfold fewer hospitalizations and deaths, but still significantly stressed the health care system. Current standards of care are not realistic in a pandemic. Hospitals and health care systems must continue to plan for handling large numbers of ill patients. Communities need to plan for ways to offload all but the most critical of patients to other community resources (traditional and nontraditional clinics, triage centers, alternate care facilities, etc.). This will entail adoption at the appropriate regulatory level of "sufficiency of care" standards prior to the need for implementation of such standards.

10.2.1 Develop Community-Level Plans to Operationalize Measures That Can Reduce Disease Spread

Potential mechanisms to reduce spread of disease involve such things as cancellation of large public gatherings, possible school closures, isolation of ill patients, voluntary quarantine of household contacts of ill individuals, and quenching with antiviral drugs. Toronto's experience with SARS showed that much of this can effectively be done voluntarily if risk communication is appropriate and basic needs are met, including assuring access to food, chronic medications, and essential supplies. Resolving issues around maintenance of income are also critical to these being effective. If not addressed adequately, potential loss of income will drive people to resume activities in spite of containment measures and could be a significant source of predictable civil unrest.

Initially, vaccination and antiviral distribution will be limited in a pandemic. Antivirals are a component of pandemic response, but not the magic bullet. There is no argument that, until the virus presents itself and reveals its vulnerability to antiviral therapy, they have limited value. Unfortunately, as a pandemic unfolds and media reports include a daily death toll, public concern along with one-sided reporting on the efficacy of antivirals may skew their value to a perception of being essential. Limited supplies will require that they predominantly be used for treatment rather than prevention. Plans to quickly get antiviral medications to targeted ill and/ or potentially exposed individuals must be operational and exercised. Discussion around drafted priority groupings is needed. These focus first on decreasing death and illness then on minimizing societal and economic impact. One cannot ignore the fact that antivirals are prescribed for the prevention and treatment of seasonal influenza. As such, conscientious application as prophylaxis must be a consideration fraught with ethical dilemmas.

A vaccine for H5N1 (clade 1) has been developed and is available in a limited quantity. Its efficacy is questionable since we do not know if it will emerge as a pandemic candidate or what variation of the parental strain we might be fighting one day. Then, what if the true pandemic threat has nothing to do with H5N1 and turns out to be a distant H2 or H7 strain? In this instance, vaccine can only be developed once the pandemic virus is identified. Vaccine will likely not be available until six to nine months after the start of the pandemic and will begin with limited supplies. It may be that two doses of vaccine will be needed to provide protection. Federally drafted priority groupings have been developed. As part of broader emergency preparedness, local health departments have been working with partners to develop priority group and community vaccination plans. Vaccine priority groupings focus on decreasing health impacts and on minimizing societal and economic disruptions. An opportunity for succeeding in our voyage through the whirlpool of pandemic influenza is to practice mitigation strategies now with seasonal influenza. Each community should re-evaluate its seasonal immunization strategy (is it morbidity or mortality based?) and begin efforts to adopt a universal immunization campaign. This gives the public confidence that your efforts are not discriminating to any demographic representation. At the very least, seasonal influenza impact is reduced, and in the face of a concurrent pandemic strain circulating, helps to reduce background clutter, making containment efforts more focused.

10.2.2 Sustain and Strengthen All Hazard Emergency Response Systems at Both State and Local Levels

The nation's approach to emergency preparedness is an all-hazard one. That way, response partners regularly work together in a variety of real events, practice using a variety of scenarios, and maintain readiness. These systems cannot be developed at the time of an event but must be a sustained part of our communities. Available and well-trained personnel, proper equipment, and jointly developed plans at the state and local levels are the most effective assets in emergencies.

Finally, if informed, aware, and involved, most people respond sensibly to disasters. Many issues in managing an influenza pandemic are complex and require public input and discussion. This is especially true around setting priorities for use of limited resources (vaccines, antivirals, medical supplies and equipment, etc.) and around effectively implementing methods of reducing disease spread in communities. What we are getting at is the involvement of all stakeholders, which leads us to the next section.

10.3 STAKEHOLDERS

Many people encompassing a broad spectrum of local society should be invited to a meeting of stakeholders to discuss the community's preparation and response to a potential pandemic influenza outbreak. In *An Introduction to Emergency Management*, Lindell, Prater, and Perry (2007) assert that community stakeholders (i.e., those members of a society that have something to gain or lose) can be divided into three separate categories: social groups, economic groups, and governmental groups. Each has members affected by potential disasters, and in some form or fashion, each has members who influence public policy.

Although Lindell, Prater, and Perry (2007) define the household as the basic social group unit, having every citizen of a community actively involved in the meeting can be impractical both for the agenda's time schedule and the meeting location's accommodations. However, allowing representatives from local public advocacy groups to be involved can be reasonable and manageable. Local print and television media must be involved and can quickly and efficiently inform the general public of the meeting's objectives and outcomes. Reporting on the forethought and prudence of local leaders to engage in disaster preparedness can help to foster a sense of well-being and security among the community in its leaders. This, in and of itself, may be sufficient reason for local politicians to engage in disaster preparedness efforts, if they sense an opportunity to stand out over an opponent. During disaster response, the media can effectively direct the public in response guidelines and directives, helping to prevent chaos and panic. Other invited representatives belonging to the social group classification should be the American Red Cross and local religious relief organizations. According to the official Web site of the Red Cross, they can contribute to a disaster response by feeding emergency workers, handling inquiries from concerned family members outside the disaster area, providing blood and blood products to disaster victims, and helping those affected by disaster to access other available resources. Religious organizations can also perform many of the same functions and view it as part of their ministerial obligations, a course not likely to be altered at the height of the pandemic storm, making them a powerful stabilizing force.

Economic groups, or businesses, organize the flow of goods and services, and a true influenza pandemic will affect almost all businesses in a community with small businesses being most at risk (Lindell, Prater, Perry, 2007). Again, along the same lines as the general public, inviting all business owners to participate can be impractical. Allowing representatives from business-related organizations, such as the local Chamber of Commerce, can be an option, as well as allowing only a select few business owners to actively participate: mainly those whose businesses contribute most to the local economy and tax base, provide support to critical infrastructure operations, and employ the highest amount of workers. Last, members of various governmental organizations and locally elected and statewide government officials should be invited. Representatives from the local emergency first-responder agencies must be included as these agencies will be some of the first to treat those affected by the outbreak, and law enforcement can be beneficial in dealing with the potential chaos and panic generated by such an outbreak. Health care facilities and the local health department are also key members in the discussion process. An outbreak on such a wide scale can easily overwhelm any medical facility's ability to care for the sick and injured, and mutual aid and other agreements for assistance and plans for mass triage and treatment must be in place. Health department staff along with epidemiologists can provide medical expertise on the cause and effects of such an outbreak and the necessary procedures for containment, and CDC officials can prove invaluable in helping with containment and treatment of individuals using its National Strategic Stockpile. Having locally elected officials and statewide legal and emergency management agency officials present would not only allow these members to share expertise on public policy, but also provides an opportunity for networking to obtain needed resources to implement such a plan. Proper networking must be capitulated by mutual aid agreements.

10.4 CONCLUSION

What communities need are operational plans to move them strategically and tactically through one to three years of pandemic influence. This plan must involve all key components of society, not just traditional response entities. Health care and business leaders, suppliers, private industry, and food and transportation representatives must be partners with the more-traditional response community of government, emergency management, police, fire, EMS, and public health entities. All these parties must be in agreement on when triggers will be pulled that result in specific actions at specific times, and what corresponding activities should be anticipated.

A dependence on paper plans can have its drawbacks, too. Resiliency, flexibility, and management by objectives are the keys to crisis management. The plan is useful; it gives opportunities to discuss possibilities, to purchase necessary materials, and to establish organizational structures for a 12-to-36 month response and rebuilding of the community. By rehearsing each role with a critical eye on the ripple effect on others, the community can begin to prepare intellectually and emotionally for a pandemic.

The arrival of a pandemic organism will set the stage for leaders across the globe to disclose their commitment to the welfare of their constituents. A clear testament to the investment each community made in recognizing the economic, security, and health threat a pandemic posed, and steps they took to mitigate them will be revealed. A pandemic will provide ample pain and suffering throughout the world even for the best-prepared communities. The time it takes for a community to rebound will be dependent directly upon the investment made today to prepare. Storm clouds are brewing on the horizon, this is a decisive point in time, and communities must act with resolve.

The greatest challenge that communities face is moving beyond general federal guidance and translating and adopting it into specific actions, programs, and policies. This involves collaboration across levels of government and among constituents that have seldom worked together against a threat. There will be disagreements and questions lacking an easy answer, yet failing to ask the questions for fear of alienating others will beg the question during the postmortem, "why didn't you?"

While it is important to consider the detailed operational tasks that will comprise a pandemic response, it is equally important to acknowledge the difficult challenges that will arise in a pandemic. All organizations, including public health and medical communities, will be affected by a pandemic.

REFERENCES

HSC (U.S.) Department of Homeland Security, Homeland Security Council). November 2005. National Strategy for Pandemic Influenza. Available from http://www.whitehousegov/homeland/nspi.pdf.

Lindell M, Prater C, Perry R. 2007. *An Introduction to Emergency Management*. Hoboken, NJ: Wiley Publications.

Index